T0304136

Gender, Mobilities, and Livelihood Transformations

In the era of globalization many minority populations are subject to marginalization and expulsion from their traditional habitats due to rapid economic restructuring and changing politico-spatial relations. This book presents an analytical framework for understanding how mobility is an inherent part of such changes.

The book demonstrates how current neoliberal policies are making people increasingly mobile – whether voluntarily or by force, and whether individually, as family, or as whole communities – and how such mobility is changing the livelihoods of indigenous people, with particular focus on how these transformations are gendered. It queries how state policies and cross-border and cross-regional connections have shaped and redefined the livelihood patterns, rights and citizenship, identities, and gender relations of indigenous peoples. It also identifies the dynamic changes that indigenous men and women are facing, given rapid infrastructure improvements and commercialization and/or industrialization in their places of livelihoods.

With a focus on mobility, this innovative book gives students and researchers in development studies, gender studies, human geography, anthropology, and Asian studies a more realistic assessment of peoples' livelihood choices in a time of rapid transformation, and the knowledge produced may add value to present development policies and practices.

Ragnhild Lund is Professor in Development Geography at the Norwegian University of Science and Technology, Norway.

Kyoko Kusakabe is Associate Professor of Gender and Development Studies at the School of Environment, Resources and Development, at the Asian Institute of Technology, Thailand.

Smita Mishra Panda is Professor at the School of Management at the Human Development Foundation in Odisha, India.

Yunxian Wang is an independent researcher, affiliated to the Institute of Sociology, Shanghai Academy of Social Sciences, China.

Routledge Studies in Development, Mobilities and Migration

Gender, Mobilities, and Livelihood Transformations
Comparing indigenous people in China, India, and Laos

Edited by Ragnhild Lund, Kyoko Kusakabe, Smita Mishra Panda, and Yunxian Wang

Gender, Mobilities, and Livelihood Transformations

Comparing indigenous people in China, India, and Laos

Edited by
Ragnhild Lund, Kyoko Kusakabe,
Smita Mishra Panda, and
Yunxian Wang

LONDON AND NEW YORK

First published 2014
by Routledge
2 Park Square, Milton Park, Abingdon, Oxon OX14 4RN

Simultaneously published in the USA and Canada
by Routledge
711 Third Avenue, New York, NY 10017

*Routledge is an imprint of the Taylor & Francis Group,
an informa business*

British Library Cataloguing in Publication Data
A catalogue record for this book is available from the British Library

Library of Congress Cataloging-in-Publication Data
Gender, mobilities, and livelihood transformations : comparing
indigenous people in China, India, and Laos / [edited by] Ragnhild
Lund, Kyoko Kusakabe, Smita Mishra Panda, and Yunxian Wang.
pages cm. – (Routledge studies in development, mobilities and
migration)
1. Labor mobility–Social aspects–Asia–Cross-cultural studies.
2. Indigenous peoples–Asia–Economic conditions–Cross-cultural
studies. 3. Asia–Emigration and immigration–Economic aspects.
4. Forced migration–Economic aspects–Asia. 5. Indigenous
peoples–Asia–Ethnic identity–Cross-cultural studies. 6. Displacement
(Psychology)–Asia–Cross-cultural studies. I. Lund, Ragnhild, editor of
compilation.
HD5717.5.A78G46 2013
331.12'7095–dc23
2013009468

ISBN13: 978-0-415-81353-2 (hbk)
ISBN13: 978-0-203-06813-7 (ebk)

Typeset in Times New Roman
by Keystroke, Station Road, Codsall, Wolverhampton

Contents

Figures

Tables

Contributors

Thomas Sætre Jakobsen is a PhD candidate at the Department of Geography, Norwegian University of Science and Technology. His research interests are human mobility, social transformations, and rural/urban relations in China.

Kyoko Kusakabe is Associate Professor of Gender and Development Studies at the School of Environment, Resources and Development at the Asian Institute of Technology, Thailand. Her research interests are on gender issues in mobility and work, especially under regional economic integration in Southeast Asia.

Ragnhild Lund is Professor in Development Geography at the Norwegian University of Science and Technology. Her research interests are related to processes of social change in the Global South, in particular mobility, gender, youth, and indigenous people.

Veena N. is a freelance researcher and writer with interests in the fields of gender, indigenous culture, and development.

Xiao'ou Ou is an assistant researcher at the Institute of Sociology, Yunnan Academy of Social Sciences, China. Her research interests are gender and development, especially focusing on ethnic minority groups.

Smita Mishra Panda is Professor at the School of Management at the Human Development Foundation in Odisha, India. Her research interests include gender issues in development, natural resource management (water and forests), governance, and tribal livelihoods.

Tanu Priya Uteng is a planning consultant at the Department of Transport and Spatial Analysis, Ramboll Consultancy Services Ltd, Norway. Her research focuses on exploring the interface between urban transport planning and mobilities.

Anitha Venkatesh is a PhD candidate at the School of Environment, Resources and Development, field of Gender and Development Studies at the Asian Institute of Technology, Thailand. Her research interests are mobility, gender, and tribal peoples' livelihoods in India.

Sengkham Vongphakdy is a researcher at the Public Works and Transport Institute, Vientiane, Lao PDR. She is trained as a planner.

Yunxian Wang is an independent researcher, affiliated to the Institute of Sociology, Shanghai Academy of Social Sciences, China. Her research interests are related to gender and development, land and rural development, mobility and livelihood, civil society development, and poverty issues.

Jing Wu is an Associate Professor at the Institute of Economics, Yunnan Academy of Social Sciences, China. Her research areas include sustainable development, environmental economy, and low carbon economy.

Hongwen Zhang is an Associate Professor at the Institute of Sociology, Yunnan Academy of Social Sciences, China. Her research interests include gender and development, HIV/AIDs, mobility particularly related to the impact of mobility on children, youth and ethnic minority people.

Qun Zhao is a Research Professor at the Institute of Sociology, Yunnan Academy of Social Sciences, China. Her research areas include gender and rural development, poverty, livelihood and technological extension, gender and climate change, gender and mobility.

Foreword

The present book is embedded in a long history of professional collaboration among the four editors from China, India, Japan, and Norway. We are: Kyoko Kusakabe, development planning and gender studies specialist; Smita Mishra Panda, anthropologist and gender studies specialist; Yunxian Wang, development economist and gender studies specialist; and Ragnhild Lund, development and feminist geographer. To date, Ragnhild has studied development-induced resettlement and changing livelihoods in Sri Lanka, Smita has studied displacement in India, Kyoko has studied labour migration in Thailand, and Yunxian has worked on migrants' labour rights and social inclusion in the practical field in China. We had all realized the importance of mobility – not only migration but also changes in daily mobility have much influence on gender relations. We have recognized that while most other studies in this field examine migration, they have focused relatively little on mobility and gender relations. For this reason, in 2009 we came together to work on a project on mobile livelihoods in three different Asian countries – China, India, and Laos.

Our collaboration rests on 20 years acquaintance, which has developed into strong relations of mutual trust and respect for each other's competency and cultural background. We are professionals, mothers, wives, daughters, and respectively members of communities in China, Australia, India, Norway, and Thailand. We all met in the early 1990s, while working at the Asian Institute of Technology (AIT, Bangkok, Thailand), where we studied gender. Since then, we have maintained contact and met at different professional events. When eventually we secured a substantial research grant from the Research Council of Norway for the period 2010–2013, our relations as colleagues deepened. We increasingly met, interacted, and communicated across borders. We also came to understand that collaboration is a resource for professional support and solidarity. In the process of our work, we have learnt how to share information, discuss, disagree, complement, and synergize existing individual merits. Hence, our collaboration has been effective in changing our intergroup attitudes and has opened up for professional reflexivity (see the methodology section in Chapter 1), and building knowledge across boundaries. At a later stage, and for the purpose of this publication, Dr Tanu Priya Uteng was invited to provide us with broader insights into the field of mobility studies, together with Thomas Jakobsen, whom we invited to strengthen the experience drawn from China, and Anitha Venkatesh, who was invited to strengthen the experience drawn from India.

We would like to express our deepest appreciation to the following partners in *China*. For the mobile livelihoods study, the Institute of Sociology, Yunnan Academy of Social Sciences supported the research collaboration and staff involvement. Students from Yunnan Ethnic Study Institute and Kunming Medical University, namely Wan Dongdong, He Jinglian, Han Yang, Sun Shuangfeng, Hu Dan, and Sun Rui, all provided assistance with administering the questionnaire survey and the latter three helped with data input and analysis. Jiang Hang helped us with the preparation of the study area map. We would like to express our gratitude to the government departments that assisted our fieldwork and carried out discussion meetings, namely Xishuangbanna Prefecture Government, Ethnicity Committee, Women's Federation, Tourism Bureau, Menghai County Government, Daluo Township Government, Simao Prefecture Government, Nanping Township Government, Yuanjiang County Government and Ethnicity Committee, and Yangjie Township Government. Sincere thanks are also due to the villagers who provided accommodation during our fieldwork and participated in the workshop. For the study in Songhuaba, Li Yunju at ICRAF, China Academy of Sciences Kunming Institute of Botany, at the Centre for Mountain and Ecosystem Studies, put in a tremendous amount of work in the design and research phase of the fieldwork conducted in Songhuaba in early 2009. Xu Jianchu at ICRAF deserves praise for his hospitality and for teaching innovative ways to do fieldwork. During the interviews in Songhuaba we had four excellent assistants, Li Lan, Duan Xiao Qian, Ni Yong Fen, and Yang Wei Xia, who gave generous amounts of their time to the project. Further, Lü Caizhen provided timely encouragement and advice during the presentation to ICRAF in November 2011.

We would like to express our deepest appreciation to the following partners in *India*. For the mobile livelihood study, Manju Prava Dhal, Director of CARD (NGO) and her team in the field, particularly Sarojini Nayak, in the villages in Khordha District helped and supported us during the fieldwork. The staff of Pragati (NGO) who worked in the study villages in Sundargarh District also helped during our fieldwork. Both organizations facilitated the identification of key respondents and with conducting the participatory workshops in the field. In particular, we would like to thank Rosaleena Mishra and Sarojini Sharma for conducting the fieldwork in the villages in Sundargarh. For the study of the villages in Karnataka district, we thank Dr Arun Kumar, co-coordinator of Vivekananda Girijana Kalyana Kendra Biligiri Rangana Hills (BR Hills) Karnataka, and his team members, especially Sharadha and Nayana Nagaraj for organizing and helping to collect data from different villages.

We would like to express our deepest appreciation to the following partners in *Laos*. The Public Works and Transportation Institute, Lao PDR for making the fieldwork possible, and the Luang Namtha and Viengphouka district offices and planning offices for their support. We also acknowledge Vongchit Mivilay, District Office, Viengphouka District; Bountharn Xayvanhthon, Office of Public Works and Transport, Viengphouka District; Bountharn Lorbanlith, Office of Public Works and Transport, Luang Namtha District; Ountham Inthavixay, District Office, Luang Namtha District; Sengsavang Soulion, Office of Public Works and Transport, Viengphouka District; Sunee Khounpaseuth, District Office, Viengphouka District; and Sika Thavi, Office of Public Works and Transport, Viengphouka District. Our special thanks go to students of ethnic higher education at the school of Luang Namtha, who served as translators during our research, and the villagers of the eight study villages for accommodating our research team.

Finally, we would like to express our deepest appreciation for the language checking and careful editing assistance carried out by Catriona Turner. We would not have managed the final stages of this work without her thorough, constructive, and helpful contribution.

1 Gender, mobilities, and livelihood transformations

An introduction

Ragnhild Lund

Introduction

In this study the authors explore how mobility as a capability translates into different livelihood strategies. In the present era of increasing globalism and transnationalism more and more people live on the move (Cresswell 2006; Rigg 2007b; King 2011). This 'mobility turn' (of individuals, commodities, disease, organizations, and knowledge) characterizes not only industrial societies but also the present development of the Global South. To date, the Global North has been the primary site of innovation, ideas, and development. Therefore, there is a need to develop a 'new mobilities paradigm' with a southern focus in the social sciences, where present forms of mobility and livelihoods are explored (Rigg 2007b). The editors of this book intend to fill in this gap by presenting the findings of our research project titled 'Mobile Livelihoods and Gendered Citizenship: The Counter-geographies of Indigenous People in India, Laos and China'. The project, which we conducted with local partners (funded by the Research Council of Norway for the period 2010–2013), explores how women and men respond to present socio-economic and spatial changes through their mobility patterns in their respective countries. We explore cross-cultural and cross-regional similarities and differences with respect to livelihood transformations.

This book represents a new approach to mobilities research in three distinct ways. First, it is neither a comparative study in the conventional statistical sense, nor a collection of isolated case studies. Rather, based on multi-sited ethnographic research in three different countries – China, India, and Laos – that are rapidly changing due to economic restructuring and neoliberalist policies, it documents contemporary changes related to how people in marginalized areas have become integrated in mainstream society, but as marginalized others. Most ethnographic research on indigenous communities is nation-specific. This book gives a cross-border perspective, thereby providing insights into common and unfamiliar differences in mobility affecting the visited communities. Second, it is a synthesis of two main discourses. Contemporary discourses within development studies and gender studies address either mobilities (the new catchword) or livelihoods (which is a broad approach in development studies). We merge these two research traditions and study how the lives of men and women in marginalized communities are in a process of dramatic change, which makes them reformulate their livelihoods and may motivate their movements. This process, we argue, is largely gendered. It expands the current area of migration analysis by studying not just the relation between place of origin and place of destination, but the whole manner in which people manoeuvre through space. Third, a common bias within studies looking at rural livelihoods is to express either implicitly or explicitly that the futures of farmers, especially indigenous people, are invariably linked to farming and land (Rigg 2006). However, with a focus on mobility, this book aims at providing a more realistic assessment of people's livelihood choices during a time of rapid transformation.

Unravelling mobility in situations of changing politico-spatial relations

With urban expansion, modernization, and industrialization in most countries in the Global South, pressure is exerted on indigenous communities, who often live in marginalized conditions in remote places. It is generally observed that roads and better access to markets with the advent of globalization and/or economic restructuring can facilitate outmigration, change in land use, and challenge original ways of livelihoods. Such developments can affect women's and men's mobility through forced displacement, long-term outmigration, commuting (or circular) migration, and longer daily mobility to collect forest products. In other cases, people have become less mobile because of better infrastructure and communication. Travel to visit kin was also a traditional form of mobility, when people attended ceremonies, moved around within forests together, and met to arrange births, deaths, marriages, and trade. Although people have travelled to other places to find work, it is a recent trend that labour migration from rural to urban areas is becoming more important than ever. There is also an opposite trend, whereby people move less in the new economy, depending on the place where they live. Different social, economic, political, and spatial structures provide different conditions for improvement to people's situations. Thus, both mobility and immobility are strategies to improve people's livelihoods. With the advent and presence of external markets and development pressures, people's mobility patterns are changing. In this book, we show how this mobility involves new practices, new choices, and different everyday lives, and affects people's perceptions of social change and identity.

Ohnmacht *et al.* (2009) argue that mobility is unequally distributed, and is therefore a result of and a contributing factor to social stratification and social inequality. People may be forced to move or stay put; hence, both mobility and immobility may take place simultaneously. Thus, different forms of mobility are not necessarily dependent on people's ability to move, but rather their competence to recognize and make use of their ability to move. Even in situations when mobility is rendered impossible, and people are forced to make choices within limited mobility regimes, mobility takes place and facilitates appropriation of particular choices that may lead to personal development and better livelihoods.

It can therefore be argued, in common with Kronlid (2008), that mobility is a capability that may explain people's ability or inability to move. In this book, immobility and mobility are considered as two different sides of the same coin; both can be forced or not, and both can appropriately explain people's choices and potential to move.

Mobility has become transnational and often detrimental to the poor and marginalized. Sassen (1998) argues that the global forces that have led to the adoption of neoliberal policies in many countries today have also led to more oppressive migration patterns (i.e. what she refers to as the counter-globalization of such change, and in which human trafficking of all kinds is an inherent part). Such forces have reinforced marginalization processes among the poorest – and increased their mobility across borders – but in enforced ways. As my own research on replaced indigenous people in Sri Lanka, namely the Veddas, has shown, women's movements abroad to serve as domestic workers is one current mobility strategy. Even more common is that young girls move to the industrial areas of Sri Lanka in search of work, while men in all age groups migrate seasonally to construction sites all over the country. However, because the position of this indigenous group in society is ethnically, socially, and economically marginal, mobility is a selective process. As people's capacity to move is embedded in livelihood strategies that reflect the Veddas' marginalized position in society, their ability to move is reduced. Hence, their ability to move is socially situated (Haraway 1988). In this perspective, we can appreciate the importance of understanding people's context of living, what practices they create in different places, and their identities.

Indigenous peoples are distinct communities: the land on which they live and the natural resources on which they depend are inextricably linked to their identity and culture. Dispossession from such land or restriction of access to natural resources therefore not only leads to economic impoverishment but also to impoverishment in terms of loss of identity and cultural survival (World Bank 2005). The World Bank's definition of indigenous peoples is related to how it weaves together territorial identity, culture, and livelihood. Other researchers show how the theory of people's everyday lives and territories can help us to understand better how cultures change, adapt to, or resist change (Scott 2009). Such reflections show how territoriality and mobility are essential dimensions of society and create people's identity (Attanapola & Lund in press; Lund in press).

Indigenous peoples have been increasingly portrayed as marginalized victims with no rights due to economic restructuring in the era of neoliberalist policies. Much research has been done on indigenous peoples and cultures and their worsened sustainability (Singh 1982; Burman 1989; Panda 1996; World Bank 2005; Kumar 2007); how they have been impacted by environmental projects that have limited their access to natural resources (Tauli-Corpuz 1995; Lund 2003; Xu & Salas 2003); how development projects have caused displacements (Vandergeest *et al.* 2007; de Wet 2008); their lack of citizenship rights (Staheli *et al.* 2004); and how development-induced displacement has affected indigenous peoples more than others and created gender disparities in resettlement operations

(Lund 1993; Baviskar 2004; Kusakabe 2012). However, there has been little emphasis on their lived realities, namely how they strategize to survive on a daily basis. One exception is James Scott (2009), who reveals that mobility is used as a weapon by such peoples to fight against forces of marginalization. He argues that throughout history, highland (indigenous) peoples in Southeast Asia have been able to manage their linguistic differences, swidden agriculture, and ethnic identity efficiently by being mobile, in order to avoid state control over agriculture, surplus, and labour. This view also conforms to those of other scholars who have claimed that indigenous peoples have always been mobile (Stepputat & Sørensen 1999; 2001). Further, it is akin to what we aim at doing here, namely unravelling how people bring their traditional mobility into new economies, creating livelihood strategies that show what can be achieved within given positions and localities. Thus, mobility is becoming a major coping strategy, and its implications for livelihoods vary according to gender (Sørensen & Olwig 2002). Instead of viewing people as victims of such transformations, we need to understand how they strategize and respond to increasing connectivities by being mobile. Furthermore, global demands for agricultural and mineral products have pushed developing economies away from producing food and wage goods for their own people, resulting in deteriorating traditional livelihoods and increasing the burden of poor women and men seeking food, shelter, and other essentials. Such processes are intertwined with other structures of inequality, such as ethnicity and class. Even though migration and its effect on community livelihoods and identities have been analysed extensively (Murphy 2002), how mobility itself (including not only labour migration but also short-term commuting migration and daily mobility) affects livelihood and identities, is not well-captured.

As we show in the various chapters, displacement of indigenous peoples has taken place repeatedly throughout history. Considering that indigenous peoples have always been mobile and aversive to state control (Scott 2009), we note that today their mobility is increasingly influenced and forced by external forces – namely, the state and the market – which they have little control over or are increasingly facing difficulties in negotiating. Hence, mobility takes place in situations of economic restructuring and changing politico-spatial relations. By politico-spatial relations (Massey 1994; Hyndman 2002), we refer to the prevailing development policies and the manner in which states and other external forces attempt to take control over people's livelihood options and strategies, and make them mobile. Although people have the ability to move, the act of moving is dependent on contextual factors at various scales and not normally on the choice of the individual alone. However, infrastructure and connectivities are not the only reasons why the lives of those living in indigenous communities are changing. Internal changes are occurring simultaneously in most indigenous communities (Rigg 2007a; Scott 2009). In the following chapters we show how variations in mobility or immobility inform us about how changing politico-spatial relations impact on people's abilities or choices to improve their lives. Like Rigg, we do not support a nostalgic notion that such indigenous communities were 'protected' and 'shielded' from the outside world prior to the advent of roads and development. Also, following Scott (2009), we see indigenous women and men as using mobility as a tool to keep respective states at arm's length, in an attempt to evade and avoid state control. This deviates from how neoliberal state policies generally understand mobility as movements made by populations to earn livelihoods, as people are considered to move due to economic pressure and because they seek economic well-being. Instead, women's and men's mobility can take different forms and occur for different reasons, such as to avoid gender-specific suppression within ethnic communities or clans that practise patriarchal customs and oppressive marriage cultures (Jin Huashan 2008).

Analytical approach

Mobility is understood as movement in a social and cultural context. It is a movement that is differently experienced by men and women, and their movements are differently coded. Inspired by Cresswell (2011), we have identified the following interconnected dimensions as important for understanding the mobility of the indigenous peoples that we present in this book: *mobility as social processes, mobility as livelihoods, mobility as voluntary to forced*, and *mobility as gendered*. Whereas our book mainly deals with two major types of mobility – labour migration and displacement/resettlement – other types of mobilities are identified that show how people (re)construct their livelihoods and lead to transformations in gendered responsibilities and practices.

Mobility as social processes

Mobility as social processes not only includes physical mobility (and hence the body), but also represents exposure to the outside world through others who enter into communities (Rigg 2006; Xu 2006). This means that mobility is a process that changes local structures and relationships. People who frequently cross geopolitical frontiers or borders also move along the edges of cultural borders, such as those created by language, citizenship, race, ethnicity, and gender ideology (Duany 2002). Such mobility contributes to the creation of new migrant identities and new politics of difference (Rigg 2007a). Those who arrive at new places are faced with challenges such as access to land and resources, a sense of belonging, and differences in ethnicity and status. Those who are left behind are faced with challenges in terms of remittances, erupting cultures in traditional communities, and changes in gender roles and responsibilities. Hence, as Cresswell (2011) says, mobility happens in places as well as through places, and some mobilities are related to or enabled by others.

The findings presented in this book indicate that mobility as social processes is transboundary and transnational. Although mobility has been a major coping strategy for indigenous peoples throughout history, it has recently been influenced by increasing geographical connectivity and market-oriented development policies. The indigenous peoples we study live on the margins of society in most

cases, despite special provisions made by their respective states. Their marginalization is also reflected in labour markets located far away from their habitats, and
in places their rights are typically violated. For example, movement to any new
destination does not always guarantee an attractive income or decent living
conditions. This becomes very clear in the case of India, where tribal women move
out of their households to seek all kinds of work outside their home villages.
Labour laws may seem just, but indigenous migrants, especially women, may find
the new place unsafe to live and work in due to the risks of being exposed to
different forms of exploitation. Similarly, as has been observed among the rural
population in China, the household registration system structures rural-urban and
rural-rural relations in general and mobility in particular. In other words, there are
several economic, social, and political barriers to rural populations interested in
going to work in cities, and the barriers have direct consequences for their
livelihood options.

The various chapters show that the outcomes of both immobility and mobility
lead indigenous men and women either into a spiral of deterioration in their well-
being or to a gradual uplift from poverty, depending on the politico-spatial
relations at work. In Laos, for example, land grabbing by overseas Chinese has
made it difficult for people to adjust to the new settlements and monoculture has
overridden traditional shifting cultivation. Living partly in traditional villages and
partly in the new settlements has made lives increasingly mobile, but has also led
to differential access to outside opportunities among the sexes. For example,
Chapter 3 cites the case of a couple in Yunnan Province who could not afford the
transport costs to travel to the prefecture city Kunming and hence had to stay in
their home village against their wish. At the same time, the household registration
system persists and forces some people, generally middle-aged women and elderly
people, to stay in their ancestral villages. By contrast, younger people are
compelled to move out in order to pay for their children's education, staple foods
(as they are no longer self-sufficient), and health care. Jakobsen (Chapter 4) shows
how the costs of education enforce mobility and affect livelihoods, thus
documenting how economic restructuring is forcing people to move due to
monetarization of daily life (Bryceson 2002; Rigg 2006). Hence, the economic
restructuring that is taking place has completely changed people's ability to be
mobile and exposed to the outside world. The experiences of mobility differ
according to gender, ethnicity, and class, and among individuals and groups.
Mobility is as much about the fact of moving as it is entangled with meaning and
the power to produce (im)mobility (Cresswell 2006).

Mobility as livelihoods

Mobility as livelihoods may vary in length from permanent to temporary, due to
changes in agricultural production, the entry of new extractive industries, industrial
development, and educational change. Mobility is thus both dependent on and
reflects peoples' capacity to create livelihoods; hence, livelihoods may be mobile.
The concept of *mobile livelihoods* was first used by Stepputat and Sørensen in

1999 to explain circulation patterns in the Caribbean and elsewhere (Stepputat & Sørensen 1999). According to Stepputat and Sørensen (2001, 770), the concept of mobile livelihoods

> connotes the social and spatial practices of people involved in migratory movements, and lifts the concept of 'livelihood' out of its locally-bounded context. It encompasses a wider understanding of mobility by looking at daily as well as long-term mobility not only migration of women and men.

The notion allows us to understand that people use location and place as resources and capital in their livelihood strategies. When people want to maintain their mobile lifestyles in pursuit of their livelihoods, mobile livelihoods may be understood as a spatial extension of people's means of subsistence to new local, regional, and national settings.

In all of the countries studied in this book, there has been a change from subsistence or semi-subsistence farming to work in the new market economy. We find that people use location and place as resources in their livelihood strategies by mobilizing resources at different places – old and new. Redundancies in the agricultural economies have completely changed the livelihoods of the indigenous peoples (and of others in the rural areas too), leading to a great variety of mobility patterns, from permanent to temporary migration, and from circular to daily commuting. Another impact is moving to new places or being resettled. In Laos, border crossing has facilitated land concessions and plantation cultivation by the Chinese, whereas in India and China new means of livelihoods have emerged, such as mining, stone crushing, and construction work, as well as human trafficking. At the same time, people in all three countries maintain some traditional farming. In India, tribal people have been compelled to leave marginal areas or have been displaced due to mining and industrial activities, effectively turning them into sedentary but poor, landless workers. In rural China, young couples with children tend to move permanently to the cities, whereas middle-aged women increasingly turn with great difficulty into the main providers through farming, and middle-aged men increasingly work outside their villages. Jakobsen (Chapter 4) particularly focuses on how it is important to understand (im)mobility during the life course of a household, thus bringing in the dynamics of socio-economic transformations across the generations of migrants. The aforementioned are all examples of people's choice and ability to move, as well as the meaning in their actions and how that eventually translates into differentiated livelihood strategies. Such findings show that the outcomes of both immobility and mobility lead indigenous men and women either into a spiral of deterioration in their well-being or to a gradual uplift from poverty, depending on the politico-spatial relations at work.

Mobility as voluntary to forced

To us (the authors), mobility as voluntary to forced refers to labour migration or displacement due to development interventions. Displacement creates harsh living conditions for many indigenous peoples. In Chapter 3, Wang *et al.* discuss such a situation, where a whole community was forced to resettle due to dam construction. The authors find that compensation was not given in due course, and even though it was properly realized, the disruption to livelihoods caused those affected to make continual comparisons between their original place and current place, and seek better compensation schemes.

Furthermore, authors of several studies caution that the notion of displacement is based on the idea that people live in one fixed place and the best solution for indigenous peoples is for them to go back to their 'place of origin' and stay there (Stepputat & Sørensen 2001; Dyer 2010; Oo & Kusakabe 2010). Such an assumption ignores the fact that many indigenous peoples use mobility as a strategy for survival, and it is because of such mobility that states want to keep them in a fixed place in order to control them. The perfect example of such a situation is the Chinese household registration system, which aims to keep people in the place where they were born. As Dyer (2010, 301) argues, mobility is too negatively understood as a 'framing of migration as a response by the poor', which covers up the fact that migration and mobility is a 'positive agency in choices' (307), and not always a response to structural inequality, preventing choices. Such opposed views indicate that the experience and meaning of mobility differ according to different people at different places: it is practised differently and does not happen unexpectedly. In this book, Venkatesh and Veena N.'s study (Chapter 6) may serve as one example of how tribal populations change their livelihoods in new settlements due to ineffective development policies and programmes, in this case in Karnataka State in India. The authors provide insights into how tribal women's commuting and temporary mobility are changing from traditional to new practices that may be mobile or not mobile in a situation of forced resettlement.

More importantly, the way mobility is practised is imbued with power at different scales – nationally as integration or expulsion, and locally by determining who and how one can move. Our study sites show great diversity in mobility patterns and livelihood options and choices. In China, mobility is strongly linked to 'national citizens' benefit', which is not extended to rural migrant workers that do not have urban household registration, and this legally binds people to fixed locations and deprives them of their rights to mobility. For those who stay put, the development pressure increases due to extensive plantations for cash crops and large-scale infrastructure expansion. Thus, the indigenous groups are squeezed in two ways, both by being deprived of their choice of mobility and, if they opt to remain, by the increasing pressure for land and resources from large agro-industries. In Laos, given the policy to relocate small and scattered hamlets into villages accessible by road, people are pressured to move away from their original place and at the same time disrupt the implementation of policies through practising mobile livelihoods, and hence living and earning in several locations. Still, mobile livelihoods are considered the norm, and following traditional livelihoods is generally considered as positive even though roadside work has become available and indigenous peoples' connectivities with their neighbours have been strengthened. By contrast, in India there are rich mineral deposits in areas inhabited by indigenous people. Several multinational and mega-national corporations operate in these regions to extract mineral resources. The indigenous people are losing water, land, and forests at an alarming rate, and displacement and outmigration are the order of the day. It is observed that their mobility and immobility are largely based on absence of choice, leading to devastated livelihood conditions for communities, while people strategize their survival mostly on the basis of increased mobility.

Mobility as gendered

The fourth interconnected dimension is of mobility as gendered. As Silvey (2006) and Harcourt (2009) have noted, spatial mobility is a social, political, and bodily process, and hence it is extremely important to understand mobility with a gender lens (Sørensen & Olwig 2002; Staheli *et al.* 2004). Traditionally, indigenous women have been mobile – engaged in swidden agriculture, collecting forest products, and engaged in long-distance trading. However, mobilities have normally been discussed in connection with a particular context (e.g. migration and travel patterns), not in a wider context involving different aspects of mobility as both physical movements and meanings, and how women's and men's shifting subjectivities are shaped by their spatial mobility. Cresswell and Uteng (2008) point out that gender both *constitutes* mobility and *is constituted by* mobility. Robeyns (2003), Uteng (2006), and Kronlid (2008) maintain that mobility should be studied as a capability. Restrictions on mobility can reinforce women's subordination, whereas for women improved mobility and access can transform unequal gender relations (Lund in press). Kusakabe (2012), who has compiled a series of case studies describing the effect of road development in the Mekong area, and focusing on women's and men's mobility, also argues that the relationship between mobility and women's empowerment and between infrastructure development and women's mobility is not straightforward and differs with context. She claims that there is a need for gender analysis in each of the road developments.

In quite another vein, in India, permanent settlement and increasing Hinduization (becoming more like the Hindu majority population) have changed gender relations within families and in the tribal communities. Increasingly, women work outside their villages; they earn cash incomes, and have gained a comparative advantage over men, who increasingly struggle to find work. As Panda shows in Chapter 5, women organize themselves in collectives for seasonal migration and construction work, while men have to stay put in their village. This shows how mobility involves the knowledge of 'potential' trips that could be made, but which are not made because of prohibiting factors (Cresswell & Uteng 2008). Thus, in the case of indigenous women and men, mobility not only shapes their gender identity, but also their capacity to move in given politico-spatial contexts.

Finally, in this book some emphasis is given to changing gender roles and relations when men and women move to a spouse, when feminization of labour in industry and agriculture takes place, as well as when new jobs can be found in the service sector in tourism and petty trade. Such processes of change take place in all of the studied countries. In China, particularly, finding a bride is an unspoken reason for mobility. Mobility also changes gender relations. In China, such changes have been to the detriment of women working in agriculture, but for those who live in the cities/new places it has resulted in more equality among the sexes. In Laos, men too have changed their work and participate more in household chores. In India, we see the same trend as in China, but we also note the increasing vulnerabilities among young women subject to prostitution and trafficking. For girls who are lured into trafficking, the mobility leads to a change from rural marginalization to urban vulnerabilities, and they have limited contact with their families and/or parents in their home village, which in turn leads to weakening of family ties. However, in both China and India, young girls particularly move outside their home environment for pleasure, whereas young men face more immobility. In China, apart from all of the macro-factors affecting and forging the mobility patterns of ethnic minorities in Yunnan, the impetus for the mobilities varies at the community, household, and individual levels. Following the implementation of the 'Go West' and agricultural vertical development strategies, economic benefit as a driver for mobility has been weakened. People have more income-generation opportunities near their home places. However, young people have been inspired and lured by developments elsewhere and want to experience such developments in person. Thus, even though their earnings would not necessarily be higher than at their home place, they try to gain exposure to the 'outside world'.

The study and methodology

The study

As mentioned, the overall objective of this mobile livelihoods study is to compare indigenous peoples in three countries – India, China, and Laos – that are rapidly being exposed to structural adjustments, neoliberal policies, and reform. Principal researchers from four partner institutions in India, China, Thailand, and Norway have come together in a project to study the gendered dimensions of such increasing connectivities and mobility among indigenous women and men. Our aim has been to understand how state policies and cross-border/cross-regional connectivities have shaped and redefined the livelihood patterns, rights and citizenship, identities, and gender relations of indigenous peoples.

Although there are many other marginalized groups who have become mobile in the new economies, we have chosen to look at ethnic groups who live at the margins of territories that are rapidly opening up to capitalist expansion and market economy. As indigenous peoples have strong traditions of mobility, their capabilities and choices may enable us to understand the complexities of their current mobility patterns and how they are gendered. Based on the study of mobile livelihoods, this book explores the transformations of indigenous peoples' livelihoods through mobility – whether forced or not – around economic restructuring and increasing market integration, to bring in the heterodox aspects of development and with particular focus on how these transformations are gendered. As most research on indigenous peoples to date has been in the form of ethnographic case studies, our intention has been to go beyond that and produce some knowledge that is transboundary and relevant for understanding contemporary social transformations in various parts of Asia.

'Indigenous people' has become a contested term. Some governments and scholars do not want to use the term indigenous people for various reasons: some find it divisive, some find it degrading, and some governments find that the use of the term leads them to accept the superior rights that such groups of people have to certain lands, as in the case of Laos. Indigenous peoples are also referred to as tribals, ethnic minorities, minority nationals, and *adivasis* in different parts of Asia. In this book, we use the general term indigenous peoples, although we use the local terms in the descriptions relating to the specific situation in India (tribals), China (ethnic minorities), and Laos (ethnic groups). We refer to all as indigenous peoples for the following reasons. First, the term indigenous is generally associated with a definite geographical area and with reference to peoples' distinctive culture that includes a whole spectrum of tribal and/or ethnic ways of life in terms of language, customs, traditions, and religious beliefs. Hence, there is a need to contextualize the mobility patterns of different places in Asia. Even though indigenous peoples have moved into their current places, we do not consider them as migrants.

Second, indigenous peoples currently suffer from dispossession from land or restriction of access to natural resources, which brings not only economic impoverishment to such people, but also results in their loss of identity and threatens their cultural survival (World Bank 2005). Since they are located in pristine forest areas with an abundance of natural and mineral resources, they have become prime losers in new economies and represent a serious development dilemma for many governments worldwide. However, and third, indigenous peoples are not a monolith and their level of deprivation and integration in mainstream society varies greatly within and among countries. In fact, it is only in the face of a collective or shared sense of identity that the term indigenous peoples has been internationally recognized. In the three countries in focus in our book there are *c*.700 Scheduled Tribe communities in India, 55 officially recognized minority ethnic groups in China, and 48 different ethnic groups registered in Laos (World Bank 2005). These communities have strong perceptions about their ethnic identities, which are not necessarily respected or recognized by the respective states. This happens even though the Universal Declaration of Human Rights, adopted by the United Nations in 1948, affirms the inherent dignity, equality, and inalienable rights of all members of human families.[1] Nevertheless, indigenous peoples are rapidly becoming marginalized in the new global economy and are subject to severe development pressures. Against this background, we find it relevant to present a cross-cultural representation of present social changes and how they lead to increasingly mobile lives and livelihoods.

Methodology

> Feminist methodology is distinctive to the extent that it is shaped by feminist theory, politics and ethics and grounded in women's experience. Feminists draw on different epistemologies, but take politics and epistemology to be inseparable.
>
> (Ramazanoglu 2002, 171)

The authors of this book use a gender lens in their analyses. According to Davids and van Driel (2007), a gender lens includes three dimensions of how one can explain and analyse observed realities: (1) the influence of institutional structures and practices; (2) how individuals deal with and negotiate these structures and practices; and (3) the influence of gender relations. Such an approach resonates with the views of other scholars regarding the need to explore people's lived realities in order to understand today's global transformations (Rigg 2007b; Harding 2008). With respect to the work presented here, by pursuing such an approach each author has been relatively free to emphasize how their male and female research participants have been influenced by these dimensions and identify what is contextually unique and relevant. The approach also gives room for analysing men's and women's subjectivity and agency and how they (the men and women) transform.

Our methodology is characterized by in situ triangulations (combinations of qualitative and quantitative methodology) and participatory approaches in multi-local sites. The authors position themselves as feminists or development professionals and hence actively relate to constructivism, thus for example, understanding gender as the social construction of male, female, and intersexual, and determining people's practices, subjectivities, and social relationships. Simultaneously, local places are also perceived as social constructions that are socially, economically, and politically unique in time and place (and therefore more than just physical locations). In the following, it will become apparent to readers that the individual authors differently understand global-local interactions and dynamics when studying mobility. This implies considering ways in which economic restructuring and neoliberalist policies are at play in constructions of social change and hence what ways gender has shaped and inflicted mobility. In this sense, having one project with multi-local subprojects may provide fresh and cumulative insights into the new complex and transnational realities of women and men in Asia.

Multiple methods have, as will become evident, been pursued in the subprojects, ranging from focus group discussions and in-depth interviews to surveys. Fieldwork was conducted in the respective countries during the period 2009–2012. Details of these methods are found in the individual chapters. The methodology of the umbrella has been to work jointly through annual participatory workshops to facilitate transparency and create processes of active participation, particularly among local research participants. This interaction has been to work towards the common goal, namely formulating an analytical approach for studying gendered mobilities, which could be applicable in several Asian countries.

In general, the umbrella methodology is characterized by three major approaches: *variety of experience and expectations*; *substantial interdisciplinary and multicultural research experience*; and *multi-sited research*. First, the project pays attention to the variety of experiences and expectations among culturally diverse Asian contexts, such as different peoples and local communities in China (Yunnan), India (Odisha and Karnataka), and Laos (Luang Namtha). By studying contemporary social phenomena it is possible to unravel what is socially and culturally unique and also identify what are contingent transformations. Hence, our concern is less about what can be generalized but instead about trying to come to terms with what can be differentiated as context-specific. For example, three participatory workshops were organized in the three countries, but very differently. The first workshop, held in India, took place in a local village with tribal leaders and NGO representatives, and was used to consult the representatives on the research design and how we should interact with them. The second workshop was held in China and took the form of a research meeting, but where the villagers we had met were invited to participate and comment on preliminary findings from the four villages. The third workshop, held in Laos, took the form of a village meeting with local authorities, where the researchers only played a role as observers while the results of our research were discussed. Hence, our participatory methodologies served different functions at different stages of the project and in different contexts for all the research participants and invited guests (researchers, members of authorities and organizations, and local villagers). We like to believe that this approach was quite innovative, and served the purpose of a mutually beneficial research process. Such collaborative research is now beginning to take place in other social science circles. However, most of our research work has emphasized the need for collaborations between researchers and research participants and how power differences need to be conflated (Jackson & Kassam 1998; Cornwall *et al.* 2008; Pratt 2012). What is new here is that researchers who are specialists in their contextual fields in some countries have been brought into unfamiliar territory and given a chance to compare and contrast. For example, we learned from participating in the Indian workshop about the differences in how indigenous people are framed by the state and how the indigenous people are utilizing this window of opportunity to advance their rights. In Laos, people avoid the state (and keep state representatives at arm's length) because there is no forum for constructive engagement. The China workshop was useful for learning of the arbitrary categorization of ethnic groups by the Chinese government. For example, the Akha are included under the Hani in China, whereas in Laos the Akha do not associate themselves at all with the Hani. This also led us to probe more into the subgroups under each official category of ethnic group.

A further benefit gained from the workshops was how they enabled us to understand to what extent mobile livelihoods have become 'a must' in rapidly changing rural communities and how complex they have become. Traditional forms of cultivation are stagnating in all three countries and affect women in similar ways as they turn to labour migration and trafficking. They also affect how elderly women play key roles in sustaining what remains in traditional agricultural practices. This participatory approach may be termed 'doing sciences from below', as Harding (2008) suggests, but without losing track of what takes place at national and global levels. As mobility transcends various boundaries and scales, we have seen the need to study not only how the local articulates with larger scales, but also how connections between places become important. This is a major rationale of our project and fits with Ong and Collier's quest for 'global assemblages' (cited in Falzon 2009, 5), which in our context are located in India, China, and Laos, but relate to national and global processes that are similar.

Second, the team of researchers behind this project bring substantial interdisciplinary and multicultural research experience. The team consists of both Asian and Nordic members, creating a productive tension in cross-cultural encounters. The collaboration itself raises problematic questions of insider and outsider, local and other, and develops insight into transnational cross-cultural encounters. The composition of the research team has thus questioned our positions as socially located researchers in two major ways: regarding how we have undertaken our research professionally, since research in itself is a process of exercising and yielding power; and regarding how we can better reflect women's and men's new 'lived realities' to inform our understanding of gender and development and to grasp the conflicting and overlapping inequalities and opportunities in a restructuring Asia.

One of the ways that we ensured accountability in our work was to develop the workshop format to allow for mutual interactions with various stakeholders of our research within the field and outside. Our primary concerns were those of power sharing by working in a more egalitarian way, and to disseminate results quickly and through information sharing at various stages of the project. Accordingly, all the project partners agreed on ethical guidelines of informed consent, anonymity, and to do no harm. We also broadly agreed on the umbrella methodology and phasing of the research.

Further, we increasingly became more reflexive about our work and collaboration. In 2011, at the Institute of British Geographers' Annual International Conference, the three female editors presented a paper on what friendship can do in research. Through collaboration on the project we were able to intensify our professional interactions. We found that being female scholars left us with challenges with respect to balancing our roles as professionals, as mothers, as wives, as daughters, and as members of a community. Such bonding recognized all these roles and provided emotional and professional support. We found that our academic ideas could not be seen in isolation from the individual emotional well-being of ourselves as researchers. Respect and mutual support strengthened our individual performances, built confidence, led to more visibility, and became a quality control from within (internal reflexivity). This process of bonding was strengthened because we ourselves had become mobile and had developed fieldwork as a practice of travelling. We found that globalization had facilitated increasing cross-border mobility and communication among us, and that our ideas travelled more effectively across boundaries in time and space. Through increasingly meeting with each other, negotiations and synergies were created that benefited our research theoretically and methodologically. We realized that academic ideas cannot be seen in isolation from the individual emotional well-being of researchers.[2] Hence, we found that our spatial routines became a route to knowledge – a 'travel practice' (Clifford cited in Falzon 2009, 9). Even though we did not do all the fieldwork in one place, we had much room for self-critical reflection. Even more importantly, our insights have gone beyond learning about 'our' individual case.

Third, our methodology may be classified as multi-sited research. Such research has become an inherent part of migration studies. Following Marcus' seminal work (cited in Falzon 2009), multi-sited ethnography is defined as when the objective is the study of social phenomena that cannot be accounted for by focusing on a single site (as in the case of moving subjects) or phenomenon (as in the case of migration or transnationalism). In such situations, fieldwork has to be conducted in multiple sites in order to follow the research subjects or to understand a phenomenon holistically. In the social sciences, this standpoint has created a critical debate, which we do not explore here. Suffice it to say, while previously the local was contextualized or compared, in ethnographic research what is normally perceived as local has now become integral to an embedded, multi-sited object of study. Falzon (2009, 1–2) states:

> The essence of multi-sited research is to follow people, connections, associations, and relationships across space (because they are substantially continuous but spatially non-continuous). Research design proceeds by a series of juxtapositions in which the global is collapsed into and made an integral part of parallel, related local situations, rather than something monolithic or external to them.

Hence, this becomes a technique of juxtaposition of data and we can unravel contingent socio-political realities. In our case, we have studied several local contexts in each country to understand how the knowledge produced this way has wider significance. Our sites were dispersed and each site exhibited different social transformations. We do not follow *the field* but we study *several fields*, which together gives us insights into the larger whole. However, the fields co-exist and social transformations may be contingent, but are at the same time situated and contextually unique. We can compare some phenomena, but not all. To us, therefore, fieldwork emerges as a process rather than a single event (Horst cited in Falzon 2009). However, without our collaboration, this process would not have been manageable. Our strength is that we knew very well what our colleagues were doing and nurtured relationships based on mutual trust, both professionally and personally.

Mobilities in China, India, and Laos

As mentioned above, all of the chapters in this book address mobility differently against the backdrop of Cresswell's (2011) four dimensions of mobility: mobility as social processes, mobility as livelihoods, mobility as voluntary to forced, and mobility as gendered. Rather than focusing on one or more of these dimensions, the chapters clearly show how the various dimensions are intertwined and reinforce each other with contextual variations.

Tanu Priya Uteng's chapter (Chapter 2), *Rethinking 'mobilities': exploring the linkages between development issues, marginalized groups, and gender*, critically explores the emerging discourse on mobility. She argues that the recognition of a new society framed by the convergence of various mobilities has been well established through understandings of 'sociology beyond societies' (Urry 2000) and the 'new mobilities paradigm' (Sheller & Urry 2006). The chapter reviews the theoretical evolvement of mobilities with particular emphasis on the sociological construct of the new mobilities paradigm. Cognizant of the fact that most literature on mobilities is based on scholarly work on the Global North, Uteng argues that the new mobilities paradigm is seamlessly percolated through all development-related issues emanating from various disciplines. She culls out the overlapping zones between development-related issues, marginalized groups, and gender. The other authors relate to these discourses in various ways and partly address some of the issues raised here in their empirical analyses. I further draw on Uteng's review in the concluding chapter.

The scale of mobility is unprecedented in China due to the present ongoing national and regional development programmes and policies. Based on fieldwork in four ethnic community villages in Yunnan Province, Yunxian Wang, Qun Zhao, Hongwen Zhang, Xiao'ou Ou, and Jing Wu's chapter (Chapter 3), *Mobile livelihoods of ethnic minorities in socio-economic transformation in China: the case of Yunnan Province*, documents a multifaceted and complex pattern of mobility in China. In the rapid economic expansion and infrastructure development, ethnic minorities in Yunnan are either attracted to or forced into mobility. The mobility patterns are closely linked to the macro-policy changes and economic restructuring, and therefore vary in their dynamism from one type to another and sometimes overlap. Mobility as capability and livelihood strategy or development coercion has very different implications and consequences for men and women. In Chapter 4, *Chinese peasants in transition*, Thomas Sætre Jakobsen investigates how the livelihoods of households in a rural area in Yunnan involve mobility and immobility throughout the life courses of family members. Further, he illuminates issues such as how transformation from a single sojourner within adolescence towards marriage and subsequently raising children affects mobility throughout the life course. This allows us to understand that transitions will transform the livelihood options and outcomes for households. Moreover, the research reveals that members of the new generation of rural migrant workers are more eager to leave their natal communities at a young age and experience city life than the former generation seems to have been. This gives an indication of the transformation taking place in rural parts of Yunnan.

The knowledge about mobilities among indigenous people in India is now rapidly becoming well-known. Recently Padel and Das (2010) documented how Indian tribals in Odisha have lost their habitats and traditional livelihoods due to mining and large-scale development projects, and their displacements have led to increasing poverty, marginalization, and ethnic violence. This has occurred in the name of development, economic growth, and even poverty reduction, despite pervasive documentation of a drastic fall in the living standards of the displaced. Smita Mishra Panda's chapter (Chapter 5), *Exploring mobile livelihoods among tribal communities in Odisha, India: gendered insights and outcomes*, examines the mobility of tribal populations in the state of Odisha which has come into the limelight in the past decade and half. There has been an increase in the mobility of tribal women and men, both within the state and outside, to seek employment opportunities. Much of the movement is predetermined. The chapter looks at the gender dimensions of mobility of tribal communities in selected regions of the state. In addition, it discusses the outcomes of mobility in terms of rights, its contribution to household income, ethnic identity, and social and economic vulnerability at familial and societal levels. The other Indian case is presented by Anitha Venkatesh and Veena N.'s chapter (Chapter 6), *Mobility patterns and gendered practices among Soliga people in Karnataka, India*, which is about the Soliga, a forest-dwelling indigenous people living in South India. For centuries, while kings, chieftains, colonizers, and politicians ruled the rest of India, the Soliga lived in the forests, where they found food, fuel, medicine, and livelihood. In 2004, the Indian government restricted their access to the forest by implementing a ban on the collection of NTFPs (non-timber forest products). As a result, the Soliga were forced to seek a livelihood outside the forest, which led to a significant change in the mobility patterns of the Soliga women and men. This research documents the profound impact that the change in mobility patterns has had on Soliga culture, society, and family life.

Laos is a small country, traditionally forest based, but today increasingly impacted by large-scale resettlement projects, agricultural modernization and Chinese interventions. Kyoko Kusakabe and Sengkham Vongphakdy's chapter (Chapter 7), *Gender vulnerabilities of resettlement and restricted mobility of ethnic groups in northern Laos*, analyses how the ethnic groups in northern Laos are forced to move their villages under the state policies to place such groups under surveillance. Under both state pressure and environmental and social pressure, people in Luang Namtha Province are constantly on the move. Their mobility, as well as their strategies to counter state pressure, has gendered impacts on their livelihoods.

In the *Concluding discussion* (Chapter 8), I briefly summarize the findings and identify some major lessons learnt about mobility in Asia.

Notes

1   The history and content of the UN's Universal Declaration of Human Rights is described at www.un.org/en/documents/udhr/ (accessed 10 December 2011)
2   R. Lund, K. Kusakabe, S.M. Panda & Y. Wang 'Being mothers, being scholars: Emotional linkages and professional support through friendship among researchers in a globalised world', paper presented at the Institute of British Geographers' Annual International Conference, London, in June 2011

References

Attanapola, C. & Lund, R. In press. Contested identities of indigenous people: Indigenization or integration of the Veddas in Sri Lanka. *Singapore Journal of Tropical Geography*.

Baviskar, A. 2004. *In the Belly of the River: Tribal Conflicts over Development in the Narmada Valley*. Oxford University Press, New Delhi.

Bryceson, D.F. 2002. The scramble in Africa: Reorienting rural livelihoods. *World Development* 30, 725–739.

Burman, B.K.R. 1989. Problems and prospects of tribal development in North-East India. *Economic and Political Weekly* 24:13, 693–697.

Cornwall, A., Harrison, E. & Whitehead, A. 2008. *Feminism in Development: Contradictions, Contestations and Challenges*. Zubaan, New Delhi.

Cresswell, T. 2006. *On the Move: Mobility in the Modern Western World*. Routledge, New York.

Cresswell, T. 2011. Mobilities. Agnew, J.A. & Livingstone, D.N. (eds) *The Sage Handbook of Geographical Knowledge*, 571–580. Sage, London.

Cresswell, T. & Uteng, T.P. 2008. Gendered mobilities: Towards an holistic understanding. Uteng, T.P. & Cresswell, T. (eds) *Gendered Mobilities*, 1–14. Ashgate, Aldershot.

Davids, T. & van Driel, F. (eds) 2007. *The Gender Question in Globalization*. Ashgate, Aldershot.

de Wet, C. (ed.) 2008. *Development-induced Displacement: Problems, Policies and People*. Berghahn Books, Oxford.

Duany, J. 2002. *Irse pa'fuera*: The mobile livelihoods of circular migrants between Puerto Rico and the United States. Sørensen, N.N. & Olwig, K.F. (eds) *Work and Migration: Life and Livelihoods in a Globalizing World*, 161–184. Routledge, London.

Dyer, C. 2010. Education and social (in)justice for mobile groups: Re-framing rights and educational inclusion for Indian pastoralist children. *Educational Review* 62, 301–313.

Falzon, M.-A. (ed.) 2009. *Multi-sited Ethnography: Theory, Praxis and Locality in Contemporary Research*. Ashgate, Farnham.

Haraway, D. 1988. Situated knowledges: The science question in feminism and the privilege of partial perspective. *Feminist Studies* 14, 575–599.

Harcourt, W. 2009. *Body Politics in Development: Critical Debates in Gender and Development*. Zed Press, London.

Harding, S. 2008. *Sciences from Below: Feminisms, Postcolonialities, and Modernities*. Duke University Press, Durham, NC.

Hyndman, J. 2002. *Managing Displac, NCement: Refugees and the Politics of Humanitarianism*. University of Minnesota Press, Minneapolis.

Jackson, E.T. & Kassam, Y. 1998. *Knowledge Shared: Participatory Evaluation in Development Cooperation*. Kumarian Press, West Hartford, CT/IDTC, Ottowa.

Jin Huashan. 2008. Domestic and international migration of Korean ethnic women in transformative China. Guocai, J. & Xingbo, C. (eds) *Discipline Building of Minority Women's Studies and the Development of Women*, 215–228. Yunnan Ethnicity Publishing House, Kunming.

King, R. 2011. Geography and migration studies: Retrospect and prospect. *Population, Space and Place* 18, 134–153. doi: 10.1002/psp.685.

Kronlid, D. 2008. Mobility as capability. Uteng, T.P. & Cresswell, T. (eds) *Gendered Mobilities*, 5–34. Ashgate, Aldershot.

Kumar, D.V. 2007. Tribal development: Issues, movements and interventions. *The Sociologist* 1, 101–124.

Kusakabe, K. (ed.) 2012. *Gender, Roads and Mobility in Asia*. Practical Action Publishing, London.

Lund, R. 1993. *Gender, Place and Social Change: Towards a Geography Sensitive to Gender, Place and Social Change* (Vol. 1); *Gender and Place: Examples from Two Case Studies* (Vol. 2). PhD thesis. Department of Geography, NTNU, Trondheim.

Lund, R. 2003. Representations of forced migration in conflicting spaces: Displacement of the Veddas in Sri Lanka. Shanmugaratnam, N., Lund, R. & Stølen, K.A. (eds) *In the Maze of Displacement*, 76–104. Norwegian Academic Place, Kristiansand.

Lund, R. In press. Mobility in marginalized spaces: Manoeuvring for survival among the Veddas in Sri Lanka. *Norsk Geografisk Tidsskrift–Norwegian Journal of Geography*.

Massey, D. 1994. *Space, Place and Gender*. University of Minnesota Press, Minneapolis.

Murphy, R. 2002. *How Migrant Labor is Changing Rural China*. Cambridge University Press, Cambridge.

Ohnmacht, T., Maksim, H. & Bergman, M.M. 2009. *Mobilities and Inequality*. Ashgate, Farnham.

Oo, Z.M. & Kusakabe, K. 2010. Motherhood and social network: Response strategies of internally displaced Karen women in Taungoo District. *Women's Studies International Forum* 33, 482–491.

Padel, F. & Das, S. 2010. *Out of This Earth: East India Adivasis and the Aluminium Cartel*. Orient BlackSwan, Delhi.

Panda, S.M. 1996. *Forest Degradation, Changing Livelihoods and Gender Relations: A Study of Two Tribal Communities in Orissa*. PhD thesis. Asian Institute of Technology, Bangkok.

Pratt, G. 2012. *Families Apart: Migrant Mothers and the Conflicts of Labor and Love*. University of Minnesota Press, Minneapolis.

Ramazanoglu, C. 2002. *Feminist Methodology: Challenges and Choices*. Sage, London.

Rigg, J. 2006. Land, farming, livelihoods, and poverty: Rethinking the links in the rural South. *World Development* 34, 180–202.

Rigg, J. 2007a. Moving lives: Migration and livelihoods in the Lao PDR. *Population, Space and Place* 13, 163–178.

Rigg, J. 2007b. *An Everyday Geography of the Global South*. Routledge, London.

Robeyns, I. 2003. Sen's capability approach and gender inequality: Selecting relevant capabilities. *Feminist Economics* 9, 61–92.

Sassen, S. 1998. *Globalization and Its Discontents*. The New Press, New York.

Scott, J. 2009. *The Art of Not Being Governed: An Anarchist History of Upland Southeast Asia*. Yale University Press, New Haven, CT.

Sheller, M. & Urry, J. 2006. The new mobilities paradigm. *Environment and Planning A* 38, 207–226.

Silvey, R. 2006. Geographies of gender and migration: Spatializing social difference. *International Migration Review* 46, 64–81.

Singh, K.S. 1982. Transformation of tribal society: Integration versus assimilation. *Economic and Political Weekly* 17:33, 1318–1325.

Sørensen, N.N. & Olwig, K.F. 2002. *Work and Migration: Life and Livelihoods in a Globalizing World*. Routledge, London.

Staheli, L.A., Kofman, E. & Peake, L. 2004. *Mapping Women, Making Politics: Feminist Perspectives on Political Geography*. Routledge, London.

Stepputat, F. & Sørensen, N.N. 1999. Negotiating movement. Sørensen, N.N. (ed.) *Narrating Mobility, Boundaries and Belonging.* Working Paper No. 99.7. Centre for Development Research, Copenhagen.

Stepputat, F. & Sørensen, N.N. 2001. The rise and fall of the displaced people in the central Peruvian Andes. *Development and Change* 32, 762–792.

Tauli-Corpuz, V. 1995. Three years after Rio: An indigenous assessment. Buchi, S., Erni, C., Jurt, L. & Ruegg, C. (eds) *Indigenous Peoples, Environment and Development: Proceedings of the Conference, Zurich, May 15–18, 1995*, 39–50. IWGIA (International Work Group for Indigenous Affairs), Copenhagen.

Urry, J. 2000. *Sociology Beyond Societies: Mobilities for the Twenty-first Century.* Routledge, London.

Uteng, T.P. 2006. Mobility: Discourses from the non-Western immigrant groups in Norway. *Mobilities* 1, 435–462.

Vandergeest, P., Idahosa, P. & Bose, P.S. (eds) 2007. *Development's Displacement: Ecologies, Economies, and Cultures at Risk.* University of British Columbia Press, Vancouver.

World Bank. 2005. *Indigenous Peoples.* Operation Manual 4.10. http://web.worldbank.org/WBSITE/EXTERNAL/PROJECTS/EXTPOLICIES/EXTOPMANUAL/0,,contentMDK:20553653~menuPK:4564187~pagePK:64709096~piPK:64709108~theSitePK:502184~isCURL:Y,00.html (accessed 21 September 2010).

Xu, J. 2006. The political, social, and ecological transformation of a landscape: The case of rubber in Xishuangbanna, China. *Mountain Research and Development* 26, 254–262.

Xu, J. & Salas, M. 2003. Moving the periphery to the centre: Indigenous people, culture and knowledge in changing Yunnan. Kaoa-sard, M. & Dore, J. (eds) *Social Challenges for the Mekong Region*, 125–148. White Lotus, Bangkok.

2 Rethinking 'mobilities'

Exploring the linkages between development issues, marginalized groups, and gender

Tanu Priya Uteng

Introduction

Gender-based variations of mobilities are an established phenomenon in both developed and developing parts of the world. However, the depth of understanding this phenomenon varies significantly. Gendered mobilities have often been studied without giving due attention to the causes and consequences of differing mobilities. The case of operationalizing gender within marginalized groups can also be posited as the same, and although a significant bank of knowledge exists on marginalized groups and related mobilities per se, very little has been explored on the changing hierarchies of gender in marginalized groups in the face of 'new' mobilities.

A recap of the development interventions undertaken in developing countries to impact gender equality, women's empowerment, and poverty reduction would highlight their limited success. Despite extensive discourse and resources that have focused on women as key actors for development, their situation has not changed considerably (Cunha 2006). Regardless of using gender as a label, most policies and programmes have failed to truly incorporate gendered issues, primarily due to lack of understanding of the contextual realities and dilution in the process of transforming goals to implementable projects. Very often, this has resulted in development programmes being run as patch-in solutions rather than as cohesive, coordinated attacks on the root issues affecting gender empowerment/ disempowerment. This is precisely the case in the development sector. Development-related projects are persuasive in their technical details but ignorant of the nexus between forced mobility and missed opportunities, context-based planning versus copying standards from the West, and the linkages between gender, mobilities, and empowerment/disempowerment.

Before embarking on the issue of the gendered mobilities in developing societies, it is equally important to highlight another big divide, that of the urban–rural dichotomy. The context at these two levels is significantly different and therefore any generalizations would be prone to great fallacy. Apart from the social, economic, political, production-related, and other tangible elements of the divide, the issue of culture vis-à-vis the positioning of women in the psyche of accessing 'outer space', 'kinds of activities', and legitimization of such access makes a deep dent on the urban–rural divide. The necessity for a stratified understanding is further augmented by the fact that today more than half of the world's population is living in urban areas, according to the *State of World Population 2007* report from the United Nations (United Nations Population Fund 2007). The urban share is likely to rise from 75 per cent to 81 per cent in more developed countries between 2007 and 2030, and from 44 per cent to 56 per cent in less developed countries (United Nations Population Fund 2007). Forecasts indicate that urbanization will occur most rapidly in Africa and Asia, doubling their urban share between 2000 and 2030. Apart from these factors, 'globalization' in the developing world is, in a nutshell, about braving the spillovers of various development activities (e.g. mining and road building), a concomitant shift in livelihood strategies, and accessing other formats of livelihood opportunities, which is evident in the huge rural–urban migrations currently taking place.

A vital question emerging out of the trends is: How are the forces of global-ization, urbanization, changing livelihood strategies, and mobilities intersecting? Further, due to the rise and intensity of disaster and conflict situations and the precarious position of women in such situations, it is important that mobility needs assessments are incorporated as vital elements of post-disaster/conflict rehabilitation processes.

The aim of this chapter[1] is twofold. It builds on highlighting the issues that have significant repercussions for gendered movements and then further explores how mobilities are either reinforcing gender norms in the frame of representation versus reality and of tradition versus modernity, or being produced as an effect of these dialectics. The following sections first discuss 'mobilities' and later deal with other equally vital trends affecting mobilities, including globalization, the existence of the informal sector, disaster and conflict situations, displacement, and issues related to governance.

Mobilities

The concept of mobilities brings forth the asymmetries of power and opportunities that might elude a one-sided focus, and therefore this book builds on the theme of 'mobilities', of which the dimension of 'development and redefining of gender' is a subset. The theme permeating all chapters in this book draws its essence from Cresswell's (2010) definition that movement itself (or lack thereof) does not possess any inherent meaning, but needs to be understood and elucidated as a socially contextualized phenomenon through both material and discursive representations and practices.

Discourses on the concept of mobility have traditionally described mobility as physical movement (operating in the domains of geography, urban planning, and transport) on the one hand and a change in social status on the other (a sociological construct). However, with growing acceptance of the perforations in different thematic areas, there has been a merging of the physical and social percepts on mobilities. This has involved addressing space, place, and locality as a cultural and social category (Gregory & Urry 1985; Featherstone 1990; Lash & Urry 1994; Latour 1999; Urry 2000; Bonβ & Kesselring 2001; 2004). These understandings have metamorphosed in the introduction of the 'new mobilities paradigm' (Hannam *et al.* 2006; Sheller & Urry 2006; Cresswell 2011a; 2011b), which posits that *movement, representation,* and *practice* are embedded in uneven socio-political relations (Cresswell 2006; 2010; Cresswell & Merriman 2011). While outlining this paradigm, Urry (2004) emphasizes the need to separate out rather carefully the nature of the five highly interdependent 'mobilities' that form and reform social life, bearing in mind the massive inequalities in structured access to each of the following:

1   Corporeal travel of people for work, leisure, family life, pleasure, migration, and escape
2   Physical movement of *objects* delivered to producers, consumers, and retailers
3   Imaginative travel elsewhere through images of places and people shown on television
4   Virtual travel, often in real time on the Internet, transcending geographical and social distance
5   Communicative travel through person-to-person messages via letters, telephone, fax, and mobile phone.

This composite set highlights that mobilities need to be studied, interpreted, and theorized in embodied and contextualized experiences of movement (e.g. Löfgren 2008), through discursive representations (Blomley 1994; Cresswell 1999; Mountz 2011), and through discerning the relationships between mobilities, inequality, and governmentality (Ohnmacht *et al.* 2009). On a similar note, Langan (2001, 459) describes the theme of mobility as a desired end, an end that is not only a function of personal achievement but also a product of several constituent and affecting parameters:

> Rousseau long ago declared in *The Social Contract* that the cripple who wants to run and the able-bodied man who doesn't will both remain where they are. But by focusing on internal resources and intentions, Rousseau forgot to mention all those whose mobility is affected by external constraints. To consider those constraints is to notice how the built environment – social practices and material infrastructures – can create mobility-disabilities that diminish the difference between the 'cripple' and the ambulatory person who may well wish to move.

Concurring with the importance of context in the production of mobility, Cresswell (2001) espouses mobility as a movement that is socially produced, is variable across space and time, and has visible effects on people, places, and things, and the relationships between them. Jones (1987) puts forth the following three components to express mobility: *individual action, potential,* and *freedom of action.* In short, the components are interpreted as:

•   *Individual action* in the form of observed movement or travel
•   *Potential action* in terms of journeys that people would like to make, but are unable to because of limitations in the transport system, and/or their own commitments restricting them in time and space, or financial restraints

- *Freedom of action* that may never be manifested in action, but gives individuals options from which to select and the knowledge that they *could* do something.

With regard to gendered movement, individual action has been studied in detail but much remains to be studied in the realm of potential action and freedom of action. Knie (1997) introduces a related understanding of the concept, and emphasizes that mobility is about the *construction of possibilities for movement* rather than actual movement. Sørensen (1999) notes that analysis of mobility is primarily about *the performance, real as well as symbolic,* of the provision of physical movement in society. In the following points, Kaufmann (2002) postulates three determining factors that shape the mobility levels and patterns of individuals:

- *Access* to mobility-scapes (representing transport and communication infrastructure as potential opportunities)
- *Competence*, referring to the skills and abilities necessary to use accessible mobility-scapes
- *Appropriation*, involving all behavioural components, such as the need and willingness to make use of '-scapes', in order to become mobile.

Kaufmann also espouses the idea of mobility as a *restricted good* where opportunities emerge as a function of market relations. Nijkamp *et al.* (1990) argue that an analysis of mobility and the underlying causes for its demand should be undertaken on a broad scale in the context of the following four themes:

1 *Socio-economic context* of analysis, which focuses attention on the influences of exogenous socio-economic conditions upon spatial patterns of interaction
2 *Technological context* of analysis, which deals with the implications of changes in the technological environment on the spatial behaviour of individuals or groups in society
3 *Behavioural analysis*, which focuses attention on motives, constraints, and uncertainties facing individuals, households, and groups when making decisions regarding transport, communication, and mobility
4 *Policy analysis*, which concerns the evaluation of actions, usually the application of policy instruments or measures of decision-making agencies regarding transport.

Sørensen (1999) builds on the theme of 'mobility regimes' in order to highlight the historical and cultural basis of mobility. A mobility regime results from a number of factors, some of which consist of the physical shaping of cities and landscapes; the available transport and communication systems; the relationship between mobility and economic, social, and cultural activities; and the meaning attributed to mobility. The coupling of social and spatial mobilities, its division into various subsets, and access to the subsets thus effectively create new terrains of deprivation, leading to disadvantaged positions, which are often most blatantly expressed in labour markets (Uteng 2006; 2009; Uteng & Cresswell 2008).

These reflections on theoretical insights suggest that mobility cannot be analysed in a purely instrumental, objectivist mode and that it remains a subjective dimension differing with the distribution pattern of the constituent resources. Differential accessibility to such resources maps out different mobility regimes that are distinguishable at the levels of people, places, and processes. *Mobility* thus emerges as an enabling characteristic, a sought-after rather than given good or commodity. Hence, the understanding of mobility has entered the wider realm of discussions of identity formation, freedom, and rights.

However, mobilities also need to be understood through an equally concentrated approach to understanding 'immobilities'. The mobilities approach facilitates this by stressing the need to understand the relationship between fixity and movement. Unpacking the relationships between society, mobilities, and politics, or rather understanding the socio-political dimension of mobility, can also aid in highlighting the nexus between mobility and immobility. It will further assist in determining how such connections are either taken into account when making development decisions or, in the absence of such positive interventions, which alternate modes are affected populaces adopting to chart out their new livelihoods and social set-ups. The gendered effects of such developments are reflected in the findings of research conducted by mobilities scholars and feminist geographers, enabling us to understand how moving between borders affects the production, effacement, or reaffirmation of social differentiation (Hyndman 1997; Dowler & Sharp 2001; Amoore 2006; Hyndman & Mountz 2006; Mountz 2011).

Mobilities have also been linked to the issue of governance (Mountz 2011) and in turn necessitate a consideration of the theme arising as a result of state policies and the associated outcomes. Several cases in this book highlight how mobilities occurring due to facilitations made by state institutions, such as the entry of multinational companies in indigenous areas for the purpose of mining, play crucial roles in forcing multiple levels of mobilities in the search for alternative livelihoods, changing gendered roles and norms, changing (or shifting) images of women who move out to seek new livelihoods, and how these multiple sites of mobilities production intersect to carve geographies of inclusion and exclusion.

Thus, the concept of mobilities has permeated areas of governance, politics, economics, history, social set-up, popular culture, livelihoods, access, travel behaviour, and movement in our understanding of the creation of identities, empowerment, and conversions into social norms, and the circulation of this composite set through time and space. The following subsections outline the social and gendered contents of mobilities for highlighting mobilities' non-negotiable position when discussing 'gender and development'.

The social content of mobility

It is widely assumed that 'the convergent effects of globalization and cross-border organizational learning have rapidly outpaced the divergent effects of cultures, national institutions and social systems' (Yeung 1998, 292). Products of unrestricted mobility and the markers of postmodern times, *time-space compression* and *social fluidification*, have become accepted as given characteristics, yet both concepts remain grossly under-examined in terms of their social distribution. Kaufmann (2002, 14), in an analysis of social fluidification, notes:

> the crux of the debate over social fluidification is whether or not the compression of time-space goes hand in hand with a decrease in certain social constraints that discourage action. It is thus a question of analysing *who has access* to which relevant technology and the *degree of freedom* afforded by the usage of this technology.

The idea of fluidification supposes that social and territorial structures take a back seat to a context that is capable of accommodating the most diverse aspirations (Kaufmann 2002). However, is that the truth? Massey, in a critique of David Harvey's (1989) all-encompassing notion of time-space compression, remarks that

> different social groups have distinct relationships to this anyway-differentiated mobility; some are more in charge of it than others; some initiate flows and movement, others don't; some are more on the receiving end of it than others; some are effectively imprisoned by it.
>
> (Massey 1993, 61)

Cresswell (2001, 25) succinctly captures this point of view, as is evident from the following quote:

> The question of how mobilities get produced – both materially and in terms of 'ideas' of mobility – means asking: Who moves? How do they move? How do particular forms of mobility become meaningful? What other movements are enabled or constrained in the process? Who benefits from this movement? Questions such as these should get us beyond either an ignorance of mobility on the one hand or sweeping generalizations on the other.

In the milieu of dissecting mobility, past research has demonstrated that access to mobility entails processes that are essentially highly differentiated along the lines of structural differences in society, with respect to, for example, gender, class, race, and caste. A similar line of research under the aegis of the Social Exclusion Unit in the UK is currently promoted under the theme of 'transport and social exclusion'. Certain key points can be gleaned from this research agenda to widen the discussion on differentiated mobilities, with reference to issues such as categorization of excluded groups, time-space interplay and its differential structure, and place-/ social-category-/person-based measures. For example (expanding on the ideas proposed by Mountz 2011), how does the state actively participate in charting out geographies of exclusion and how can researchers employ the literature on mobilities to examine immobilities critically? According to Mountz (2011, 320),

'One answer is to bring into relief a number of time–space trajectories at once: not only those of migrants, but of mobile states whose authorities, policies, practices, and enforcement infrastructure also migrate.' This position can be further strengthened by analysing the dialectic and operationalization of moorings and mobilities (cf. Urry 2003, who expands on this theme).

The gendered content of mobility

The interaction between spatial mobility for negotiating daily lives and other forms of mobility (e.g. social, economic, and political), has not been substantially explored in the literature. Specifically, a focus on the operationalization of gender norms and consequently gendered mobility permits an inquiry on the theme of development, democracy, equity, and their distribution through the resource of mobility offered by different societies. To expand on this understanding, it becomes essential also to evaluate the differential claims on genders due to *cultural beliefs and norms* being an equally important factor or, in some cases, the most important factor dictating mobility and how these beliefs and norms are changing. Are these changes supportive or detrimental to the cause of gender development and empowerment? Which issues can be corrected through policy interventions to aid positive changes?

Further, such an inquiry will also lead to a better formulation of space-making attributes. Tracing the shifting and contested meanings of 'good girls', 'obedient daughters', 'virtuous women', and 'respectable places' in the developing world brings into focus the ways in which the cultural struggles over gender norms influence the causes and consequences of mobility (Silvey 2000, 145).[2]

'Space, whether sacred or profane, is not produced in vacuum, but rather through a web of cross-cutting power relations that are themselves forged at multiple scales from the local to the global' (Massey cited in Secor 2002, 7). In order to build up a mobility profile of the developing world, the research arena provides a good foundation to enumerate the gender differences and build a case for redesigning methods, analyses, and policies.

Understanding the issues that impact gendered mobilities in the developing countries

As discussed above, *gender* operates in myriad different ways in developing countries and rather than being a given state of being, it is in constant formation. Certain key discernible points with reference to operationalizing gender in the developing world are the existence of huge disparity between the 'urban, educated, middle-class' versus 'urban, uneducated, low-income' women; access to activities/ urban spaces and socially sanctioned movements in 'rural and semi-urban areas' versus 'cities and metropolises'; and the existence of slums and deep permeation of religious beliefs in society placing tangible boundaries to women's participation in the outside world. Importantly, the developing world is characterized by a high demand for and low availability of accessible mobility regimes for women.

Despite this, these elements of differentiation between the genders do not form part of mainstream government-run development planning policies and programmes, for example, procuring loans and for regularization of basic services. Further, gender division of labour in urban areas is different to that in rural areas. Keeping these aspects in mind, the key features governing gendered mobilities in the developing world are presented in the following sections.

Social and cultural norms

Understanding gendered mobility outside the patriarchal system and the social-cultural norms dictating the visible movement of women is tantamount to segregating the body and the mind. The concept of gender is constructed through performative reiterations and assertions, which historically, geographically, culturally, and politically have always been and will continue to be in a state of flux. This dynamicity is central to the current analysis of how mobility enables/disables/modifies exclusionary processes affecting women in particular. Even in the active, technological world of today, opposition of relative flow and fixity of women is widely practised in many non-Western cultures, thereby affecting women's access to central services such as education, work, and health, as well as to the intangible entitlements of participation and information. Any modification to the element of access should be treated with due respect to persuasive social norms, otherwise the attempts will be in vain.

The reasons for evaluating mobilities in the light of pervasive social and cultural norms are first that such an approach will allow a cohesive inquiry into the themes of development, democracy, and equity, and their distribution through mobility as a resource offered by society. It will aid in evaluating the differential claims on genders due to *cultural beliefs and norms* since they are in some cases the most important factor dictating mobilities.

Second, such an inquiry would also aid a better formulation of space-making attributes. For example, Amir-Ebrahimi (2006) quotes the case of post-revolution Iran to emphasize how frequent presence in different public spaces gave women a new consciousness about themselves and their rights as individuals and citizens in society. Through his focus on the methods employed by Iranian women to conquer enclosed public spaces, Amir-Ebrahimi was able to elucidate the direct linkages between entering public spheres as social actors and gaining power, albeit in silence, in different socio-political and cultural fields.

Third, the inquiry would facilitate a grasp of 'the scale of the problem' owing to cultural traditions that are difficult to measure. For example, the extreme yet socially acceptable and widely practised 'honour killings' in many parts of the developing world elude any official records in the majority of cases. Bringing basic human rights to the segment of female population subjected to such norms is not an easy task. It is possible only through consistent efforts taken in all development-related sectors by addressing development in a gradual, deliberate, and percolative manner. However, by incorporating culturally appropriate interventions, development sectors can make a direct impact on the access and visibility afforded to women, without making any direct attack on developing countries' social norms. This requires a conscious insertion of the acceptable 'modes', 'spaces', and 'timings' of women's movements and designing policies and programmes with these specifics in mind. The analogy of the development sectors is used here to evoke all the branches of governance – prima facie the state, development organizations and institutions such as the World Bank, advocacy groups, networks, non-governmental organizations (NGOs), and community-based organizations (CBOs).

Mobility has always been linked with progress, and how the subtleties of various forms of mobility imprint on the psyche of a society is an important point of entry into making any meaningful and long-lasting changes in the behaviour of their populations in general, and women in particular. The cases presented in this book run counter to simplistic assertions that insurmountable cultural biases prevent women in developing countries from gaining access to meaningful roles. It is evident that rather than being an issue of power struggles within the confines of the household, women's access to different roles and spaces are primarily dictated by local cultures and general social practices.

Globalization

The business of globalized services has settled on the international trade scenario and is likely to remain there for a long time to come. In order to compete in a deregularized, neoliberal, open-market, world trade set-up, companies need to internalize (on a global scale) a range of specialized competencies (Perera 2007). A significant and consistent outcome of globalization has been the *feminization of labour*, a sudden and withstanding change affecting the social, cultural, economic, and political fabric of developing societies (Luke & Munshi 2011). Given gender as the variable to be analysed, Held *et al.*'s (1999, 16) definition of globalization –

> a process (or a set of processes) which embodies a transformation in the spatial organization of social relations and transactions – assessed in terms of their extensity, intensity, velocity and input – generating transcontinental or interregional flows and networks of activity, interaction and the exercise of power

– highlights the following four elements to be further analysed with reference to the gendering aspect of globalization:

- The extent of transformation
- The intensity of transformation
- The velocity of transformation
- The inputs furling the above-mentioned transformations.

Mobilities (comprising the dimensions of flows and networks of activity) thus revolve around the core theme of transformations in socio-spatial organizations (see the discussion on 'transmigrants' in Frändberg & Vilhelmson 2003).

Both low-income and middle-class Asian women are subject to the effect of rapid globalization and their lives are dramatically being altered by this phenomenon. However, rather than being a win-win situation, globalization has brought new gendered issues to the forefront. For example, the *positive* mobility of skilled women is taking place at the cost of the immobility of the gendered service class in the form of domestic workers, who are forced to adopt mobile livelihoods and shift to urban areas due to changes made in their original habitat by interventions such as those made by mining industries (Friedmann & Wolff 1982; Sassen 1999; 2001). Thus, as several cases in this book highlight, mobilities in the form of forced migration, and immobilities in the form of being situated in an alien context with either partial or no knowledge of the context can be experienced simultaneously by a group and it would be erroneous to analyse for the very same group the mobilities element or the immobilities element of isolation. Gill *et al.* (2011) reiterates this point by highlighting Germann Molz & Gibson's (2007) comment that the concepts of migration, mobility, and hospitality are assumed to exist as a cohesive group but are rarely brought together in a sustained way in academic literature. The fluid notion of hospitality varies according to the cultural context and social climate in which it circulates, with profound consequences for migrants in terms of the bundles of rights and responsibilities that they are entitled to if they move to different places (Ruhs & Chang 2004). Understanding the spurts of globalization through its associated mobilities and immobilities will highlight the ways in which mobility, uncertainty, risk, and fear interact (Day & White 2001; De Genova 2002; Cwerner 2004; Peutz 2006; Gill *et al.* 2011).

When referring to development, the trend is to quantify in terms of, for example, GNP (gross national product), poverty reduction, reducing adult illiteracy, and reducing infant mortality rate. However, the linkages between 'mobilities' and these assessed factors are still not undertaken seriously. This issue becomes magnified in the light of the processes initiated by 'globalization'. Therefore, in order to allow the benefits of globalization to permeate the different strata of developing societies, it is necessary to analyse the mobilities context, history, and culture of the country in question. Differentiated mobility seems to affect women at a much deeper level than men, even in the case of globalization's 'emancipatory' effects.

Mobility as a 'quantifiable' factor of progress

International commitments such as the Beijing Platform for Action (1995) and the Copenhagen Programme of Action (1995) addressed some of the problems arising out of globalization, but given that globalization's effects are vast and varied, it is not surprising that many of these effects are left unexamined. Solutions proposed for women in such documents are largely microeconomic, with particular focus on enabling poor women to obtain access to credit, presumably to begin small businesses. In January 2000, a total of 116 UN members had submitted national action plans to fulfil government commitments to the Beijing Platform for Action, with the majority of the action plans focusing on education and training, women in power and decision-making, women and health, and violence against women. Few plans have established comprehensive, time-bound targets for monitoring such progress, and most have not referred to sources of financing for the actions agreed. Sandrasagra (2000) quotes Social Watch, an NGO watchdog system aimed at monitoring the commitments made by governments at the World Summit for Social Development in Copenhagen and the Beijing World Conference on Women, as stating:

> Indicators show that 13 countries – of which Albania, Burundi, Iraq, Liberia, Myanmar, Nigeria, Somalia and Tanzania are a few – are in the same shape or worse off today than they were in 1990, and for almost 40 countries the data is insufficient to say anything, which probably reflects an even worse situation for women.

The issue of mobility is largely missing from discussions of these action plans.

In capturing the gendered employment effects of globalization, Seguino and Grown (2006) contend that, theoretically, job access for women can improve their level of well-being and that of the children they care for, if it provides more income and if women can find a way to juggle their care responsibilities. Are there measurable effects that show up in measures of well-being or household bargaining power? We need to answer this question in order to determine whether economic and trade liberalization provide the conditions for women to achieve equitable standards of living and power with men over time, even if, in the short term, women's incorporation into labour forces is under unfavourable conditions. Further, what role does mobility play in accessing these 'new' employment opportunities? This area still remains grossly unexplored.

There are still no clearly established trends indicating that access to paid employment in developing countries has resulted in sufficient leverage to alter social norms that devalue women. This leads to the question of whether the conditions under which women are incorporated into the paid economy are adequate to transform conditions of gender inequality into gender equity. Some studies find that as women's access to outside income increases, they are better able to renegotiate the distribution of resources within their household to the benefit of themselves and their children. However, the source and stability of such income appears to play a role in influencing women's bargaining power. For example, Kabeer's (2000) study of Bangladeshi garment workers found that women employed as home workers with insecure and intermittent earnings were less able to renegotiate their position in patriarchal households than women with higher and more stable income. Seguino (2002) considers these questions for Asian economies where rapid growth was fuelled by low-cost female labour in a period of otherwise global economic stagnation.

The *World Development Report 2012* (World Bank 2012), too, with its novel move of uplifting the theme of *gender equality and development*, has come under critical scrutiny for its partial examination of the factors affecting empowerment of women. Razavi (2011, 4) voices similar concerns when she reiterates that 'despite the welcome attention to labour markets, employment issues, and persistent gender-based segregation . . . the analysis of these critical and timely issues falls short in several important respects'. Razavi mentions that beyond the obligatory mention of *gender wage gaps* and *informality*, the *World Development Report 2012* fails to genuinely engage with these issues and examine the structural and discriminatory forces that could provide a meta-analysis to the existing gaps between the genders.

A focused study on the role of mobilities, especially in the lives of women operating at the lowest strata of production and the interlinkages of mobilities with higher and stable earnings and employment opportunities, will allow development policies to be based on a quantified study of a structural and hitherto discriminatory force. This approach can be used to distinguish if, and under what conditions, 'mobilities' are beneficial and what changes are required to better the chances of women's employment and access to higher and stable earnings. This issue is also closely tied with the existence of the informal sector in developing countries, which is examined further in the next section.

Some relevant governance issues

Governance and its impact on mobilities and the resultant position women occupy in a given society at a given point in time is a further vital area for examination. Given that governance is a very broad thematic area and full justice to the topic is rendered impossible as a subsection of a chapter, I have focused on only the following two vital elements of governance that bear direct and significant impacts on the mobilities and the consequential bargaining power of women in the lowest strata of developing societies:

- Formal-informal interplay in the new globalized economies
- Conflict situations and displacement.

Formal-informal interplay in the new globalized economies

The prevalence of employment in the informal sector[3] is noteworthy in developing countries, and accounts for 50–75 per cent of non-agricultural employment: specifically, 48 per cent in northern Africa; 51 per cent in Latin America; 65 per cent in Asia; and 72 per cent in sub-Saharan Africa (Carr & Chen 2004). It is further reported that if South Africa is excluded, the area of informal employment in non-agricultural employment rises to 78 per cent in sub-Saharan Africa, and if comparable data were available for other countries in southern Asia, including India, the regional average would probably be much higher (Carr & Chen 2004). Clearly, the informal sector economy comes with a big set of risks and agendas, including insecurity of tenure, no pension or other kinds of benefits, payments below the stipulated minimum wages, all of which make it hard for the working poor to carve their way out of poverty. In an economic sense, it would be correct to posit that informal sector workers are in many ways a marginalized group, deprived of, for example, access to credit, pension schemes, stable earnings, and access to welfare grants. Given that women are more exposed to such risks than men, it behoves the research and policy-making community to unearth different ways in which these problems can be mitigated. Constrained mobility, especially in the case of women, can reduce women's economic opportunities by limiting, for example, their choice of work location, access to finished goods and markets, access to information relevant to their work, and the freedom to combine jobs in the informal sector. At the same time, by evoking 'forced mobilities', caution needs to be exercised when sieving through movements that might be best described as negative and harmful, such as young girls falling into the trap of human trafficking. Such varying nuances need to be understood in order to avoid the fallacy of designating movement as 'positive' and fixity as 'negative'.

This point is illustrated through elaboration of the case of microcredit schemes. Following the lead from the World Bank, during the 1970s it was recognized that one of the main reasons why the poor in developing countries failed to benefit from development (the 'trickle-down' problem) was that they lacked access to resources and opportunities, thus leading to the formulation of the 'target group' oriented development strategy. The strategy emphasizes the promotion of specific target groups that have failed to benefit from development, by implementing *direct* allocation of resources and channelling opportunities. However, judged by the current levels of poverty in many of the countries, the new approach appears to have had only a limited success after more than two decades (i.e. since the 1990s). As Sethuraman (1998) notes, although the presence of women in the informal sector in developing countries is markedly high, current strategies towards women in the informal sector do not seem to recognize the existence of market imperfections in developing countries, especially in the area of credit, and accordingly they have not focused on easing women's access to credit. There is also growing recognition that credit and other markets in developing countries are not user-friendly or accessible to the poor and illiterate, particularly to women. As a proactive response to this state of affairs, the trend has been to address the constraints that the informal sector in general and women in particular have faced through the advocacy of microcredit schemes. Consequently, multiple microenterprise credit programmes have sprung up in recent years, which have endeavoured to develop 'informal' financial mechanisms to reach women in a friendlier environment. However, as Omorodion (2007) contends, although much research has been done on the effectiveness of microcredit programmes in improving the economic situation of women (Ahmed *et al.* 2001; Amin *et al.* 2001; Perry 2002; Pitt *et al.* 2003; Izugbara 2004), the findings have been inconclusive. For example, Pitt *et al.* (2003) found that women's participation in microcredit programmes increased their empowerment. However, in a separate study, Perry's (2002) analysis shows that although capital was useful to the participants, they were unable to make repayments as they were forced and cajoled by their spouses to hand over money meant for repayment to reinvest in their own economic activities, thus questioning the assumption that empowerment is simply a matter of handing over credit.

Conflict situations and displacement

Conflict situations and the associated displacements present unique opportunities to analyse the various destabilizing processes. There are three discernible aspects: first, conflict situations provide an opportunity to make a dent in the pre-determined gendered roles in a society at a given point in time; second, they provide an apt platform to analyse a state's mobility with reference to post-conflict rehabilitation; and third, they allow us to sieve through a state's response to creating dialectics of mobilities and immobilities.

It is often noted that humanitarian and rehabilitation programmes continue to favour men (Trujillo 2000). Even in the field of research, the vast majority of the available literature on 'mobilities' is found within the development discourse and the link with conflicts/emergencies/displacement is either absent or perfunctorily mentioned (an exception being the special issue of the journal *Mobilities*, Vol. 6, Part 3, published in 2011). Despite a consistent focus on equal access and full participation of women by international agencies, there remains a gap in the translation of this focus. This could be simply due to lack of understanding of the importance of mobility per se. In order to do justice to the rehabilitation process in the aftermath of conflicts or displacement, one needs to study the relationship between mobilities, immobilities, and the developmental issues. Further, the relationship needs to be guided at the levels of respective genders and the scale of conflicts.[4] A brief review of the rehabilitation processes highlights the lack of such insight. For example, although tremendous pressure is exerted in the post-disaster reconstruction stage to showcase the progress being made, the key challenge lies in reconstructing with change, avoiding mechanisms for constructing new vulnerabilities or exacerbating those that already exist. In this respect, the International Forum for Rural Transport and Development (IFRTD 2005, 1–2) states that:

> prioritising the rehabilitation of rural road networks to enable small farmers to access markets could potentially discourage post-disaster migration to vulnerable rural areas and urban slums. By continuing to listen to the needs of the poor in the post-disaster context, the development sector has the potential to avoid creating new societies with even greater vulnerability.

In essence, post-conflict rehabilitation is prima facie much wider in scope than a matter of building infrastructure alone. Lahai (2010, 5) touches upon the depth of this issue in an examination of the nature of women's participation in ongoing and recently concluded armed conflicts in 15 countries in Africa:

> It is evident in the literature that the end of conflicts, or the signing of peace accords, does not represent the end of violence against women. Countries in the data set of 'recently-ended' civil wars share this feature of increasing levels of post-war gender-based violence. In Sierra Leone, for example, after the war the dashing down of the optimism of former male combatants to reclaim their

lost status in society has resulted in more cases of domestic violence. In Southern Sudan, it has been pointed out that the violence that existed in pre-war years – such as arranged marriages, battering of women, and wife inheritance – is closely related to the prevailing culture of violence that escalated during the war, with multiple cases of rape of women . . . Right across the African continent, Bop . . . contends that the loss of identity, bodily integrity, the distortion of agency, economic losses, loss of leadership, losses in education and health, amid the increase in domestic responsibilities define the precarious condition of women's post war lives – hence the validation of Cockburn's . . . argument that violence against women is a gendered continuum.

However, post-conflict situations offer women opportunities to change the pre-war gender stereotypes and subordinations (Lahai 2010). In Chad, as a consequence of the civil war that started in 1965, there has been a change in the patriarchal social outlook, because 'the social disorder brought by the war transformed gender relations' and 'enabled women to leave the private sphere and participate extensively in the public domain' (Women's Commission of the Human Rights League of Chad and the Editors 1998, 118–128). In Nigeria, Ibeanu (2001) found that the Ogoni conflict raised the profile of Ogoni women.

Turning to the issue of displacement and states' reaction to it, Mountz (2011) contends that the intersecting trajectories of mobilities and displacement, as exerted by the displaced and the state governing such mobilities, need to be studied concurrently. The mobilities of states as actors in the production of mobilities, immobilities, and moorings of displaced populaces need a better review and analyses of this facet have been largely overlooked by the burgeoning literature on mobilities (e.g. Urry 2005; Cresswell 2006; Hannam *et al.* 2006; Sheller & Urry 2006). The point that Mountz (2011) attempts to make is of paramount importance in unpacking the event of displacement – mobility of the state enforces, encloses, precludes, or enables the mobility of the other (the displaced) and thus the dialectical relations between mobilities and moorings continue apace in situations of conflicts and displacement. The only way of understanding the interplay between the state and the affected populace then lies in unpacking mobilities in the full spectrum of civil, cultural, economic, political, and social rights, since they relate to the right to life, health, food, and an adequate standard of living and many more rights (as proposed by Leckie 2009). For this reason, Leckie argues that that 'there is a reasonably strong basis from which to demand positive and well-planned actions by states and others to develop the means necessary to protect and secure all of these rights for climate displaced persons' (Leckie cited in Blitz 2011, 440). Leckie (2009) uses this particular format of displacement to illustrate the ways in which the state can positively mobilize displacement. For example, at the national level, he proposes identifying 'land banking remedies', whereby states seek out the possibility of expropriating land for resettlement purposes (Leckie 2009). This theme can be further expanded to address displacement in a more functional manner than has been done in many parts of Asia, as highlighted by the cases presented in this book.

In conclusion, post-conflict and associated displacement often presents slippages in existing societal set-ups where women may become mobile, and there is a possible reduction of the gap between private and public spaces. For development planning, this presents opportunities for facilitating women's mobility to readdress gender-based discrimination in pre-conflict eras, and ideally the process should be integrated in the fabric of recovery and rehabilitation. Essentially, rather than being a linear process of establishing the pre-existing set of situations, rehabilitation in the aftermath of conflict situations offers a unique opportunity to correct development and gender-related imbalances. Vulnerability reduction measures can become an asset in post-conflict relief and rehabilitation situations with regard to the positive impact of targeted policies for community-level advocacy, aware-ness, preparedness, education, and training. Longer-term measures that assist in reducing vulnerabilities to hazards by ensuring the important role of civil society are therefore of fundamental importance in order to operate an effective transition from relief to development (Graham 2001). Tackling the boundaries of women with regard to mobility needs to be inbuilt when conducting the well-established stages of community-based risk mapping, contingency planning exercises, and damage and needs assessments in the event of a crisis.

Discussion and concluding remarks

In this chapter I have attempted to broaden the discussion on 'mobilities' to incorporate some important determinants of women's mobility in developing countries. The attempt is based on the assumption that a sole focus on development will give a diluted picture of women's position in the wider setting, since mobilities are structured differently for the respective genders due to differential access to resources, social norms, issues related to safety, and the dictates of various social/political/development policies and programmes. A consistent finding that emerges from developing countries is that there is a gap in the inclusion of gender in the development sector. It is frequently the case that 'gender' as a development priority does not percolate down to the lowest level of implementation hierarchy.

At the micro-level pertaining to the physical mobility dimension, it should be acknowledged that physical mobility is highly charged to make significant changes in women's lives. However, it would be unwise to broach upon it through an attack on any established culture and the concomitant prescriptions around women's movement. Incremental and thoughtful measures can eventually empower women through their newly found mobility. Improvements in safety nets for women who adopt a mobile livelihood strategy have the potential to dilute gender-based segregations and eventually help the cause of women's empowerment. However, it seems that the understanding of this fact is extremely limited and only operational within the domains of research studies and development organizations. Thousands of case studies and a general overview of the development process in developing countries highlight that mainstream planning still remains blatantly ignorant of the connection. Whether the development planning processes and mechanisms intentionally choose to do so, or are simply hindered by bureaucracy to cater to any new creative ways of thinking, demands further inquiry.

A final suggestion of this chapter is to create feedback systems on gendered mobilities that can be incorporated in mainstream planning. Åström and Murray (2008) define *feedback* as the interactions of two (or more) dynamic systems that are connected together in a fashion where each system influences the other and their dynamics are thus strongly coupled. A system is *closed loop* if the systems are interconnected in a cycle and *open loop* when this interconnection is broken. Two key properties of feedback are its ability to provide *robustness to uncertainty* and its use in *design of dynamics*. For example, by measuring the difference between a plan's actual and desired outcomes, we can provide a corrective action. This measurement can be obtained through combining the various indicators of mobilities at both micro- and macro-levels into a robust set. This action can signal if the plans deviate from the desired goal, and can be used to modify the natural dynamics of the mobilities taking place – physical, cultural, economic, political, and social. The following five critical questions and key criteria can be made part of this feedback system (Lucas & Currie (2012) outline a similar structure with regard to understanding social exclusion):

*   What is the nature of the mobilities taking place? Conceptualizations, definitions, theoretical perspectives
*   Reasons for the various facets of mobilities? Market effects, public policies, funding structures, service provision, capacities and constraints of individuals
*   Who is affected or at risk? Demographic breakdowns, distribution across different income groups, behavioural analyses
*   Where is it happening? Geographies, spatial distributions, affected areas, settlement types
*   How can it be addressed? Action pathways, strategies and timescales, tools, resources and capacities, institutional arrangements, delivery agencies, existing good practices.

In the beginning, attempts will definitely increase the overall complexity of understanding 'mobilities' by coupling different parts of various topics. However, as long as their dynamics are dependent on one another, they can be combined to create a feedback system on 'gendered mobilities' which can inform future planning decisions.

Future works could concentrate on expanding this feedback system by looking into different groups, different places, and the different processes which might be affecting gendered mobilities. Another way to approach this problem could be through concentrating on one group alone, for example: a particular tribe, and tracing the details of their mobilities at all levels – data collection; problem formulation; kinds of analysis needed; various policies that should consider mobilities as a vital input; and finally framing of implementable programmes to facilitate development. The scope and possibility of developing such a feedback system should be further explored in different countries. The cases presented in this book facilitate such nuanced understandings.

Notes

1   This chapter builds on a paper written for the *World Development Report 2012: Gender Equality and Development* (Uteng 2011).
2   Referring to this theme, 'moral geographies' is defined as the ways in which gendered normative ideologies operate in place-making and shaping spatial mobility and spatial relations.
3   'The *informal* sector is an oxymoron – on one hand it is an unorganized "nuisance" sector whose members, for example, do not pay any form of tax; on the other hand, it provides jobs and increases the incomes of the most vulnerable groups in a city – the very low-income group' (The Global Development Research Center 2010).
4   The issues are different when the disaster or conflict situation entails displacement:

> Displacement has different consequences for women and girls than for men and boys. There is often a dramatic increase in the number of women heads of households, and they bear additional responsibilities for meeting the needs of children and ageing relatives, since the male family members have either joined the warring groups or been captured. Women face new demands in providing for themselves and their children, with increased workloads and limited access to and control over the benefits of goods and services.
>
> (Gururaja 2000, 13)

References

Ahmed, S.M., Chowdhury, M. & Bhuiya, A. 2001. Micro-credit and emotional well-being: Experience of poor rural women from Matlab, Bangladesh. *World Development* 29, 1957–1966.

Amin, R., Pierre, M., Ahmed, H. & Haq, R. 2001. Integration of an Essential Services Package (ESP) in child reproductive health and family planning with a micro-credit program for poor women: Experiences from a pilot project in rural Bangladesh. *World Development* 19, 1611–1629.

Amir-Ebrahimi, M. 2006. Conquering enclosed public spaces in Tehran. *Cities* 23, 455–461.

Amoore, L. 2006. Biometric borders: Governing mobilities in the war on terror. *Political Geography* 25, 336–351.

Åström, K.J. & Murray, R.M. 2008. *Feedback Systems: An Introduction for Scientists and Engineers.* www.cds.caltech.edu/~murray/amwiki/Main_Page (accessed 19 May 2011).

Blitz, B.K. 2011. Statelessness and environmental-induced displacement: Future scenarios of deterritorialisation, rescue and recovery examined. *Mobilities* 6, 433–450.

Blomley, N. 1994. Mobility, empowerment and the rights revolution. *Political Geography* 13, 407–422.

Bonβ, W. & Kesselring. S. 2001. Mobilität am Übergang vom Ersten zur Zweiten Moderne. Beck, U. & Bonβ, W. (eds) *Die Modernisierung der Moderne*, 177–190. Suhrkamp, Frankfurt.

Bonβ, W. & Kesselring, S. 2004. Mobility and the cosmopolitan perspective. Bonβ, W., Kesselring S. & Vogl, G. (eds) *Mobility and the Cosmopolitan Perspective*, 9–24. Workshop at the Munich Reflexive Modernization Research Centre, 29–30 January

2004. SFB 536. www.mobilitypioneers.de/Dokumente/download/November%202004/ B3_Workshop_0104_Dokumentation.pdf (accessed 5 February 2013).

Carr, M. & Chen, M. 2004. *Globalization, Social Exclusion and Work: With Special Reference to Informal Employment and Gender.* Working Paper No. 20. Policy Integration Department, World Commission on the Social Dimension of Globalization, ILO, Geneva.

Cresswell, T. 1999. Embodiment, power and the politics of mobility: The case of female tramps and hobos. *Transactions of the Institute of British Geographers* 24, 175–192.

Cresswell, T. 2001. The production of mobilities. *New Formations* 43, 11–25.

Creswell, T. 2006. *On the Move: Mobility in the Modern Western World.* Routledge, London.

Cresswell, T. 2010. Towards a politics of mobility. *Environment and Planning D: Society and Space* 28, 17–31.

Cresswell, T. 2011a. Mobilities I: Catching up. *Progress in Human Geography* 35, 550–558.

Cresswell, T. 2011b. Mobilities II: Still. *Progress in Human Geography* 36, 645–653.

Cresswell, T. & Merriman, P. (eds) 2011. *Geographies of Mobilities: Practices, Spaces, Subjects.* Ashgate, Surrey.

Cunha, C. 2006. *Bicycles as a Lever for Rural Women's Empowerment: Lessons Learned from Bicycle Projects in Sub-Saharan Africa and an Alternative Approach in Southern Mozambique.* www.benbikes.org.za/namibia/pdfs/Bicycles%20and%20empowerment %20Paper.pdf (accessed 30 January 2013).

Cwerner, S. 2004. Faster, faster and faster: The time politics of asylum in the UK. *Time and Society* 13, 71–88.

Day, K. & White, P. 2001. Choice or circumstance: The UK as the location of asylum applications by Bosnian and Somali refugees. *Geo Journal* 56, 15–26.

De Genova, N. 2002. Migrant 'illegality' and deportability in everyday life. *Annual Review of Anthropology* 31, 419–447.

Dowler, L. & Sharp, J. 2001. A feminist geopolitics? *Space and Polity* 5, 165–176.

Featherstone, M. 1990. *Consumer Culture and Postmodernism.* Sage, London.

Frändberg, L. & Vilhelmson, B. 2003. Personal mobility: A corporeal dimension of transnationalisation. The case of long-distance travel from Sweden. *Environment and Planning A* 35, 1751–1768.

Friedmann, J. & Wolff, G. 1982. World city formation: An agenda for research and action. *International Journal of Urban and Regional Research* 6, 309–344.

Germann Molz, J. & Gibson, S. (eds) 2007. *Mobilizing Hospitality: The Ethics of Social Relations in a Mobile World.* Ashgate, Aldershot.

Gill, N., Caletrío, J. & Mason, V. 2011. Introduction: Mobilities and forced migration. *Mobilities* 6, 301–316.

Graham, A. 2001. *Gender Mainstreaming Guidelines for Disaster Management Programmes: A Principled Socio-Economic and Gender Analysis (SEAGA) Approach.* Paper for the Expert Group Meeting on 'Environmental management and the mitigation of natural disasters: a gender perspective', 6–9 November 2001, Ankara, Turkey. www.un.org/womenwatch/daw/csw/env_manage/documents/EP1-2001Oct 22.pdf (accessed 5 February 2013).

Gregory, D. & Urry, J. 1985. *Social Relations and Spatial Structures.* Palgrave Macmillan, London.

Gururaja, S. 2000. Gender dimensions of displacement. *Forced Migration Review* 9, 13–15.

Hannam K., Sheller, M. & Urry J. 2006. Mobilities, immobilities and moorings. *Mobilities* 1, 1–22.

Harvey, D. 1989. *The Condition of Postmodernity*. Blackwell, Oxford.

Held, D., McGrew, A., Glodblatt, D. & Perraton, J. 1999. *Global Transformations: Politics, Economics and Culture*. Polity Press, Cambridge.

Hyndman, J. 1997. Border crossings. *Antipode* 29, 149–176.

Hyndman, J. & Mountz, A. 2006. Refuge or refusal. Gregory, D. & Pred, A. (eds) *Violent Geographies*, 77–92. Routledge, London.

Ibeanu, O. 2001. Healing and changing: The changing identity of women in the aftermath of the Ogoni crisis in Nigeria. Meintjes, S., Pillay, A. & Turshen, M. (eds) *The Aftermath: Women in Post-Conflict Transformation*, 198–209. Zed Books, New York.

IFRTD (International Forum for Rural Transport and Development). 2005. Reconstructing Vulnerability or Reconstruction with Change? *Forum News* 12:1. http://ifrtd.gn. apc.org/en/full.php?id=567 (accessed 5 February 2013).

Izugbara, C.O. 2004. Gendered micro-lending schemes and sustainable women's empowerment in Nigeria. *Community Development Journal* 39, 72–84.

Jones, P.M. 1987. Mobility and the individual in Western Industrial Society. Nijkamp, P. & Reichman, S. (eds) *Transportation Planning in a Changing World*, 29–47. Gower, Aldershot.

Kabeer, N. (2000) *The Power to Choose: Bangladeshi Women and Labour Market Decisions in London and Dhaka*. Verso Books, London.

Kaufmann, V. 2002. *Re-thinking Mobility*. Ashgate, Aldershot.

Knie, A. 1997. Eigenzeit und Eigenraum: Zur Dialektik von Mobilitat und Verkehr. *Soziale Welt* 47, 39–54.

Lahai, J.I. 2010. Gendered battlefields: A contextual and comparative analysis of women's participation in armed conflicts in Africa. *The Peace and Conflict Review* 4, 1–24.

Langan C. 2001. Mobility disability. *Public Culture* 13, 459–484.

Lash, S. & Urry, J. 1994. *Economies of Signs and Space*. Sage, London.

Latour B. 1999. *We Have Never Been Modern*. Harvard University Press, Cambridge, MA.

Leckie, S. 2009. Climate-related disasters and displacement: Homes for lost homes, lands for lost lands. Guzman, J.M., Martine, G., McGranahan, G., Schensul, D. & Tacoli, C. (eds) *Population Dynamics and Climate Change*, 119–132. UNFPA and IIED, New York and London.

Löfgren, O. 2008. Motion and emotion: Learning to be a railway traveller. *Mobilities* 3, 331–351.

Lucas, K. & Currie, G. 2012. Developing socially inclusive transportation policy: Transferring the United Kingdom policy approach to the State of Victoria? *Transportation* 39, 151–173.

Luke, N. & Munshi, K. 2011. Women as agents of change: Female income and mobility in India. *Journal of Development Economics* 94, 1–17.

Massey, D. 1993. Power-geometry and a progressive sense of place. Bird, J., Curtis, B., Putnam, T., Robertson, G. & Tickner, L. (eds) *Mapping the Futures: Local Cultures, Global Change*, 59–69. Routledge, London.

Mountz, A. 2011. Specters at the port of entry: Understanding state mobilities through an ontology of exclusion. *Mobilities* 6, 317–334.

Nijkamp, P., Reichman, S. & Wegener, M. (eds) 1990. *Euromobile: Transport, Communications and Mobility in Europe: A Cross-national Overview*. Averbury, Aldershot.

Ohnmacht, T., Maksim, H. & Bergman, M.M. (eds) 2009. *Mobilities and Inequality.* Ashgate, Aldershot.

Omorodion, F.I. 2007. Rural women's experiences of micro-credit schemes in Nigeria: Case study of Esan women. *Journal of Asian and African Studies* 42, 479–494.

Perera, O. 2007. *The Globalisation of Services and its Implications for Sustainable Development: A Preliminary Discussion Document.* International Institute for Sustainable Development (IISD), Winnipeg, Geneva, Ottawa and New York. www.iisd.org/pdf/2008/globalisation_services_sd.pdf (accessed 5 February 2013).

Perry, D. 2002. Micro credit and women money-lenders: The shifting terrain of credit in rural Senegal. *Human Organization* 61, 30–35.

Peutz, N. 2006. Embarking on an anthropology of removal. *Current Anthropology* 47, 217–241.

Pitt, M., Shahidur, R.K. & Cartwright, J. 2003. *Does Micro-Credit Empower Women? Evidence from Bangladesh.* The World Bank, Policy Research Working Paper Series 2998. The World Bank, Washington, DC.

Razavi, S. 2011. *World Development Report 2012: Gender Equality and Development An Opportunity Both Welcome and Missed.* United Nations Research Institute for Social Development (UNRISD). www.unrisd.org/80256B3C005BE6B5/search/7F6321E556 FA0364C12579220031A129 (accessed 5 February 2013).

Ruhs, M. & Chang, H.-J. 2004. The ethics of labour migration policy. *International Organisation* 58, 69–102.

Sandrasagra, M.J. 2000. *Globalisation Heightening Gender Inequalities.* www.twnside. org.sg/title/height.htm (accessed 5 February 2013).

Sassen, S. 1999. *Globalization and its Discontents: Essays on the New Mobility of People and Money.* New Press, New York.

Sassen, S. 2001. *The Global City: New York, London, Tokyo.* Princeton University Press, Princeton, NJ.

Secor, A.J. 2002. The veil and urban space in Istanbul: Women's dress, mobility and Islamic knowledge. *Gender, Place and Culture* 9, 5–22.

Seguino, S. 2002. Gender, quality of life, and growth in Asia 1970 to 1990. *The Pacific Review* 15:2, 245–277.

Seguino, S. & Grown, C. 2006. Gender equity and globalization: Macroeconomic policy for developing countries. *Journal of International Development* 18, 1081–1104.

Sethuraman, S.V. 1998. *Gender, Informality and Poverty: A Global Review, Gender Bias in Female Informal Employment and Incomes in Developing Countries.* Poverty Reduction and Economic Management Department, The World Bank, Washington, DC.

Sheller, M. & Urry, J. 2006. The new mobilities paradigm. *Environment and Planning A* 38, 207–226.

Silvey, R.M. 2000. Stigmatized spaces: Gender and mobility under crisis in South Sulawesi, Indonesia. *Gender, Place and Culture* 7, 143–161.

Sørensen, K.H. 1999. *Rush-Hour Blues or the Whistle of Freedom? Understanding Modern Mobility.* STS Working Paper 3/99. Department of Interdisciplinary Studies of Culture, Norwegian University of Science and Technology, Trondheim.

The Global Development Research Center. 2010. *The Informal Sector.* www.gdrc. org/informal/index.html (accessed 30 April 2011).

Trujillo, M. 2000. Rural farming systems, plant genetic resources and disasters. *Forced Migration Review* 9, 26–28.

United Nations Population Fund. 2007. *State of World Population 2007: Unleashing the*

Potential of Urban Growth. www.unfpa.org/webdav/site/global/shared/documents/publications/2007/695_filename_sowp2007_eng.pdf (accessed 31 January 2011).

Urry, J. 2000. *Sociology Beyond Societies: Mobilities for the Twenty-first Century*. Routledge, London.

Urry, J. 2003. *Global Complexity*. Polity, Cambridge.

Urry, J. 2004. Connections. *Environment and Planning D: Society and Space* 22, 27–37.

Urry, J. 2005. The complexities of the global. *Theory, Culture & Society* 22, 235–254.

Uteng, T.P. 2006. Mobility: Discourses from the non-western immigrant groups in Norway. *Mobilities* 1, 435–462.

Uteng, T.P. 2009. Gender, ethnicity, and constrained mobility: Insights into the resultant social exclusion. *Environment and Planning A* 41, 1055–1071.

Uteng, T.P. 2011. *Gender and Mobility in the Developing World*. Background Paper: *World Development Report 2012: Gender Equality and Development*. https://openknowledge.worldbank.org/bitstream/handle/10986/9111/WDR2012-0010.pdf?sequence=1 (accessed 5 February 2013).

Uteng, T.P. & Cresswell, T. (eds) 2008. *Gendered Mobilities*. Ashgate, Aldershot.

Women's Commission of the Human Rights League of Chad and the Editors. 1998. Women denounce their treatment in Chad. Turshen, M. & Twagiramariya, C. (eds) *What Women Do in Wartime: Gender and Conflict in Africa*, 118–128. Zed Books, London.

World Bank. 2012. *World Development Report 2012: Gender Equality and Development*. The World Bank, Washington, DC.

Yeung, H.W. 1998. Capital, state and space: Contesting the borderless world. *Transactions of the Institute of British Geographers* 23, 291–309.

3 Mobile livelihoods of ethnic minorities in socio-economic transformation in China

The case of Yunnan Province

Yunxian Wang, Qun Zhao, Hongwen Zhang, Xiao'ou Ou, and Jing Wu

Introduction

Arriving at Baliu Resettlement Village (excerpt)
Riding on a term called 'Poverty Alleviation Migration',
you came from mountains, from dense jungles . . .
to the bank of a river running whole year around;
to a land vehement in all seasons;
to a place with no terraced field, but rubber tree forest;
to a blue print designated for construction and development . . .
along with a red letterhead.
Overnight, many ways of living have become stories,
many legends have become realities.
Will the hands used to hold the plough and harrow,
be good at rubber tapping?
Will the bare feet fond of walking in the terraced fields,
be used to coffee field?
Who is born a rubber worker?
As you are here, you let go those rice fields you keep on nagging,
days and nights in four seasons.
The offspring of the terraced farming ethnicity,
wherever they go, can cultivate a new life,
harvest new fragrant rice.
As long as the smoke is rising, do not care how it is lighted.

Mo Du (2005, 122–123)[1]

China is currently experiencing rapid economic expansion and restructuring, which has led to mass mobility. The scale of mobility is unprecedented and incomparable with that in any other country. Prior to the 1980s, people's mobilities were restricted, particularly from rural to urban areas and from economically poor regions to the prosperous eastern coastal region. With the relaxation of the household registration system (*hukou*) and shrinking welfare attached to urban residential registration, there has been a large-scale population mobility in China, the largest mobility pattern being the rural–urban migration of 230 million by 2011 (NPFPC 2012).

Ethnic minority people in Yunnan Province have traditionally had different mobility patterns with various resource endowments, i.e. shifting cultivation and herding, and cross-border tea trade. With the advent of market expansion, tourist development, and state and corporate intervention, the mobilities of ethnic minority groups have developed beyond ethnic community and agrarian boundaries. The global productions of cash crops, soaring energy and infrastructure demands, and tourist developments have generated various waves of mobility. Whereas there is outmigration of the rural population to cities and coastal regions in the east, and into neighbouring countries, the influx of business and people from inner China has resulted in net in-migration to Yunnan Province (Bao & Mo 2007), and the lands of the local people have been put under contract farming and estate development. The ethnic minority people of the province are also driven to move from their home places either by the infrastructure development or in the name of disaster preparedness and poverty alleviation in ecologically fragile areas. Different mobilities have varied social implications and consequences. This chapter attempts to capture the varieties of mobility patterns in Yunnan under the rapid economic expansion and infrastructure development. It aims at understanding how the mobilities among the ethnic minority people resonate with the national and regional economic development paradigms, whether mobilities have created options or disruption to ethnic minority people's livelihoods, and whether mobile livelihoods have affected women's and men's entitlement to resources and their social and cultural identities.

The chapter is structured in five sections. After this introduction, we discuss Chinese concepts of mobilities and give a historical account of ethnic minority groups' mobilities, mainly based on vernacular literature. Thereafter, the research methodology and introduction to four village cases are presented. The fourth section starts with the macro socio-economic and policy contexts linked with the mobility patterns, followed by an elaboration on mobility as a livelihood strategy and social differentiation process. The chapter ends with a brief conclusion.

Chinese concepts of mobilities

The Chinese language contains several terms to reflect the concept and patterns of mobility in different contexts. In the history of population movements, terms such as *qianxi* (迁徙), *liuxi* (流徙), *qianyi* (迁移), and *yimin* (移民) have been used to reflect mainly relocation, resettlement, or migration for better access to natural resources or to escape from war, diseases, or suppression (Wang 2008). In modern China, the term *yimin* covers the meanings of various types of domestic and international migrations and migrants in English expressions (Li 1999). Although the term reflects small-scale temporary movements or households moving away from their original places of residence, particularly under the Chinese household registration system, along with *qianyi*, it also suggests forced migration and permanent relocation from household's original homes due to the implementation of official policy (Wang 2011). Therefore, the term *yimin* has at least two meanings to refer to different contexts and types of mobilities: organized involuntary relocation by the government or driven by development projects, and voluntary migration by individuals. By contrast, the term 'floating populations' (or 'mobile populations') (*liudong renkou*, 流动人口) is widely used to describe mobile people and migrant workers. In contrast to *qianxi* (迁徙), *qianyi* (迁移), and *yimin* (移民), the term *liudong* (流动) has the connotation of movement back and forth, and more closely represents the situation of rural–urban mobility, which is often expressed as migration in English. Nevertheless, all of the above-mentioned terms overlap in their meaning to some extent. Where we use the concept of mobility in this chapter, it refers to several types of voluntary movements and involuntary relocation. Hence, terms such as mobility, migration, relocation, and resettlement are used interchangeably in some contexts in this chapter.

A major part of the vernacular literature on mobility in China has focused on labour migration, while two other types of mobilities – namely involuntary or government-organized relocation for the purpose of infrastructure development, ecological and disaster preparedness, and poverty alleviation;[2] and international migration – are also covered in mobility studies (Li 1999).

Labour mobility from farm to non-farm work has generally been regarded as a progressive livelihood option and an opportunity, and until recently men have been the major force in labour mobility. In the absence of mobility opportunities for women and the feminization of agriculture, women's development would be hindered (Gao 1994; Jin 1998).

In relation to the propensity for mobility, studies of impacts of mobility often focus on families' labour allocation and economic returns (Cai 2007). However, Tan (2004) argues that household livelihood strategies cannot fully explain the complexity of outmigration; rather, individual and non-economic factors are more convincing variables. In the Chinese context, individuals *seeking development opportunities* through mobility has the connotation of *improving one's qualification and capability* (Jin 1998), as similarly perceived by Western scholars such as Uteng (2006) and Kronlid (2008). In the process, traditional family and gender relations are shaken up, particularly with respect to other dimensions of capabilities such as access to resources, land, and education.

Historical accounts and features of mobilities among ethnic minority groups

It has been recognized that ethnic minority people have been mobile historically, despite the remoteness of their habitats. Nicholas Tapp (2010) illustrates from a historical perspective the economic and trading relations of ethnic minority groups in Yunnan that have existed for a long time due to the province's geographic border with neighbouring Asian countries. He synthesizes the different relations and integration as markets and mobility, such as cross-border trading, commercialization and consumption of ethnic culture in tourism, Han immigration into ethnic minority areas through marriage and engaging in plantation work, and military forces.

Yunnan's outward-facing character is not only due to its geographic location, but also to historical and ethnic connections with neighbouring countries such as Laos and Myanmar (Tapp 2010). Until the 19th century, various ethnic minority groups were able to move freely across the borders of China, Myanmar, Laos, and Vietnam, and to Thailand (Xu *et al*. 2006). As Michaud and Forsyth (2011) claim, the livelihoods of ethnic minorities are best understood on a transnational basis in relation to the existence of cultural and trading links across borders.

Typically, discourses on the mobility of ethnic minority groups hold that population growth and pressure on resources led to internal conflict and stratification, and both internal and external suppression had forced ethnic minority groups into constant migration in order to seek alternative livelihoods (Wang 1999; Zhao 2001; Li 2004). For example, Wang Qinghua, in his ethnographic study of the Hani ecosystem of terraced fields, shows that mobility has strongly characterized Hani ethnic history (Wang 1999). The Hani people developed a highly complicated farming system after they were forced to relocate to the Ailao Mountains and they survived as a result of their unique ecosystem (Wang 1999). The Bulang ethnic group evolved from the Mon-Khmer and developed into a separate group. The Bulang people do not have a written language. The mobility legend clearly records the footprint of the Bulang people's mobility history, their original habitation, and routes of mobility. The mobility of Bulang people was very frequent, but not long-distance or large-scale (Feng 2001, 4). The Bulang used to mix with Dai ethnic people in Xishuangbanna (Figure 3.1), but due to conflicts they were finally forced into deep mountains from lowland areas (Zhao 2001; Zhang 2005). Due to wars, conflicts, and natural disasters, the Dai ethnic people were also frequently mobile. Nevertheless, Dai people always moved along rivers, searching for more fertile and richer land with water (Zheng 2005).

Historically, Han immigration into minority areas was encouraged for reasons of political control, frontier border stability, and civilization (Xu 2006; Tapp 2010; Wang 2010). Xu sees the rubber plantations in Xishuangbanna since the 1950s as a classical manifestation of state power to introduce modern industry and a political ideology. During the 1960s and 1970s, Han Chinese farmers from inner China were recruited as state workers in rubber plantations in Xishuangbanna because they were considered a more educated and advanced labour force compared to primitive ethnic minority labour in Yunnan. The ideological landscape of rubber plantations was thus believed to embody 'the transformation of society from a feudal mode of production into a socialist society by eliminating classes, mobilizing the masses and centralizing productivity and land use decisions' (Xu 2006, 256). The Han Chinese settlement, along with rubber plantation in Xishuangbanna, changed not only the ecological landscape but also the local social networks and the political landscape between locals and outsiders (Xu 2006).

Currently, mobilities in Yunnan reflect the common patterns of mobility in China as a whole, but also have unique features due to the province's geographical location bordering several countries and associated ethnic connections. Yunnan has 16 cross-border ethnic minority groups and strong ethnic connections and kinship exist, which made cross-border mobility a traditional practice. Nevertheless, businessmen and labourers from inner China are also involved in the cross-border mobilities (Lu 2006). The cross-border mobility since the 1980s has included trafficking in women.[3] Many of the women were trafficked for the sex industry (Tong *et al.* 2005).

Research has shown that ethnic minority women who are mobile in Yunnan tend to be young, unmarried, and of reproductive age (Yang 2008). Different ethnic cultures, traditions, and gender roles have influenced the mobility patterns. For example, Dai women have stronger attachments to land and their home village and tend not to leave, and therefore those who work outside their village are looked down upon by other villagers. In addition, Dai women have higher status in the family and less dependence on men in terms of inheritance and control over property and land resources, and men often marry into women's families and share household chores (Dong & Yu 2003). Hani women do not enjoy the same status in their own ethnic community and families. The perception of men's superiority is strong and girls are born for the benefit of others, and therefore it is acceptable for Hani women to marry and live far away from their own family. However, M. Wang (2008) argues that nomads' and ethnic minority groups' mobilities enable them to break various spatial, social, and ideological boundaries, and this is particularly reflected in their division of family labour.

Research methodology and village cases

The research presented in this chapter was conducted under the common framework of the research project 'Mobile Livelihoods and Gendered Citizenship: The Counter-geographies of Indigenous People in India, China and Laos' funded by the Research Council of Norway for the period 2010–2012. Based on methodological triangulation, the field study took place in Yunnan during the period October 2010–July 2011. The field study methods included a reconnaissance visit, questionnaire interviews, in-depth interviews with key informants, and focus group discussions.[4] After the reconnaissance visit, four villages along the Kunming–Bangkok Highway were selected for case studies: Ge Cun in Yuanjiang County; Bulang Resettlement Village in Nan Cun (an administrative village) in Pu'er Prefecture; and Zhao Cun and Xi Cun in Xishuangbanna Prefecture. All four villages are located on or adjacent to the Kunming–Bangkok Highway.

A total of 216 questionnaire interviews were conducted. The in-depth interviews included village leaders and village group heads, youths and women members, veteran village cadres, small traders, land and plantation contractors, and the organizers and agents of frequent outmigrations. The focus group discussions were held with youths, women, and elders. Observations were also made in the Bulang resettlers' original village to gain insights into their former livelihoods and resource situation. A two-day workshop was held, with the participation of village representatives, scholars, and practitioners, in order to verify the information and

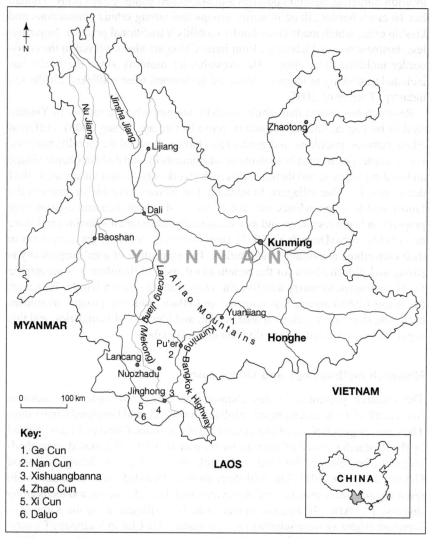

Figure 3.1 Location of the study area in Yunnan Province, China.

to gain different perspectives on mobility and livelihoods from the stakeholders. The comprehensive research methodology enabled us to understand the multidimensional facets of mobilities and related changes in livelihoods among the ethnic people living in the study villages.

The rationale for choosing the villages was that they represented ethnic variety and diverse mobility patterns. Xi Cun is a Bulang ethnic village bordering Myanmar, 3 km north of the border gate Daluo to Myanmar and 120 km west of Jinghong, the district capital of Xishuangbanna (Figure 3.1). The village was formerly located in mountainous upland. Early in 1958, the local government encouraged the villagers to move to lowland. The movement of the people was gradual and circular until 1980, when a big fire destroyed the whole village. In the 1990s, some villagers relied on the support of their relatives in Myanmar and Thailand, and moved to Thailand to work as horticultural workers or motorcycle taxi drivers and remained there for eight or nine years either without status or with only semi-legal status. Most of the migrants were unmarried young men. The border gate with Myanmar opened in 1991, ushering in a tourist boom in Daluo, and the villagers took the opportunity to work as tourist guides, assistants in souvenir shops, or cultural performers. During the period 2002–2005, a new wave of mobility arose, and the villagers travelled around performing cultural shows (folk songs and dances) in cities and tourist sites within China – a practice known as 'roaming performance' (*zou xue*). After 2006, the villagers started cross-border cultivation of cash crops and established rubber plantations (interviews with key informants, October 2010 and May 2011). As the rubber plantation and harvesting the latex demands huge labour forces, the villagers ceased their practice of roaming performances on a large scale. The rubber plantation and smaller banana plantation in rice fields have attracted inflows of labourers and investors from both within Yunnan and other parts of China.

Ge Cun is inhabited by the Hani ethnic people. It is located 33 km east of the county town of Yuanjiang. The villagers live on the uppermost parts along the Ailao Mountains. Hani people are regarded as having been the most mobile in the history of ethnic minorities' movement (Wang 1999; Li 2004).[5] Due to limited land resources, prior to 2005 young women villagers in Ge Cun had practised out-marriage, and were later joined by their relatives. After 2005, the villagers initially migrated to work in nearby towns and then gradually to cities in the province and beyond. In 2008, outmigration for work reached a peak, and was mainly practised by young unmarried women and men as well as married Hani men (interviews with key informants, October 2010 and May 2011). Yuanjiang is located at the northern limit for growing tropical products such as flowers and fruits. Large numbers of flower companies and horticulture nurseries have moved into Yuanjiang and villagers are hired as agricultural labourers for permanent or seasonal work in flower, vegetable, and horticultural fields.

Bulang Resettlement Village was relocated to Nan Cun in 2007. It was originally located on the bank of Lancang River, 200 km west of the current resettlement village. The original village on the riverbank had relocated from a site 10 km higher up in the mountainous area. The villagers' movements began in 1965, but the majority of them moved to the place close to the river in 1980, and the process of movement lasted until 2004. Not long after that, due to the construction of the Nuozhadu Dam, the village was scheduled to be submerged. Therefore, 67 households were relocated to Nan Cun, seven to other locations, and 12 were unwilling to relocate. In the resettlement site in Nan Cun, however, only limited lowland was allocated to the newcomers and no upland was available (interviews with key informants, May 2011). Many of the households found it necessary to return to their original village to cultivate the unsubmerged uplands

Table 3.1 Land resources and income sources

Village	Number of households	Lowland/upland per capita (mu*)	Mobility pattern	Income source
Xi Cun	178	0.6/0.4	Daily and circular mobility, with roaming performances in the past	Rubber, rice, tea, wage labour
Zhao Cun	186	1.5/0.3	Immobility	Rice, tea, sugarcane, paper, bricks
Bulang Resettlement Village	66	0.7/0**	Relocation, daily and circular mobility	Rice, maize, hired work, wage labour
Ge Cun	70	0.5/0.9	Outmigration	Tobacco, maize, rice, wage labour

Notes: *1 mu = 667m²; ** Large areas of uplands available in the former place, 200 km distant.

for their living at least twice a year. With limited land resources, many of the resettled villagers also had to engage in daily mobility as hired agricultural labourers in coffee fields owned by companies or local people.

Compared with Xi Cun, Ge Cun, and Bulang Resettlement Village, the villagers in the Dai village Zhao Cun are not very mobile. The village is located 59 km to the west of Jinghong. In 2010, the net income per capita was CNY 4800.[6] With relatively large and fertile landholdings, the villagers' livelihood sources are mainly rice, tea, vegetables, traditional handmade paper, bricks, and tiles (Table 3.1). With the exception of some business people, very few of the villagers work outside Dai village.

Socio-economic environment affecting mobilities in Yunnan

In China as a whole, factors that are endorsed by the state and have influenced mainstream mobility include labour demand in the economically booming eastern coastal provinces, massive infrastructure projects for energy extraction, poverty alleviation programmes, and ecological conservation. Yunnan did not escape any of these influencing factors. Instead, as part of the western region, Yunnan has had very specific reasons for having vibrant and varied mobilities.

Globalized production and urban expansion

Despite Yunnan's remote and border-frontier location, the impacts of globalization are no less felt than in eastern coastal regions. On the contrary, the globalized production model was manifested in Yunnan even earlier than in other provinces. When neighbouring countries such as Thailand marched into industrialization in the 1990s and needed huge amounts of cheap labour, Yunnan's ethnic minority population joined the labour forces in horticulture and informal services in the peri-urban and rural areas of Thailand.

When massive industrialization took place in China in the late 1990s and wages started to rise, Yunnan's ethnic minority migrant workers returned to Yunnan. To meet the needs of global production, particularly in the east and coastal regions, large-scale industrial development has attracted migrant workers from inner provinces. Prior to the 1980s, mobility was restricted, especially from rural to urban areas. When restrictions based on household registration were relaxed, and at the same time there was little profit to be gained from small-scale farming, outmigration was an important means of generating income for families in rural areas.

The export-oriented economy also promoted border trade, which in turn attracted the inflow of inland Chinese and border residents' relatives living in countries with poorer economies, such as Myanmar and Laos, to migrate to Yunnan to work or trade on a small scale. Further, the offspring of rubber plantation workers who migrated to Yunnan, particularly to Xishuangbanna, from, for example, Hunan and Sichuan, in the 1960s and1970s, became the new wave of inflow of Han populations and a major force in the border trade and small businesses. The intensity of the mobility is reinforced by the price of commodities in the international markets. When international market prices of rubber and coffee rise and the demand for fresh-cut flowers and greenery increases, the inflows of both investors and labourers into plantations increases. Available studies show that Yunnan has a net inflow migration (Bao & Mo 2007).

In addition to global production, rapid urbanization is taking place all over China and has a direct impact on population movements. In 2011, urban residents for the first time accounted for more than 50 per cent of the total population in the country (NPFPC 2011). Massive urbanization has also induced production to serve its purpose, i.e. related supporting services have expanded from big urban centres to suburbs, satellite towns, and to other adjacent cities. The infrastructure development and urban expansion in the western provinces under the Go West development strategy[7] are happening at an even greater rate. The suburb areas of Kunming used to be the biggest supply depot of fresh flowers and greenery, grains, and vegetables. When Kunming expanded to include the suburb areas, towns further to the south became the production bases and depot centres for flowers, greenery, grains, and vegetables for Kunming and other big cities in China and for the region. Much of the production of fresh agricultural produce has even been shifted to Yuanjiang. The surrounding areas of Yuanjiang have attracted investors in the production of flowers, tropical fruits, and greenery. The Hani people from within Yuanjiang County and Honghe Prefecture are the major source of labour for the agro-businesses.

Official policy and mainstream perception see outmigration and non-farm work as a better livelihood option compared to staying behind and depending upon farming for a living. As part of the poverty-alleviation strategic plan in the new era after 2001, a nationwide vocational training programme for rural labour migrants was launched. Members of the rural labour forces from poor provinces, who intended to migrate and work outside, received subsidies for their attendance at skills training courses. The subsidy and promotional policy encouraged rural labourers to be prepared by acquiring some skills and knowledge of industrial life. As a remote and economically poor province, Yunnan became a place where rural labour force destined for the eastern provinces were sent.

At the same time, vertical integration of agriculture became another pillar for poverty alleviation, and because the agro-business is intended to be inclusive, small producers are integrated into cash-crop production and enjoy a fair share of profit in the value chain. Thus, apart from the inflow for agro-business, Yunnan population movements are mainly seasonal and within the province (Yunnan Association of Expertise and Yunnan Training School of Township Enterprises 2009). In some areas of Yunnan Province, where land is relatively more spacious, vegetables, fruits, tea, coffee, and fresh flowers have become the major produce in agricultural integration through company-organized 'cooperative' or contract farming. The higher value-added produce discouraged rural labourers from moving out and attracted rural labour to return from outside the province. Staying put and engaging in agro-business related production became more profitable in some contexts than working away from home in construction, manufacturing, or services.

Tourism development

In the Go West development strategy, the national and provincial government have diverted resources to develop road infrastructure, such as the Kunming–Bangkok Highway and the railway system. Road improvements have made it much easier to travel around in Yunnan and for the villagers to visit their relatives across the borders. In 1991, the provincial government approved Daluo Town as a provincial-level border gate, and since then border trade, tourism, and related services have boomed. With the whole country prospering, domestic tourism has developed rapidly since the turn of the 21st century. Until 2004, the cross-border tourist programme especially attracted domestic tourists to experience exotic cultural lifestyles, including performances.

With the vast varieties of presentations and prevailing exotic feeling towards ethnic cultures and traditions among the Han population, the ethnic cultures are seen as adding value to tourism development and are therefore exploited from market and productive force perspective. The tourist sites in other parts of Yunnan and China have started to add ethnic cultural components and recruit ethnic staff from Yunnan ethnic communities to promote ethnic cultural activities as commodities. Xi Cun villagers were drawn into the practice of roaming performances to showcase their familiar roles as singers or dancers in many of the big cities and tourist sites within China.

Infrastructure and development programmes

Village relocations among ethnic minority people have been common in the past. Since landownership is fixed at village collective level, any village relocation has to involve the intervention of higher levels of government administration. Nevertheless, such relocations continue. Regardless of its peripheral location, Yunnan is a miniature version of China in terms of development. It is a typical example of mass-mobilized developmentalism (McGee 2011), where popular poverty alleviation and development programmes under the Go West development strategy are concentrated. Ample water resources in Yunnan have attracted a number of dam constructions for hydropower generation, which have led to involuntary relocations of ethnic minority people (Guo 2008).

The state power in China restricts people from total freedom of movement under the household registration system, which in principle fixes a person in a place where his or her household identity registration is held, but also makes people move or relocate. In the period between 1949 and 2008, economic construction resulted in more than 70 million involuntary relocations nationwide, and the number relocated immediately due to dam construction alone reached 19.3 million (Wang 2011). Further, it has been believed that resettlement is the most rapid way to reduce poverty (Lin 2003), despite the reality that among the millions of resettlers nationwide caused by dam construction, one-third of them and their offspring are still living in absolute poverty (Liu 2012). There is often little space for negotiation for either compensation or access to land resources in new resettlement places. Partial compensation for relocation, insufficient resources, and difficulties in adjusting to social and community relations in new places lead to further mobility and unsustainable livelihoods. The affected people's rights to sustainable livelihoods have been neglected under the state power intervention (Hu & Huang 2010). There is a strong appeal for legislation on involuntary relocation to minimize the effects of the abusive administrative power (Hu & Huang 2010; Wang 2011).

Mobile livelihood patterns among the studied ethnic minority groups

From the above presentation, it is evident that there are varieties of mobilities in the four study villages and that various types of mobility can exist within one village. Still, we can draw very rough lines to understand the mobility patterns among different ethnic groups. It has been noted that the Bulang ethnic people in the border area had been mobile due to their production modes, such as shifting cultivation and herding across the border, as well as relocation from ethnic conflicts and connections. From the field study, it was apparent that Bulang villagers in Xi Cun were the most mobile minority group and took maximum advantage of opportunities in various waves of mobility. Their mobility patterns were rather dynamic within a short period of time.

Although belonging to the same Bulang ethnicity in general, people living in Bulang Resettlement Village did not experience similar vibrant mobile livelihoods. If they had not had to relocate to the resettlement village due to dam construction, they would have been the same as other ethnic minority groups living with a sustainable but semi-subsistence economy along the banks of Lancang River.

However, the dam construction totally changed their livelihood. Ultimately, they have had to live by practising long-distance mobile cultivation in their original village lands in order to produce food and animal feed for home consumption and future cash income.

Hani people in Yuanjiang, in common with their ancestors, evidently prefer to be mobile, even to very distant and alien places. Their mobile livelihoods are relatively homogenous in terms of occupations, social strata, and economic returns. They are pushed out more by their limited resource endowments and increasing population pressure. By contrast, villagers in Zhao Cun have experienced very limited mobility due to better land resources and a traditional attachment to land.

Cross-border mobilities

Due to Xi Cun's location on the border between China and Myanmar, in the 1990s the villagers engaged in cross-border migration to Thailand via Myanmar. According to key informants in the village, there were *c*.100 migrant workers in Thailand in 1994. They were mainly young and unmarried men, some families, and a few single mothers with children. Due to their illegal status, it was not possible for them to return home frequently, and they had to stay there for many years.

The second type of cross-border mobility has been brought about in the wave of tourism promotion. Cross-border tourism since 1991 created prosperous job opportunities for Xi Cun villagers as, for example, performers, guides, illustrators, and shop assistants. In the period 1998–2003, *c*.70–80 villagers were involved in tourism and related services. The cross-border tourism was halted in 2004 and gradually replaced by trade with border residents and cross-border cultivation of cash crops:

> [At that time] I was a junior middle school student. During the school holidays, I worked as an enumerator and earned 300 yuan, 10 yuan per day ... My second sister worked in a jade shop in a border town in Myanmar for three years. My elder sister was also an enumerator in the border street, for four years.
>
> (YSA, female, Xi Cun)

Border trade has gradually become dominated by men. Before the rubber plantation, their border resident status allowed them to carry out small and medium trading activities and to collect agricultural products or forest products from Myanmar villagers. Those with clan connections were able to do better than just earning some money for cigarette and liquor: 'My family has many relatives in Myanmar and Thailand. When I do business, I contact my relatives there directly and I can get whatever goods I need. It is convenient to do everything' (AKW, male, Xi Cun).

The third type of cross-border mobility emerged when the cultivation of rubber trees became widespread. Although there was not enough land for growing rubber trees in the village, the villagers in Xi Cun utilized their ethnic and clan links in Myanmar and received the land concession. It is estimated the villagers received more than 10,000 mu (667 ha)[8] land concessions and planted 300,000 rubber trees. According to the village statistics, there are 170 households in Xi Cun, which leased land in Myanmar, where each family planted 700–6,000 rubber trees. The villagers travel by motorbikes daily to cultivate the plantation.

Domestic migration

With the exception of villagers in Zhao Cun, school leavers and young people mainly worked away from home, in the prefecture and provincial capital cities and in eastern coastal cities. In Xi Cun, when the border tourism was stopped, the villagers opted for roaming performances, to showcase their traditional Bulang ethnic singing and dancing in exotic tourism locations and entertainment sites. According to the village informants, c.340 villagers were involved in such roaming performances in the peak period 2003–2005. In 2005, the number reached 400 people. The performers, men and women, old and young, moved from one city to another and stayed there for a month or so. They went to many parts of the country, and some even went to Vietnam. Each group performed the traditional roles according to their age and gender roles:

> In June 2007, I went to Shenyang and provided massage services [to the performers]. In January 2008 I went to Cangzhou, Hebei for three months and then to Zibo, Shandong; and then to Zhengzhou, Henan in May for five or six months. I moved back and forth in Shanxi, Hebei and Shandong, dancing and providing massages. It was very tiring. Between 2009 and 2010, I moved between Kunming and Gejiu, Dali, one month in one place. I returned home last November [2010].
>
> (YZK, female, Xi Cun)

Due to fewer opportunities for cash-crop cultivation in the village, the Hani villagers in Ge Cun tend to emigrate for work. The villagers move to the prefecture city, Kunming, and the eastern coastal regions to work in manufacturing, road construction, mining industry, or as coolies. In the resettlement village of Nan Cun, mainly young graduates migrate to the cities to work in the service sectors and assembly lines in the coastal regions.

Relocation

In the process of the Bulang Resettlement Village being relocated in 2007 to allow for dam construction, the villagers proposed they move higher up to their original farm houses where they had lived until the 1980s. Their argument was that they would not have to move to distant places and hence the cost of relocation would be much less, and they could look after their vast areas of uplands. However, the local government insisted that by living in the mountainous area they would not become prosperous, and instead they would benefit from moving nearer to towns and roads, where they would have easier access to schools and transportation. In relocation mobilization, the local government officials tempted resettlers with the prospect of a bright future for development: 'Prior to the relocation, the government officials brought us here and showed us, the mountain is there, the land is here, the water is there' (YWZ, male, Bulang Resettlement Village).

Eventually, the villagers had to move and disperse to three locations, without sufficient land allocated to them. In Nan Cun, the amount of compensation received for loss of crops, houses, and land was barely enough to build a new house for a family. Many of the families were unable to make a sustainable living from the reallocated wetland. The reduction in land resources pushed the resettled villagers to return to their original village to practise circular cultivation.

Seasonal and circular mobility for cultivation

Villagers in Xi Cun and Bulang Resettlement Village practised shifting cultivation between their new village and the upland farms where they had farmhouses. Following the relocation of Bulang village to Nan Cun, the villagers had to start another type of mobile cultivation. Each year, at various stages of the crop growth, they had to travel between two and four times to their former village to cultivate their uplands. Families that practised circular cultivation spent an average of 47 days per year at their original village and upland farms. Furthermore, women and elderly villagers stayed at their farms for longer periods and spent more time looking after subsistence crops such as corn and sweet potatoes compared to men, who took more responsibility for cultivating rubber trees, coffee plants, and trees planted as cash crops. In the study area as a whole, daily mobility and engaging in work as hired agricultural labour are practised on a considerable scale (Table 3.2).

Xi Cun villagers cultivate rubber trees, tea plants, upland rice and corn in their former village, and also have land concessions to cultivate rubber trees in Myanmar. Hence, the villagers have to travel between their new village, their uplands in their former village, and rubber plantations in Myanmar. Tapping the latex is labour-intensive and consequently the work is not only done by men and women but also children and hired labour from other ethnic groups with no prior experience of cultivating rubber trees. Due to the need for labour, the practice of roaming performances on a large scale has ceased. At the same time, other types of mobility, such as cross-border and circular mobility, have led to the expansion of the rubber plantations (Table 3.3), even into neighbouring countries. Thus, for Xi Cun villagers, daily life is characterized by frequent circular mobility according to crop cycles.

In the case of Ge Cun, where terraced wetland is scarce, the majority of families relied on labour mobility and earned their income from engaging in waged labour. Another major type of mobility practised by the Hani villagers is seasonal mobility to Yuanjiang and other parts of the area in Yunnan where cash crops are cultivated. Among 52 women, 40 were involved in hired agricultural work. The wages for such work are paid on daily or piece-rate basis, and often women can earn more than men.

Table 3.2 Main work of respondents and spouses in the four study villages

Main work	Men*		Women*	
	No.	%	No.	%
Farm work (own)	34	16.4	8	3.8
Domestic work	7	3.4	14	6.5
Small business	3	1.5	1	0.5
Off-farm outside	11	5.3	3	1.4
Hired agricultural work	41	19.8	79	37.1
Farm & domestic work	12	5.8	23	10.8
Farm work, hired agricultural work	13	6.3	3	1.4
Farm, domestic, hired agricultural work	9	4.4	16	7.5
Farm, off-farm, hired agricultural work	4	1.9	3	1.4
Farm, domestic, small business	17	8.2	14	6.6
Farm, domestic, off-farm outside	22	10.6	3	1.4
Farm, domestic, paper making	28	13.5	42	19.7
Farm, domestic, paper, business	6	2.9	4	1.9
Total	207	100	213	100

Note: *Men includes male respondents and the spouses of female respondents; women includes female respondents and the spouses of male respondents.

Table 3.3 Land use and cropping pattern in Xi Cun in 2005 and 2010

Land use	Crop area (mu*)			
	Number of responses	Minimum	Maximum	Mean
2005:				
Rice	42	1	13.5	4
Fruit	2	1	1	1
Rubber trees	44	5	165	29.7
Sugarcane	2	2.5	3	2.8
Tea	32	1	30	7.3
Vegetable	6	0.5	15	3.3
Other upland crops**	11	0.3	20	7.7
2010:				
Rice	17	1	7.5	3
Fruit	8	1	53	15.5
Rubber trees	47	6	225	60.7
Sugarcane	0	0	0	0
Tea	36	1	32	8.4
Vegetables	5	0.5	2	1.1
Other upland crops**	16	2	26	7.8

Notes: *1 mu = 667 m^2; ** Other upland crops are intercropped with young rubber trees.

Inflow investment in agri-business

Under the vertical agricultural integration scheme, investors lease lands from villagers or sign farming contracts with smallholders. In Xi Cun, paddy land has been leased for banana plantations due to lack of water and shortage of labour, as most of the labour force is employed in the rubber plantations. In contrast, in Nan Cun, coffee companies have contracted more than 200 mu (13.3 ha) for coffee plantation. In Yuanjiang, there has been an inflow of investments to plant fruits, green plants (for greenery), and flowers, not only for the domestic market but also for overseas consumption. Investors either lease land or purchase it illegally from the villagers at a low rate.

Permanent and seasonal agricultural workers

As a result of cash-crop production and inflow investments in all four study villages, hired agricultural labour has become common. In addition to the landless and landowners who lease out their land and become hired labourers, there are migrant labourers from the poorer regions of inner China and Yunnan Province, such as Lancang and Zhaotong – the Miao, Lahu, and Hani ethnic minority people, and the Han people. Many of the migrant labourers are young or middle-aged men, but also include couples. They are introduced to the families or companies that employ them through their ethnic and kin networks. In Xi Cun, it is estimated that each family has to hire labour equivalent to seven or eight persons to work 4–5 days per year on their rubber plantations:

> In the last four years, there has been no labour exchange. We have to hire people from outside and pay them cash to work on banana and rubber. It costs me over 10,000 yuan a year. I have five permanent contacts who introduce me to the labourers. I make a phone call to ask for five workers and prepare 600 yuan cash. Most of them are couples. Both husband and wife come to work together.
>
> (ALL, male, Xi Cun)

With only partial realization of relocation compensation, the resettlers in Nan Cun have also had to join the ranks of hired agricultural workers who assist the cultivation of coffee. In Yuanjiang, the cultivation of fruits, vegetables, and flowers on lower lands attracts seasonal and permanent ethnic Hani workers from the mountains. The Hani are the major source of hired agricultural workers in vertical agricultural development.

Immobility

Due to the use of communication technologies, market network development, and road facilities, immobility is prevalent among women who run small businesses in Nan Cun and the county town Yuanjiang because wholesalers deliver groceries and various goods to their doors (Wang & Zhao 2012). By contrast, immobility in Zhao Cun is related to the villagers' resource endowments and their cultural identity and attachment to the land, which is high-quality lowland. Historically, Dai people have occupied the lowlands and due to their cultural value they seldom leave their home places. Some key informants in the region commented that due to their adherence to their lowlands, Dai people missed the opportunity of adventure and the benefits to be gained from being mobile, and gradually they have been left behind other ethnic groups that formerly were much poorer.

Mobilities as livelihood strategy and social process

The external factors described above have affected the landscape of the mobilities of ethnic minority people in Yunnan. At community and household levels, access to resources, educational needs, household labour, and time-allocation strategies reflect the agency and capability as well as the vulnerability of the ethnic people with respect to mobility. In the following subsections, we demonstrate how mobilities have created options or caused disruption to ethnic minority people's livelihoods, and how the impacts on women's entitlement to resources and identities have differed compared to those of men.

Family labour and time-allocation strategies

With the exception of relocation in Bulang Resettlement Village, mobility and immobility in the study villages have been used as family livelihood strategies and collectively seen as capability. The ethnic minority groups are often under pressure due to resource constraints. In the other three villages, villagers have on average less than 1 mu (667 m²) of wetland per capita. Many families remain at subsistence or semi-subsistence levels due to limited resources and limited access to markets. With marketized public services, such as health and education, the meagre amounts of cash earned from a semi-subsistence economy are not sufficient to live on. In addition, modern lifestyles lead to increased demands for cash. Thus, earning cash incomes to meet household expenses such as marriage, house construction, and school fees, is the immediate push factor for villagers to migrate for work.

Different mobilities have led to varied income levels in the study villages in Yunnan. For example, in the period 2006–2010, among those who worked as labourers and provided services, the highest incomes were earned from roaming performances (CNY 3000), especially for agents and the team leaders, followed by outmigration to eastern coastal regions (CNY 2000–2500), work in services in the local prefecture and county towns (CNY 1000), and agricultural labour close to their villages (CNY 40–60 per day or piece rate). The survey revealed that the majority of families (*c.*70 per cent) had increased their income within a period of five years, particularly in Ge Cun and Xi Cun. Approximately 65 per cent of the respondents reported that their family living conditions had improved due to mobility.

Mobility as household livelihood strategy was most clearly observed in Xi Cun, where the villagers utilized their language and identity, ethnic network, and cultural resource for early cross-border migration to Thailand for better income, to border tourism and trade, domestic roaming performances, and cross-border rubber plantations. All of these mobilities were (and are) intertwined, due to the close link between labour and time with respect to households' mobility for their livelihoods.

In Ge Cun, the majority of outmigrants worked in services, the agricultural sector, and other low-paid jobs, and very often they were not able to earn a living wage. Consequently, the villagers struggled to survive if the most able-bodied members in the family worked away from home. Men were usually the first to suggest migrating for work and had the authority when it came to decision-making:

> My wife did not want me to go and said I did not have good health. My three sisters also came to tears to persuade me not to go. I told them not to cry. I would go out even if they cried.
>
> (CMH, male, Ge Cun)

> I raised the idea [of working away from home] and I made up my mind myself. I only discussed it with them [family members], mainly with the parents.
>
> (LDB, male, Ge Cun)

In addition to considerations of when to migrate and when to return, there were many other factors that restrained members of some families from working away from their home and village. For example, transportation costs and educational level restricted some villagers from finding work elsewhere, as claimed by several Hani women in Ge Cun: 'We have no money for transportation fares'; 'We both [husband and wife] have never been to school. We cannot go out [to work].' A further factor is the opportunity cost of mobility, which is not only related to the comparative income earned at home and outside, but also to family relations and community responsibility in the village. As one of the above-quoted Hani women expressed, 'When parents are getting old and children are too young, we cannot go out. Without hands at home, one has to hire labourers to do the rice cultivation. It is not worthwhile [going out to work].'

Thus, the process of deciding who should work away from home was a process of family labour division. It was not only determined by the desire to maximize family income, but also by the expectation of gender roles in ethnic culture. The gender relations in households and the respective communities were expressed by the villagers in Ge Cun as follows: '[Among the couple] one goes out to earn money for children's schooling, another stays back and cultivates the land. Young people, both boys and girls, go out; for the married, usually men go out and women stay back.'

In response to the question concerning why a woman did not join her husband, the woman said: 'If all went out, who look after the home? It needs people to repair road and canal and to help with money and time when old people pass away. Moreover, children also need care for their schooling.'

Women who returned from outside to the villages confirmed that they had had to work away from home before marriage; after marriage, a woman's family responsibilities and gender roles would not allow them to do so. Married women are expected to take on responsibilities of caring for the family members, and engage in more agricultural work and community affairs when men work away from home. Thus, in the study villages, marital status was a determinant of women's freedom to be mobile.

Agency in ethnic network and cultural inheritance

Social and ethnic networks played a crucial role in facilitating and accommodating the various types of mobilities in the study villages. In each wave of mobilities in Xi Cun, ethnic connections and identity have overridden the importance of national identity and state control. By exercising their agency in the various types of mobilities, the Xi Cun villagers had gone to Thailand without legal identity, yet they were able to remain, live, and work there for many years due to the support of their ethnic network. The issue of villagers leasing land in Myanmar is sensitive and plantations are subject to potential risks linked to national territories and political instability in the border areas. However, land concessions have been possible through the strong ethnic networks. Similarities in language and skin colour serve to camouflage their identities in foreign lands: 'My aunt's grand-children are in Thailand and run a horticulture nursery. I can understand and speak the languages in Myanmar and Thailand. I was never held up at the checkpoints' (ASK, male, Xi Cun).

The ethnic solidarity not only among the Bulang in Xi Cun, who engaged in roaming performances throughout China, but also among the Hani in Ge Cun, played a significant role in their decisions to work away from home: they are mobile when there are acquaintances at their destination that will provide support and solidarity in times of difficulty. The spontaneous nature of the mobilities of ethnic minorities is largely attributable to their strong sense of attachment and trust in their ethnic network:

> I, together with others, developed a Southeast Asian Tribe programme in Dali Butterfly Spring Resort. I was in charge of recruiting performers. All the performers should be ethnic minority. I took eighty-eight performers along with me, ten were Wa ethnic, [and] the rest were all Bulang from Xi Cun.
>
> (ANX, male, Xi Cun)

As observed by others, ethnic minorities do not just passively accept state delineation of ethnicity, but rather they learn to assert their rights and make use of their identity while finding solutions to their basic needs and economic benefit (Guo cited in Xu & Salas 2003; Michaud & Forsyth 2011). In the marketization of ethnic and cultural elements in tourism development, villagers use their ethnic culture and identity as main assets in mobile livelihoods beyond their daily life and production boundaries. They take pride in their respective ethnic identities and their presentation and commercial success in larger, urban places. Whenever they have faced misunderstanding from tourists and felt insulted due to their culture and norms, they have learned to fight back. If any members are treated unfairly, all other members of their group collectively protest by going on strike.

Individual choice and development illusion

The impetus of mobilities varies at community, household, and individual levels. Particularly for young people, economic benefit as push factor for mobility has weakened since the Go West and vertical agricultural development strategies were implemented. People have more opportunities for income generation near their homes. However, young people have been inspired and lured by developments outside their communities and want to experience such developments. For example, after attending a vocational school for six months, one girl from Ge Cun dropped out of school and started to migrate for work:

> When I saw the returnees from outside were wearing nice clothes, I changed my mind and also wanted to go out. My parents did not agree and I was even hit when I told them my idea. I then quietly quitted school and went to Kunming . . . I did not regret [my decision]. My classmates in the vocational school did not earn more than me.
>
> (LLB, female, Ge Cun)

In three villages where the villagers practised outmigration, the new graduates from schools did not want to work on land but neither could they expect to be supported by their parents. At the same time, they were also attracted by life outside their home places and therefore wanted to migrate in order to experience the 'outside world'. When the parents of young villagers and the young villagers themselves described their reasons for working away from home, they used expressions such as 'eye opening' and 'exposed to world perspectives' to describe their aspirations. Many young people experience hardship when they work in cities and consequently become closer to their parents. From the perspective of those who are affected, the family benefits and maturity that young people gained from mobility were thus one type of capability.

Individual choice with respect to mobility also reflected young girls' resistance to traditional marriages. Two Hani girls, who worked for a flower company near Yuanjiang, explicitly expressed that they did not want to return home to marry Hani men from their village. Evidently, mobility had afforded them some degree of freedom to choose their husbands. Prior to 2005, women in Ge Cun mainly left their home village in order to marry. They had developed the initial network that led to the trend of outmigration by villagers seeking spouses. Mobility has given women freedom and opportunities to escape traditional confinement. It is a means to resist gender suppression within ethnic communities or clans that have patriarchal customs (Jin 2008).

Men, too, utilize mobility as a way to find a bride. In Xi Cun, which has some elements of matrilineal culture, some of the men who had migrated from places in inner China, such as Sichuan and Hunan, had married Bulang women and settled down in the village, thus breaking with tradition and the custom that did not permit intermarriage between members of different ethnic groups.

The imbalanced sex ratio at birth in China and Yunnan has been a negative demographic feature (Li & Yan 2010). Young girls of marriageable age from poorer places are drawn to regions that are economically better-off but have disproportionately few potential brides. When more girls move out and do not return to their villages, men of marriageable age in poor and remote villages find it even more difficult to find a partner (Ma 2004; Yang 2008). Young men leave remote mountainous villages to work as hired labourers for cash-crop farming, not only to earn an income but also to look for a wife. In Nan Cun, we met three Lahu men who were single and had been hired as agricultural labourers. They reported that from their village, which had 32 families, *c.*40 men had left to work as hired agricultural labourers and half of them were single or did not have brides of marriageable age. Thus, finding a bride was an underlying reason for mobility.

Mobility as a differentiation process

While some types of mobilities have enhanced some villagers' capabilities and improved their livelihoods, other types of mobilities have become a process of differentiation. With the relaxation of the household registration system, people have gained a certain degree of mobility and some young people are free to choose whether to be mobile. However, Chinese rural populations have never had total freedom of choice about their mobility and the ability to settle permanently in cities.

Prior to 2003, members of rural populations had to present documentary evidence of their eligibility to work and live in the cities, and such documents related to their work and residential permit, and family planning regulations. Although physical movement has become relatively free, mobile populations' access to public services such as healthcare, education, unemployment relief, and pensions is restricted, due to the fact that their eligibility for welfare and social security benefits are still attached to their household registration, thus hindering them from permanent settlement in urban areas. Although the majority of rural people join the rural healthcare cooperative scheme, they can only have their expenses reimbursed in their hometown, where their household registration is held. Hence, when they are away from their hometown, they cannot claim expenses if they have to attend hospitals elsewhere until they return to their hometown.

In addition, children's education is a concern for migrant families. Although migrant children do not have to pay tuition fees to attend public schools in receiving communities, they are discriminated against because they are treated differently when they have to pay other kinds of fees, such as school selection fees and temporary or transient fees as 'visiting' students. There is bias in class allocation and in the attitudes of teachers, and local students and their parents, who look down on migrant children. Further, in order to receive senior secondary education after Year 9 (equivalent to Grade 9 in lower-middle school), migrant children have to return to their hometown because the entrance examination for university is still fixed to household registration.[9] Thus, in the absence of access to public services, labour migrants' capabilities for mobility are hampered and often their mobilities are vulnerable and volatile, resulting in discontinuity and family separation. Due to the household registration system and restrictions in urban areas, rural–urban migration in China is characterized by a high level of circulation (Davin 2005).

However, the inflow of investors and capital captures a big share of the revenue from ethnic minority groups' resources by changing land use and reinforcing the transition from subsistence crop farming to cash-crop cultivation. These circuits of mobilities show that mobilities with varied possession of resources (e.g. labour, land, and capital) have resulted in differentiation processes. Ethnic minority people from Yunnan migrate to larger, urban places to earn subsistence incomes, yet lack access to public services, and their lands are leased to investors to grow cash crops for substantial profit. This reflects the counter-geographies of production, survival, and profit-making, as Sassen (2000) claims. Much greater differentiation is manifested in involuntary relocation resulting from development coercion. The involuntary relocation of Bulang Resettlement Village to Nan Cun and the different understandings of land categories and utilization have led to varied compensation and rates. The relocated villagers only received 0.7 mu (467 m²) of wetland per capita, and no upland in the new place. Out of 54 respondents, 42 explicitly said their family income had decreased. Due to shortages of land in their new place, the members of c.40 households in Bulang Resettlement Village had to return regularly to their former village to cultivate the land there. The marginalized families, such as sporadic members from other village groups (*cha hua hu*) and women, were deprived of land reallocation and compensation by their own community and families:

> The village group argued the land did not belong to us, but to the village collective; so the compensation should not merely come to us. They were not willing to give an endorsement to the compensation plan. Without this endorsement, the Migration Bureau would not allocate the compensation to us. The reallocated land is occupied by others.
>
> (DXZ, female, a representative of sporadic
> families, Bulang Resettlement Village)

Women who marry outside their village are the first to have their names deleted from the list of relocated populations. China's Rural Land Contract Law stipulates that the land contract shall remain unchanged for 30 years. Accordingly, a woman who marries outside her natal village, and therefore does not receive a new share of land in her husband's village, still holds a land share in her natal village. If she was not relocated, her share of land would be cultivated by either her parents or brothers, otherwise compensation for her share of land would be decided *ad hoc* by the village committee in her natal village and by her parents or brothers. In some cases, women do not receive land in their husbands' place or a share of compensation from their natal families. Further, their identity, belonging, or village membership would be cancelled and they would not be counted as members of the resettled population. Thus, the possibility of future compensation would be eliminated.

The resettled population in Bulang Resettlement Village moved from abundant uplands to a place with limited lowlands, where their traditional skills in cultivating upland rice, corn, and fruits, trees grown as cash crops, and rearing animals were not applicable. Dramatic reduction in land possession and space affects people's ability to rear animals. In turn, this has strong implications for women's household responsibilities, as they have to make additional efforts to plant maize in the original village in order to rear a few pigs for home consumption. During the research workshop held in Kunming, one woman representative expressed:

[in the original village] we had sufficient corn and we women used to rear many pigs. After we came to this new place, we have no land and [therefore] have to buy feed for our pigs. We women need corn to rear pigs. So, we have to come back.

(WZH, female, Nan Cun)

Although travelling to the original place and transporting the produce was costly and women reportedly felt uncomfortable about travelling, women spent more time than men living in the field houses and maintaining the crops. Travelling to the original village and cultivating the land helped to ensure that families had basic food supplies and animal feed for a period of time before the dam started to fill up. Such circular mobility is a matter of forced choice. Thus, relocation from infrastructure projects and the induced circular mobility has become a process of disempowerment for marginalized people in the study area.

Conclusions

With globalized production, regional development integration, and a liberal development policy, the mobilities of the ethnic minority populations in Yunnan are unprecedented. Closely linked to the macro-policy changes and economic restructuring, the mobility patterns among the ethnic minority people in Yunnan have become comprehensive, reflecting both the overall situation in China in economic expansion and the unique features of Yunnan as a border front province with diverse ethnic minority groups. The mobility patterns include not only domestic rural–urban migratory work, cross-border trading, and agro-business, but also circular and daily mobility, inflow investments and labour, and involuntary relocation under development coercion.

Mobilities as a capability and livelihood strategy have provided people with an opportunity to earn better incomes. By exercising the agency role of ethnic connections and cultural inheritance, the ethnic minority groups in general and women in particular are able to gain a certain amount of individual freedom and choice. However, mobility has also resulted in social differentiation. Such differentiation is clearly manifested in the access to public services, the possession of assets such as land resources and capital, and the effects of land use change. Further, relocation as involuntary mobility is not just a matter of compensation but also of disruption to livelihoods. Involuntary relocation has further disempowered the powerless and marginalized groups and women. The different circuits of mobilities in the study villages in Yunnan Province thus confirm the counter-geographies of production, survival, and profit-making, as conceptualized strongly by Sassen (2000).

Notes

1   The quoted parts of the poem and quotes from the interviewees have been translated by Yunxian Wang.
2   This type of relocation is often categorized as voluntary resettlement, although it is noted that the distinction between voluntary and involuntary is ambiguous (Lin 2003).
3   Q. Zhao and H. Zhang, 'A case study of cross-border female migrants from Simao, Yunnan', internal report 1998, funded by UNICEF.
4   To preserve the anonymity of the villages and interviewees, the village names have been changed and codified letters such as XCF and LFD are used in place of the interviewees' names.
5   Most of the information on Hani mobility history is derived from the epic *Hani Apei Congpopo*, a 5000-line record of the Hani ethnic group's development and mobility history based on the singing and chanting of Hani scholars.
6   CNY 1 = USD 0.16
7   The Go West development strategy was initiated in 2000 to develop the western regions of China. The strategy aims at improving infrastructure such as transport, irrigation, electricity, and communication facilities, enhancing ecological and environmental conservation, restructuring industries and specialty sectoral development, advancing science and technology, human resource development, institutional innovation, and opening up borders for trade and investment. The strategy is operational for a period of 50 years, in three stages: 2000–2010, 2010–2030, and 2030–2050. In the first stage, emphasis was placed on infrastructure development and poverty reduction.
8   1 mu of land is equivalent to 667 m^2.
9   In recent years, there has been a strong appeal from the concerned scholars and migrants to reform the system that restricts migrant children's university entrance exam to their household registration hometown. This has stimulated interest and given rise to confrontation between urban residents and migrant families.

References

Bao, G. & Mo, G. 2007. Characteristics and trend of population mobility and relocation. *Journal of Yunnan Finance and Trade Institute* (Social Science Edition) 6, 96–98.
Cai, F. 2007. *Issues on Mobile Population in China*. Social Sciences Documentation Publishing House, Beijing.
Davin, D. 2005. Women and migration in contemporary China. *China Report* 41, 29–38.
Dong, H. & Yu, Q. 2003. An empirical study on out-migration of ethnic minority rural women. *Guizhou Ethnicity Studies* 1, 115–124.
Feng, C. 2001. Foreword II. Zhao, Y. *A Cultural History of the Bulang Ethnic Nationality*, 3–6. Yunnan Ethnicity Publishing House, Kunming.

Gao, X. 1994. Rural labour migration and trend of agricultural feminization in contemporary China. *Sociological Studies* 2, 83–90.

Guo, J. 2008. *Rethinking Development – Anthropological Studies on the Development of the Ethnic Groups in the Lancang-Mekong River Basin*, Yunnan People's Publishing House, Kunming.

Hu, E. & Huang, D. 2010. The state's role in involuntary relocation from infrastructure projects. *Henan Social Sciences* 18, 137–139.

Jin, H. 2008. International and domestic migration of Korean ethnic women in transitional China. Yang, G., Chen, X., Li, R. & Wu, Q. (eds) *Curriculum Development in Ethnic Minority Women's Studies*, 215–228.Yunnan Ethnicity Publishing House, Kunming.

Jin, Y. 1998. Rural women in non-farm work. *Sociological Studies* 5, 106–114.

Kronlid, D. 2008. Mobility as capability. Uteng, T.P. & Cresswell, T. (eds) *Gendered Mobilities*, 15–34. Ashgate, Aldershot.

Li, J. & Yan, P. 2010. Problems of sex ratios at birth and measures in Yunnan. *Chongqing Polytech Science Institute Journal* (Social Sciences Edition) 6, 58–60.

Li, M. 1999. Attributes of Chinese in the Netherlands: Are they Huaqiao or Huaren? *IIAS Newsletter* 18 (Pink Pages), 45. International Institute for Asian Studies, Leiden.

Li, X. 2004. *A Cultural History of the Hani Ethnic Nationality*. Yunnan Ethnicity Publishing House, Kunming.

Lin, Z. 2003. *Voluntary Resettlement in China: Policy and Outcomes of Government-organised Poverty Reduction Projects*. PhD Dissertation, Wageningen University, Wageningen.

Liu, J. 2012. The Voices of the Locals Need to be Heard. Special Column. Sina Commentary, 15 March 2012. http://news.sina.com.cn/pl/2012-03-15/130124120199.shtml (accessed 16 March 2012).

Lu, G. 2006. Cross-border population movement on China-Myanmar borderline. *Yunnan Ethnicity University Journal* (Philosophy and Social Sciences Edition) 23, 1–5.

Ma, J. 2004. Sex ratio, marriage squeezing and female migration. *Journal of Guangxi Ethnicity Institute* 26, 88–94.

McGee, T. 2011. Foreword. Michaud, J. & Forsyth, T. (eds) *Moving Mountains: Ethnicity and Livelihoods in Highland China, Vietnam, and Laos*, ix–xvi. UBC Press, Vancouver.

Michaud, J. & Forsyth, T. (eds) 2011. *Moving Mountains: Ethnicity and Livelihoods in Highland China, Vietnam, and Laos*. UBC Press, Vancouver.

Mo Du. 2005. *In and Outside Villages*. Yunnan Ethnicity Publishing House, Kunming.

NPFPC (National Population and Family Planning Commission of China). 2011. *China's Mobile Population Development Report*. NPFPC, Beijing.

NPFPC (National Population and Family Planning Commission of China). 2012. *China's Mobile Population Development Report*. NPFPC, Beijing.

Sassen, S. 2000. Women's burden: Counter-geographies of globalization and the feminization of survival. *Journal of International Affairs* 53, 503–525.

Tan, S. 2004. Household strategy or individual autonomy? Gender analysis of decision making on out-migration. *Zhejiang Scholars' Journal* 5, 210–214.

Tapp, N. 2010.Yunnan: Ethnicity and economies – markets and mobility. *The Asia Pacific Journal of Anthropology* 11, 97–110.

Tong, J., Zhang, J., Zhao, J. & Zhang, H. 2005. Learning by doing, practice in learning, Yunnan GAD Group (ed.) *Gender Footprint in Participatory Development*, 363–381. Chinese Social Sciences Publishing House, Beijing.

Uteng, T.P. 2006. Mobility: Discourses from the non-Western immigrant groups in Norway. *Mobilities* 1, 435–462.

Wang, M. 2008. *The Nomad's Choice: The First Encounter between Northern Nomads and Imperial China.* Guangxi Normal University Press, Guilin.

Wang, N. 2010. Changes in ethnic identity among Han immigrants in the Wa Hills from the seventeenth to nineteenth centuries. *The Asia Pacific Journal of Anthropology* 11, 128–141.

Wang, Q. 1999. *The Culture of the Terraced Field: Hani's Ecosystem*, Yunnan University Press, Kunming.

Wang, W. 2011 *Da Yimin* (Grand migration): A suspense of 2.8 million migrants in Shaanxi. *China Newsweek* 517:19, 22–30.

Wang, Y. & Zhao, Q. 2012. Gendered impacts of road infrastructure development along the Kunming-Bangkok highway. Kusakabe, K. (ed.) *Gender, Roads and Mobility in Asia*, 67–71. Practical Action Publishing, Rugby.

Xu, J. 2006. The political, social, and ecological transformation of a landscape: The case of rubber in Xishuangbanna, China. *Mountain Research and Development* 26, 254–262.

Xu, J. & Salas, M. 2003. Moving the periphery to the centre: Indigenous people, culture and knowledge in a changing Yunnan. Kaosa-ard, M. & Dore, J. (eds) *Social Challenges for the Mekong Region*, 123–145. Chiang Mai University, Bangkok.

Xu, J., Fox, J., Melick, D., Fujita, Y., Jintrawet, A., Qian, J., Thomas, D. & Weyerhaeuser, H. 2006. Land use transition, livelihoods, and environmental services in montane mainland Southeast Asia. *Mountain Research and Development* 26, 278–284.

Yang, G. 2008. The features and change in ethnic minority women's mobility in border areas. *Journal of Yunnan Ethnicity Studies* (Philosophy and Social Sciences Edition) 25, 46–52.

Yunnan Association of Expertise and Yunnan Training School of Township Enterprises. 2009. Transfer rural surplus labour orderly and promote sustainable agriculture: Special investigation report on rural labour mobility in Yunnan. *Experts' View* 1. Yunnan Association of Sciences and Technology. http://222.221.5.103/DisplayPages/ContentDisplay_89.aspx?contentid=1606 (accessed 8 August 2012). In Chinese.

Zhang, X. 2005. *Transformation and Development: Social Research on Yunnan Bulang Ethnic People.* Ethnicity Publishing House, Beijing.

Zhao, Y. 2001. *A Cultural History of the Bulang Ethnic Nationality.* Yunnan Ethnicity Publishing House, Kunming.

Zheng, X. 2005. The Dais' water culture and sustainable development. *Thinking* 31, 76–81.

4 Chinese peasants in transition

Thomas Sætre Jakobsen

Introduction

This chapter provides insights into how transitions within the life courses of migrant workers in Yunnan Province, China, involve periods of mobility and immobility that impinge on livelihood resources and illuminates how life-course transitions differ between two generations of rural migrant workers. One of the most visible features of '[n]eoliberalism with Chinese characteristics' (Harvey 2005, 122), commonly referred to as 'open-door' policies or reforms, is the increasing mobility of the rural population as migrant workers (Davin 1999; Solinger 1999; Murphy 2002; Chan 2008). Migration from rural to urban areas has been a strategy for livelihood diversification for rural households in China since the early 1980s and has become a permanent and increasingly important factor in China's economic success by supplying the manufacturing sector, export processing zones, and urbanized areas in general with cheap and unyielding labour (Hare & Zhao 2000; Liang 2001; Pun 2005; Chan 2008). At the same time, due to the household registration system, rural migrant workers have been denied the opportunity to settle permanently in urban areas, access to educational and health services, and basic social rights such as pension allowances (Solinger 1999; Whyte 2010).

What is termed the new generation or second-generation migrant workers, a demarcation of rural migrant workers born after 1980, now makes up 85 million of the *c.*145 million rural labour migrants in China (Hu 2012). It is argued that the new generation of migrant workers travel further to work compared to the old generation born before 1980, that they do not necessarily return to assist their household in the harvest season because they remain in the vicinity of the factories and urban areas where they work, and that their goals and motivations for migration differ from those of the old generation of migrant workers (Pun & Lu 2010; Zhu & Chen 2010).

This chapter begins with a conceptual clarification of the relationship between migration, life courses, and generations. Thereafter, the reader is led through a description of the methodological approach to fieldwork carried out within four rural working teams (*zu*)[1] before reaching the analysis. It is argued that household members' mobility and their livelihood resources are structured around transitions within their life courses, especially with respect to raising children, and that the life courses involve continuities and discontinuities between two generations of rural migrant workers.

Migration, life courses, generations, and social change

This study draws upon a branch of literature on migration and the livelihoods of rural households that argues that migration is one component of the livelihood diversification of such households (Massey *et al.* 1993; Skeldon 1997; Ellis 2000). When the 'new economics of labour migration' (NELM) model emerged in the mid-1980s, the household was identified as the primary social agent in decisions of whether to move (Stark & Bloom, 1985; Massey 1988). Households are often characterized, both in terms of NELM and by the literature on rural livelihoods, as risk averse and actively engaged in practices and strategies aimed at managing risk (Ellis 1998; De Haas 2010). An increasingly common way for households to minimize risk is by allocating resources in a diverse portfolio of activities, captured by the term livelihood diversification (Ellis & Freeman 2005).

A steady critique emerged in the mid-1990s, especially from feminist scholars, on conceptualizations of the household as a unitary rational actor (Elmhirst 2002). Objective relations dividing members of households along gender and age hierarchies conspire to make households contested domains. Put differently, rural migrant workers have a will of their own and the relationship between household priorities and that of individual migrant workers involves struggles, remorse, and shared interests in different situations (Pun 2005). In recent years, there has been increased interest in studying how different transitions within the life courses of households and individuals shape the mobile livelihood options and fortunes of rural households and the individuals comprising those households (De Jong & Graefe 2008; Thao 2013). With the concept of *life courses*, in contrast to the concept of life cycle, the focus shifts from analysing a fixed set of stages that families go through to how both the practices and circumstances of families and individuals change throughout transitions within life courses (Bryman 1987). For the purpose of the present study and the focus on life courses, *time* and how we understand migration as involving movement from one place to another and taking place more frequently at certain periods than others, is of particular interest. Thus, we move from seeing migration as a timeless practice as it appears to the observer (Bourdieu 1977) to migration 'as an "action in time"' (Halfacree & Boyle 1993, 337).

The shift in perception allows us to conceptualize migration as not just movements to somewhere else, but as involving different degrees of immobility and mobility throughout the life courses of individuals and households. It follows that such transitions within the life course will have important consequences for the livelihood options and outcomes of migrant households (De Jong & Graefe 2008). The term 'migrant households' refer to households in which one or more family members are migrant workers. Conceptualizing mobility within different times in the history of a household, i.e. transitions within the life courses of the individuals comprising the household unit at various times and places, enables us to illuminate issues such as how transformation from a single sojourner within adolescence towards marriage and subsequently raising children is situated relatively along the mobility–immobility continuum. It also allows us to understand that transitions transform the livelihood options and outcomes for households, especially with respect to how having children incurs high expenditure for many years, as demonstrated by both this chapter and Chapter 3 by Wang *et al.*

Further, when looking at life courses and the transitions within them in terms of their significance for the immobility and mobility of household members as well as how they shape the material resources of households, we also need to acknowledge that they are taking place within a specific historical time (Pilcher 1994). Thus, transitions within the life courses of rural migrant workers who grew up before the reforms were set in motion in China might have been completely different from those who grew up in the reform era. Whereas the concept of generation is often used to refer to parent-child relations, the concept of cohort is commonly understood within the social sciences 'as those people within a geographically or otherwise delineated population who experienced the same significant life event within a given period of time' (Glenn 1977, 8).

Underscoring the importance of conceptual rigour and common ground, Jane Pilcher (1994) argues that we should make a distinction between *generations*, understood as the structural kinship relation between parents and children, and *social generations*, understood as people who grow up with shared experiences in the same socio-historical time, which is how Karl Mannheim defined the concept in 1923 in his seminal essay *The Problems of Generations* (Mannheim 1952). In his understanding of social generations, Mannheim both stresses the continuity of certain social structures such as class relations and how an analysis of social generations could reveal how social change comes about through changed life events between social generations. Hence, for him it was not external time that defined generations (e.g. people born before or after 1980) but 'a subjective condition of having experienced the same dominant influences' (Pilcher 1994, 486).

Moreover, Mannheim recognized that although people that are born in the same year grow up during the same time, live through adolescence during the same decade, and so forth, they do not necessarily share the same history (Pilcher 1994). Recognizing the subjective formation of social generations does not sidestep the factual issue of dealing with generations as quantitative cohorts – people existing within the same time span and qualitative social generation, i.e. people who share experience and have been subject to the same or similar influences through common events. In the case of Chinese rural migrant workers, the decisive year of 1980 is not arbitrary because it refers to the commonly accepted year of the initiation of reforms after more than 30 years of Maoist rule and the initiation of rural and urban market transformation. It could be argued that by looking at life courses and how they are constituted differently between social generations, we are exploring the social spaces inhabited in personal and historical time (Harris 1987). In other words, rural migrant workers experience transitions in their lives and at the same time they are part of a generation that has shared similar experiences and influences. By looking at differences between generations of rural migrant workers it is possible to develop an index of the social transformations taking place.

The study area and methods

Yunnan Province is situated in southwest China, bordering Myanmar in the west, Laos and Vietnam in the south, Guizhou Province and Guangxi Province in the east, and Sichuan and Tibet to the north (Figure 4.1). Yunnan covers an area slightly larger than Japan and has a land size of 394,000 m^2 and a population roughly the same as that of Spain or Colombia, with 45.4 million in 2008 (Donaldson 2011). Approximately 7 per cent of the land is considered arable, and there is an average of 0.15 ha of arable land per capita. In 2003, the population of Yunnan Province was 43 million people and urban residents had an average disposable income of CNY 7,643.57 (USD 1,226.56),[2] while farmers had a per capita net income of CNY 1,697.12 (USD 272.337) in 2003 (*Yunnan Statistical Yearbook* 2004). Although the figures for the respective incomes are not directly comparable, they are the closest comparable numbers available for rural and urban households in Yunnan. Yunnanese farmers earned less than the national average for farmers in 2003, which was CNY 2,622 (USD 420.752) (*Yunnan Statistical Yearbook* 2004). According to the *Yunnan Statistical Yearbook* (2004), the agricultural population of the province totalled 36.6 million people in 2003. Although many people in Yunnan are involved in other income-generating activities in addition to farming, the majority of Yunnanese are farmers.

The fieldwork for this chapter was conducted in the Songhuaba watershed area (Figure 4.1), situated 15 km north of Kunming city, where the activities and the way that farmers carry out their livelihood activities affect the water of residents in Kunming, the provincial capital. For this reason, Songhuaba was designated a special environmental preservation area in the early 1980s (Bureau of Environmental Protection of Kunming City 1988). In 2004, there were 74,382 people living in the area, which spans two counties, Songming and Panlong, which come under the administration of the Kunming city government. Due to the special status of Songhuaba, there are heavy restrictions on the kind of local off-farm businesses that can be set up. There are very few local off-farm working opportunities to be found other than in small shops, restaurants in the nearby towns, or within local government offices. Hence, prior to the study it was expected that migration would be an important livelihood option for many households seeking to diversify their livelihood activities.

The Songhuaba watershed area contains five towns and 44 administrative villages. Within each village, there is usually 3–10 teams (*zu*), hereafter referred to as village groups, ranging from 20 to 200 households (conversations with Kunming World Agroforestry Centre staff, December 2008). In 2004, there were *c*.270 village groups in the Songhuaba watershed area and the annual average income per person in 2004 was CNY 1,662 (USD 266.701), according to the local government.[3]

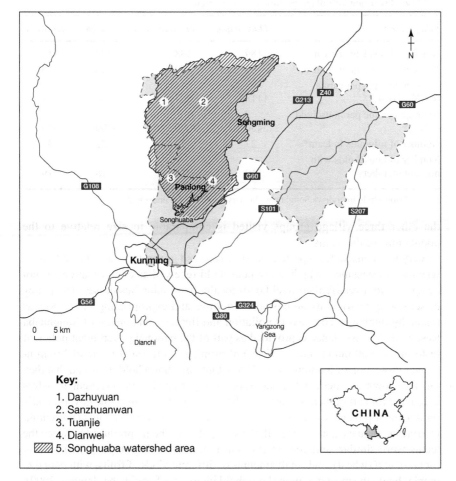

Figure 4.1 Location of the study area, the Songhuaba watershed area in Yunnan Province, China.

Household interviews were conducted in four village groups within four villages: Dazhuyuan, Sanzhuanwan, Tuanjie, and Dianwei (Table 4.1). In order to preserve the village groups' anonymity, they are referred to by their collective village name.

In Dianwei, there are relatively high numbers of migrant workers in proportion to the number of households and the apparent reason for this is that the village group is located close to Songhuaba Reservoir. The government has expropriated most of the land contracted by the Dianwei village group. Since there are few or no local wage labour opportunities, local farmers have increasingly made their living by engaging in migration (household interviews Dianwei, January 2009). The main livelihood activities practised by members of the households in the village group are agriculture and migration. The number of migrant workers within

Table 4.1 Overview of village groups (teams) visited

Village name	Dazhuyuan	Sanzhuanwan	Tuanjie	Dianwei
Number of residents in team*	189	188	200	115
Number of households in team*	41	50	70	26
Average income per capita (CNY) (2004)**	1118	867	—	2311
Average income per household (CNY)*	3430	2000	3000	3300
Number of migrants in team*	27	22	22	35
Number of households with migrant members*	19	15	18	19

Notes: *Household interviews Songhuaba, January 2009; ** See endnote 2.

the other three village groups visited is comparable in size relative to the populations of the teams.

Very few households reported that they received government assistance beyond water area assistance, which every household received as compensation for not being able to diversify their livelihoods locally by running businesses. The policy of setting up restrictions on business activities and expropriating farmland was reputedly implemented to avoid pollution and further containment of Songhuaba Reservoir. The assistance is provided as part of the national government policy of restoring 40,000 mu (1 mu = 667 m²) of farmland to forest (Bureau of Environmental Protection of Kunming City 1988). Only one household informed that they ran their own business. Other households reported that government transfers accounted for part of their income, which they received as part of the government's fight against poverty through poverty assistance to poor households (household interviews, January 2009). Overall, the stock of crops being produced between the teams were similar, and consisted of *cai* (Chinese cabbage), *gu* (corn), *tu dou* (potato), *mai* (wheat), and small amounts of different kinds of fruits, with *ping guo* (apple) being the most common (household interviews Songhuaba, January 2009).

The village groups were chosen after we had made some phone calls to village leaders in order to find villages with substantial numbers of migrant workers. Knowledge of the area possessed by my colleague, who was conducting his doctoral research in the area at the time, was crucial for deciding who and where it would be beneficial to visit. We wanted to conduct household interviews within households with migrant workers and households without migrant workers at the time of the study. In addition, to ensure representativeness within the village groups visited, at least two-thirds of the households in each village group were targeted for interviews and in total 85 out of 91 interviews were completed.[4] Thus, the sizes of the village groups were also important to allow for the target number of interviews to be reached.

Household interviews were carried out to identify characteristics of demography, assets, livelihood activities, and migration. In addition, the interviewees were asked for their perceptions on why migration was initiated, how it affected work relations within the household with respect to gender and age, the role of networks, and their plans for the future. After the initial phone calls, we identified six villages that we considered suitable in terms of the numbers of households and migrant workers that we wanted to visit. In two of the villages, no one was at home and therefore we ended up holding household interviews in four village groups in four different villages; one member of each household who was above the age of 15 years was interviewed.[5] We used a snowball method during the interviews to ensure that we targeted households with migrant workers especially, and to ensure that we visited houses where people were present. Moreover, when we arrived in the village groups, we gathered members of the community to make a participatory map of the village to enable us to identify households with and without migrant workers, the location of water supplies, agricultural land, grassland, and nearby institutions such as schools, post offices, and stores. The mappings were done to make the purpose of our visits known to the community members and to prepare them for the possibility that we might knock on their doors to ask some questions, and to ensure that we could return to specific households at a later time if we had any follow-up questions. The method was also a means of validating the numbers of migrant workers in the village groups at the time of our visit and the number of members in each household.

During the interviews we used a semi-structured questionnaire and during the participatory mapping we gathered either in an open space or in the home of the village group leader. I was accompanied by four research assistants who were trained in fieldwork and a colleague who was writing his doctoral thesis on the quality of the soil and water in Songhuaba. Some villages were difficult to access due to limited public transportation and poor quality gravel roads, which meant we had to hire a car and a designated driver to reach them. Hereafter, the household survey is referred to as the Yunnan household survey and the participatory mapping is referred to as the Yunnan participatory mapping.

The reason why this chapter focuses on migration solely undertaken for work is to explore the impact of migration on the livelihoods of the households inter-viewed.[6] At the time of the household survey, a considerable number of rural migrant workers had returned to their village group, either with the intention of remaining permanently or to stay temporarily with their family during the Spring Festival (the Chinese New Year) celebrations. All except one of the households visited identified themselves as belonging to the Han majority. Of the 54 migrant worker households that we visited, 43 told us that they had left to find jobs in Kunming city (15 km to the south) because it is situated close to the Songhuaba watershed area. It is almost impossible to commute on a daily basis between Kunming and most destinations within the Songhuaba watershed area due to poor quality roads and fixed working hours. Most of the informants said that the fact that they knew someone in Kunming, either from the family or from the same village group, was an important consideration when taking up work in the city. Hence, social networks and physical distance, as well as financial and personal costs, are important when deciding where to become migrant workers (Lee 1966).

Rural migrant workers in the reform era in China

Any analysis of internal migration in China should take into account the specific institutional mechanisms that regulate mobility in general and settlement in particular. Following the culmination of the present *hukou* system at the end of the 1950s, in 1958 the government established the current mobility regime (Cheng & Selden 1994; Whyte 2010). Under the system, at birth every person inherits their mother's or father's agricultural or non-agricultural registration status, which in practice means they have either a rural or urban citizenship. Although the *hukou* system was reformed at the beginning of the 1980s, provisions from 1985 to allow for temporary residence permits in cities were especially important, and the *hukou* system remains integral in constituting settlement opportunities, work relations between urban employers and rural residents, and welfare provisions for both rural and urban residents (Chan & Buckingham 2008; Xu *et al.* 2011; Solinger & Hu 2012).

There were *c.*100–115 million rural migrant labourers (*minggong*) in China at the beginning of the 21st century (Chan 2008), and the most recent official data suggest that the number had surpassed 200 million by 2010 (Sun & Fan 2010). Most of the migrant workers are not able to retain their urban registration, despite certain reforms to the *hukou* system since the turn of the 21st century to allow some privileged groups, such as overseas entrepreneurs, to settle permanently in urban areas and hold temporary residence permits in urban areas (Chan & Buckingham 2008; Sun & Fan 2010). Rural migrant labour refers to 'the working population without local *hukou* in the destination and from the countryside' (Chan 2008, 97).

Traditionally, rural migrant workers in China have been characterized as seasonal workers returning to the countryside during the most intense periods in the agricultural cycle, but their mobility seems to have become characterized by long-term circular movement, whereby they return to their place of origin once or twice a year. Their circular movement should also be understood in relation to the limited settlement opportunities in urban areas created by the *hukou* system. Moreover, rural migrant workers retain links to their place of origin by sending money and commodities, and by returning to their farm at busy times of the year, as well as during the Spring Festival in January or February (Murphy 2002). The main reasons why rural migrant workers retain strong links with their natal community are social exclusion in the cities, the search for social acceptance at home, their upbringing and a continued sense of 'belonging' to the land through the *hukou* system, diversification of risk by having land as a livelihood safety net, and the expectation of benefits upon return (de Haan 1999; Murphy 2002).

Cindy Fan (2008) implies that the transitions over the life courses of women are important in constituting the livelihood options available for rural households. Young, single women have become an important group of rural migrant workers over the years in China, and have given rise to the concept of *dagongmei* (working girls) (Pun 1999). Whereas adolescence may constitute a time of much mobility for many young women from rural areas in China, the time after marriage often involves long periods of immobility as they are left with the task of managing farm work, childcare, and taking care of their parents-in-law (Fan 2008).

Pun Ngai and Lu Huilin make a distinction between what they name first-generation rural migrant workers, born before the reform period was initiated in the beginning of the 1980s, and who migrated for work during the 1980s and 1990s, and second-generation rural migrant workers, born in the reform period, i.e. after 1980, and who ventured out to work during the late 1990s and in the 2000s (Pun & Lu 2010). Others have made a distinction between new-generation migrants and old-generation migrants (Liu *et al.* 2012). The division between migrant workers born before and after 1980 has thus become commonly accepted within Chinese scholarship on this issue, as ardently argued by Wang Xingzhou (Wang 2008). The concept of a newly emerging generation of mobile rural populations was coined as early as 2001 by Wang Chunguang (cited in Wang 2008). Despite being unsatisfactory, the conceptual couple of new-generation and old-generation rural migrant workers is used in this chapter because it avoids the confusion arising from the use of the terms first generation and second generation.

Yan Hairong makes the case that perceptions concerning personhood have changed dramatically from one generation to another between those that grew up before the reform era and those that grew up within it (Yan 2003). She found that young women interviewed between 1998 and 2000 were impatient to escape their rural origins in Anhui Province and they anticipated that their goals and desires would be achieved in urban areas in the future. Yan Hairong traces the process of change in the perceptions and outlooks between two cohorts of female rural migrant workers to the discursive violence that the countryside has been subjected to in the post-Mao (1976) era (Yan 2003). Similarly, Pun Ngai and Lu Huilin argue that not only do the new-generation migrant workers lack opportunities to take up permanent urban residence, but also, due to rural-urban inequality, they cannot envision fulfilling their goals and desires by returning to the countryside (Pun & Lu 2010). Not being able to settle in the city due to the *hukou* system and not being willing to return to the countryside and work as farmers gives rise to a sense of quasi-identity among the new-generation migrant workers, who are 'neither *nongmin* (peasant) nor a *gongren* (worker)' (Pun & Lu 2010, 498). In addition, it should be noted that the new-generation migrant workers seem to be deskilled in terms of farming, which may distance them further from the traditional subsistence type of farming practised by their parents (Pun 2005). In short, we should expect that members of the new generation of rural migrant workers do not necessarily share the motivations or the mobility patterns of the old generation of rural migrant workers when heading to the city to work.

Migration and the life course

When we asked a woman of 28 years, who formerly had worked in Kunming as a waitress, about her reasons for returning to work on the household farm, she replied that she planned to marry (Yunnan household survey, 2009). It is a common notion that many women return to their natal villages when they are to marry and settle down, both in China and elsewhere (Fan 2008; Thao 2013). In China, this practice is related partly to patriarchal values that guide events throughout the life courses of men and women and partly to the low status assigned to rural women in the urban marriage market (Fan 2008). After marriage, men are expected to continue their breadwinning activities, including leaving their village to find wage work and farm, whereas women are expected to stay at home to take care of children and farmland (Fan 2008). Despite the rules and expectations, they do not fully determine, nor is it possible to predict, the practices and interests of men and women over their life course, as this study shows. In total, there were 29 female and 78 male labour migrants in the studied four village groups in Songhuaba (Yunnan participatory mapping, 2009). The households that we visited accounted for 23 female and 52 male migrant workers, and the average age of the sample was 33 years (Yunnan household survey, 2009). We visited 55 out of 69 migrant worker households in the village groups, which comprised 187 households in total. Hence, more than one-third of the households had one family member working away from home at the time of the investigation. Migrant worker households were defined as those with one or more members working in off-farm sectors.

With regard to mobility during the course of a year, we were often told that members of households working in urban areas returned home for at least a couple of months each year and more often than not their return coincided with the time of the Spring Festival. The proximity of Songhuaba to Kunming, at least geographically, enhanced their opportunities to be mobile in terms of participating in both life back home and wage labour in the provincial capital. They could return home several times each year to assist their household at busy times in the agricultural year, especially during the autumn, and to participate in major life events such as funerals or weddings involving close family.

A closer look at how mobility was practised by men and women in the households visited in Songhuaba revealed that men had longer tenures as migrant workers compared to their female counterparts. Women typically worked as migrant workers for between two and four years, although a few had spent as much as ten years of their lives working in the same place (Yunnan household survey, 2009). It should be borne in mind that for many migrant workers, 2008 was the first year they had worked outside their household and it thus marked the start of their mobility. For example, a father told us that his daughter aged 19 years had started working in a restaurant in Kunming early in 2008 and although at the time of the interview she had returned for the Spring Festival, it was likely that she would migrate for work afterwards. A comparison of the amount of time that migrant workers spent working as an employee revealed that 29 out of 52 men worked away from home for more than five years, while the corresponding figure for women was nine out of 21 (Yunnan household survey, 2009). Thus, the men in the households visited in Songhuaba typically spend longer periods of time as rural migrant workers. A woman aged 39 years told us that her husband, aged 43 years, had been working away from the village for 13 years and that in his absence she had had to take care of their two children, aged four and 12 years respectively, as well as her father in-law. In addition, their farmland was reduced when her husband went to work in Beijing, because the land was regulated and distributed according to the number of adult labourers in the household. The woman's burden of farming and housework had increased. She stated that she was willing to go out to work if an opportunity arose because the income gained from farming was not sufficient to support the household. Similar stories were told to us by several women who had been left with the responsibility of taking care of children and parents-in-law as well as farming while their husbands were working away from home (see also Chapter 7 by Kusakabe and Vongphakdy).

Typically, men are in the age group 17–22 years when they start migrating to work in urban areas (Yunnan household survey, 2009). In addition, a considerable number of able-bodied men have their first experience of migration in their thirties. Interestingly, very few men and women first migrate when they are in their late twenties. However, in Songhuaba, men tend to marry in their late twenties, whereas women often are younger at the time of marriage, and these findings are similar to those from elsewhere in China (Fan & Huang 1998).

Thao (2013), who studied how life-course transitions affect mobility and immobility in a rural area in Vietnam, found that after marriage women typically stay at home for several years. There are reasons to believe that there may be a similar pattern in Songhuaba. First, in accordance with the patrilocal marriage custom, women are expected to settle with their husband in his natal home. Second, with an agricultural *hukou* the responsibility for some of the farmland is inherited by the son and leaving farmland idle is considered a criminal offense as well as socially unacceptable in China (Fan 2008). Thus, either the daughter-in-law or the son is expected to continue the agricultural work and be interested in it. Third, following marriage, it is quite evident that many couples soon become parents, which also inhibits women's and men's mobility in different ways (Fan 2008). The study conducted in Songhuaba revealed that women were most likely to be single when they migrated for work and did not marry until they returned to their place of origin. This was mainly due to their young age at the time of becoming mobile (Pun 1999). Men tended to follow a similar pattern, although some of them remain unmarried in their late thirties. One man aged 39 years told us that there was a possibility that marriage or finding a partner would motivate him to leave his farm in the future. Thus, the life-course transition from being a single young adult into forging conjugal ties renders both women and men less mobile.

Whereas marriage may initially alter the mobility practices of both men and women, having children can further alter their mobility in terms of either their ability or interest in being migrant workers (Thao 2013). During the household survey it was discovered that both men and women were more mobile before having children and after their children had grown up, i.e. after their children had reached the age of 16 years. For example, a father aged 40 years and his wife aged 32 years informed that they could not go out to work as they had to take care of their two children who were aged 11 and 16 years. However, 24 out of 52 of the men who were mobile had children at the time of migration, whereas only three women were mobile. By contrast, in response to the question of whether they would want to migrate to work if they had the possibility, both men and women who had reached their sixties stated that they were too old. Hence, the time after children had grown up was not necessarily considered a transformation towards increased mobility for older villagers, although it often was for their children.

Fewer women who had transitioned from being single sojourners or married without children were mobile compared to men, suggesting that gender plays an important role in terms of mobility practices throughout the different life-course transitions in the study area. A woman aged 28 years said that she had migrated for work when she reached 16 years and had continued the practice for seven years. However, when she became pregnant she had returned to her place of origin and at the time of the study she was settled with her husband and their son, aged five years. In another family, the husband and father, aged 30 years, worked away from home while his wife took care of their two children, aged four and seven years, thus demonstrating that having children does not necessarily affect husbands and wives in the same way. Thus, in Songhuaba, both women and men are most mobile during adolescence and/or before marriage. This is further illustrated by a woman who informed that her husband had left to work in Kunming 13 years earlier, but when their son was born (in 2004), her husband had started working locally so that he could be closer to his family (Yunnan household survey, 2009).

To summarize, while many migrant workers from Songhuaba continue to work in urban areas after marriage, men are more mobile than women following the transition within their life course. Following the birth of their children, many parents opt to stay at home and farm while the children grow up. However, many still go out to work after having children and in such cases fathers are more mobile than mothers in Songhuaba, which points to the gendered formation of different transitions of their life course.

Mobility and immobility – livelihood outcomes

It is to be expected that different transitions within the life courses of families will affect their well-being, livelihood options, and priorities, as argued convincingly by Gordon De Jong and Deborah Graefe (2008) in their study of the economic consequences of life-course transitions for internal migrants in the USA. In other words, household resources, such as human capital, the level of education and number of adult labourers, and social networks, open up or restrict opportunities in the mobility–immobility continuum. At the same time, the ability, interest, and practices of being mobile or staying put affect household resources. In the case of Songhuaba, transitions within a household affect the members' capability and interest for mobility or staying put, as exemplified in the preceding section by the case of the family with two children of school age. Arguably, the transition from having children of school age to the time when the children become single sojourners, after they have completed their education or have dropped out of school, has the most impact on the mobility–immobility continuum. The process can be understood with reference to the family with two children below the age of ten years, who stated that they might want to go out to work later but for the time being needed to be at home to take care of their children. However, quite a large number of households with children had one or two family members who were migrant workers. A son, aged 16 years, stated that since his father had started working in Kunming he did not get enough assistance with his school homework. The remittances received from the father, aged 42 years, were used for the boy's education and his sister's education, which in 2008 cost approximately CNY 5,000 (USD 802.350). Households with grandparents in good health had flexibility in terms of mobility because parents could ask their parents to assist with childcare while they worked away from home. It was also observed that children of pre-school age stayed with their grandparents while their parents worked away from home, which meant there were differences in immobility and mobility among the household members. Hence, when the research participants embarked on their life-course transition, they found that raising children affected their practices and interests with respect to their mobility.

Below, I outline a typology of households based on gross income, owner-ship of livestock, and ownership of durable consumer goods (Table 4.2). The typology serves as an index of class relations in the village groups visited, and was designed to reveal the relationship between mobility and immobility and resources available at the time of the investigation. In addition to these measures, indicators such as receipt of poverty assistance, a large proportion of income derived from borrowing, lending money to others, saving surplus money, and business ownership are included to show the relative status of the households. This typology was inspired by Rachel Murphy's (2002) household survey conducted in Jiangxi Province, based on the recommendations set out by the International Fund for Agricultural Development (IFAD). The latter approach can be used when no longitudinal household data are available, as was the case for Songhuaba. Thao (2013, 87) makes an analogous case when she compares what she terms 'mover' and 'stayer' households with regard to income and ownership of durable consumer goods and livestock.

To a large extent, the size of land allocations and number of adult labourers correspond to the level of resources found at the time of the investigation (Jakobsen 2009). Hence, the study confirms the findings from Murphy's (2002) study conducted in Jiangxi Province in the mid-1990s, namely that wealthier households consolidate their position by migrating, as they already enjoy the benefits of many labourers, larger land allocations, and access to local, off-farm labour sources. However, both the study in Songhuaba and Murphy's (2002) study found that, in general, migration leads to a better standard of living for households that participate, thus suggesting that both poorer and wealthier households benefit from outmigration (Table 4.3).

Looking beyond the numbers presented in Table 4.3 gives some clues about the relationship between household resources, life courses, and mobility. In several of the households categorized with low resource endowments, all members of the family were above 60 years, which meant they were less entitled to land resources and their mobility was more likely to be halted by both age and requirements in the urban labour market. In the case of a wife aged 50 years and her husband aged

Table 4.2 Household typology

Category	Number of households	Characteristics
Low resource endowments	13	Net annual income less than CNY 1000* the previous year
		Own a few animals
		Own 1 or less durable consumer goods**
		Receive poverty assistance from the government***
		More than 80% of the income derived from borrowing money in the previous year
Low to medium resource endowments	18	Net annual income CNY 1000–1300 the previous year
		Own fewer than 2 pigs and have few animals in general
		Own 2 or less durable consumer goods
		Relatively large proportion of total income is from borrowed means, *c.*50–70% of total income in the previous year
Medium resource endowments	24	Net annual income CNY 1300–2000 the previous year
		Fewer than 3 pigs and 10 chickens
		Own between 3 and 4 durable consumer goods
		Utilized approximately CNY 3000 on durable consumer goods in the last 10 years****
Medium to high resource endowments	16	Net annual income CNY 2000–3000 the previous year
		Fewer than 3 pigs, 10 chickens, and have sheep or cattle in addition
		Own 4 or less durable consumer goods
		Utilized approximately CNY 4000–5000 on durable consumer goods in the last 10 years
High resource endowments	16	Net annual income more than CNY 3000 the previous year
		Own more than 4 pigs, 10 chickens, and cattle or sheep in addition
		Own more than 5 durable consumer goods and utilized more than CNY 5000 on durable consumer goods in the last 10 years
		Save money due to surplus in household income in the last year
		Own a business
		Lent other people money in the previous year

Source: Yunnan household survey, January 2009 (derived from Jakobsen 2009, 16).

Notes: *See endnote 2.

    **Some durable consumer goods are scarcer than others and most households in the survey owned a TV and washing machine, while a few owned a motorbike and a solar panel. Few households received poverty assistance and few households save money, own their own business, or lend money to other people.

    ***In the survey we asked about ownership and spending on housing, TVs, cars, motorbikes, washing machines, solar panels, and additional durable consumer goods.

    ****The average spending on durable consumer goods for the studied households was CNY 3000 in the period 1999–2009.

Table 4.3 Relationship between household resources and mobility (by household)

Household members who were migrant workers	Low resource endowments	Low to medium resource endowments	Medium resource endowments	Medium to high resource endowments	High resource endowments
None	7	9	7	4	4
One	5	7	13	8	7
Two or more*	1	2	4	4	5

Source: Yunnan household survey, 2009.

Note: *Only one household had more than two migrant workers at the time of the survey.

60 years, who were asked about their plans for the future, they informed that they would have liked to have gone out to work but they were too old. Hence, they perceived their transition towards old age as impinging on their mobility.

Mobility and immobility thus shaped the livelihood outcomes for the households in four villages in Songhuaba. Remittances are arguably the most direct way that households gain from having someone working as a migrant worker. Some parents in the study area stated that pressure on their household economy was relieved when their children were able to support themselves as a consequence of migrating for work (Yunnan household survey, 2009). Hence, for some families, the life-course transition from having children of school age to the children becoming migrant workers and leaving their parents' home, means that they gain control over more resources than previously. At the same time, some parents complained that they had had to pay for their children's migration, as there had been some initial costs involved, yet they had not received any remittances.

As indicated earlier in this chapter, since the early 1990s, rural families in China have experienced significant increases in the costs of their children's education (Lü 2012). There are several reasons for this, but the reduced transfers from central government to local governments in the 1990s created incentives for local governments to introduce fees and levies on schools. Further, due to the policies of centralizing schools and merging schools in urban and rural areas at the turn of the 21st century, many local schools were shut down and therefore many rural schoolchildren were faced with having to use transportation for long journeys, which proved costly for many parents. In addition, due to the long distances between home and school, many children have to live at their school during the week and therefore their parents need to pay for staff, materials, and other costs at the boarding houses (conversation with World Agroforestry Centre Kunming staff, 2011). Thus, although the government has boosted public spending in recent years, removing most fees paid to public schools, the cost of boarding still remains. The net result is an increased monetization of daily lives analogous to what structural adjustment policies have done to subsistence farmers in sub-Saharan Africa (Bryceson 2002). In Songhuaba and elsewhere in Yunnan, the policies place pressure on parents to engage in migration to support their household while their children attend school. Thus, we are reminded that mobility and immobility is not just a question of strategic manoeuvring within the livelihood options available but for households it is just as much negotiation between needs and priorities.

Some parents are not content with public schools and spend heavily on private schools or extra private tuition for their children, which are an important priority when it comes to spending remittances and cash income in general (Yunnan household survey, 2009). Most parents said that they valued education for their children highly and one worried father told us that when he went away to work, his children, aged 11 and 17 years, needed to do more work on the farm, which could impinge on their school efforts and results. Another parent, aged 35 years, with two children aged 11 and 17 years, stated that when he migrated for work, the income of the household increased and therefore they could afford to spend money on their children's education. He longed for another life for his children and education was seen as a key to achieving it (Yunnan household survey, 2009). Thus, motivation of earning money to sustain children's education was important for migrant workers.

The levels of education shown in Table 4.4 are based on The International Bureau of Education's information about China's educational system (UNESCO 2006). Under the system, primary education is considered to correspond to the age range 6–12 years, secondary education 12–15 years (lower) and 15–18 years (upper), and higher education from 19 years onwards. Only a few of the interviewees told us that either they or their family members had continued their education after they had reached the age of 19 years. The households were asked about their current state of affairs and those in the previous calendar year. In China, the new school year begins in March. Therefore, for the purpose of the study, if a child was aged 12 years at the time of the household survey they were recorded as being a primary education pupil. Ideally, we would have liked to collect data on the socio-economic status of each household in a number of different years, in order to see how transitions had affected their well-being. Nevertheless, the data in Table 4.4 provide an idea of the relationship between having children of school age and a household's resource endowments.

Although the effect on households' resources of the extra costs of children's education varies, there is undoubtedly a link between household resources and both the number of children attending school and the level of education they are receiving (Table 4.4). Some households were heavily burdened by the cost of education and it was quite common for households with children, especially those in secondary or higher education, to have spent more than 50 per cent of their previous year's income on education (Yunnan household survey, 2009). Evidently, spending as much as CNY 15,000 (USD 2,407.05) on children's education was not uncommon. Most households with children in primary education told us that in 2008 they spent CNY 1,500 (USD 240.705) on their child's education. Parents often told us that in 2008 they had spent more than CNY 5,000 (USD 802.350) on their children's education when they were enrolled in upper secondary or higher education. In addition, grandparents made significant contributions towards their grandchildren's education. They contributed by caring for the children while their parents were working away from home and they helped with farming activities,

Table 4.4 Household resources according to the number of children attending school

Educational status for school-aged children in households	Households with low resource endowments	Households with low to medium resource endowments	Households with medium resource endowments	Households with medium to high resource endowments	Households with high resource endowments
None	4*	2	7	2	6
Do not attend school	1 with 1 child** and 1 with 2 children	1 with 2 children**** and 1 with 1 child	2	0	1
Primary education	2	2 with 1 child and 1 with 2 children	2 with 2 children and 6 with 1 child	1 with 2 children and 2 with 1 child	2 with 2 children and 3 with 1 child
Primary and secondary education	2 with 2 children	4 with 2 children and 1 with 3 children	4 with 2 children	4 with 2 children	3 with 2 children
Secondary education	1	3 with 1 child and 2 with 2 children	1	4	1
Secondary and higher education	1 with 2 children***			3 with 2 children	
Higher education		1	2		

Source: Yunnan household survey, 2009.

Notes: *Unless stated otherwise, the figures refer to the number of households with one child attending school.
**The child worked as a migrant worker.
***The family informed that they had spent CNY 25,000 (USD 4,011.75) on education fees in 2008. Although the amount may have been exaggerated (as was usual when referring to expenditure figures), clearly a large proportion of the family's income was spent on the children's education.
****Both children in the household worked as migrant workers.

most often subsistence farming, which relieved their grandchildren of their responsibilities for agricultural labour. Hence, it is reasonable to conclude that education was highly prioritized among parents even though it put a strain on the household economy. Among the expenditures mentioned by interviewees during our household survey, education far exceeded any other costs for households with children attending school. It could therefore be argued that spending on children's education represents a long-term accumulation of livelihood resources (Thao 2013).

In general, households with high resource endowments had few children receiving secondary or higher education (Table 4.4). More than one-third of the households did not have any children enrolled at school at the time of the household survey. It should be borne in mind that most of the households had at least one member who worked away from home. Hence, households leaning towards the mobile end of the mobility–immobility continuum were relatively well off and had yet to experience or surpass the stage within their life course of having children enrolled at school. Despite the relationship between mobility, children's education, and household resources, it is also evident from Table 4.4 that a substantial number of the households in the medium to high resource category had children of school age. Furthermore, those households quite often had children who were receiving upper secondary or higher education. Considering the high costs incurred by the households, this reflects their ability, interest, and resources within the community. The relationship between mobility and household resources is demonstrated by how the households in the medium to high resource category were just as mobile as the high resource category in terms of having migrant workers.

By contrast, in the case of households in the low to medium resource category and some households with the least resources, having children enrolled at school was a heavy economic burden on their livelihoods (Table 4.4). Among households in the two lowest resource categories were a couple in their seventies without children and a couple in their seventies with an unmarried son in his forties. They experienced increased daily cash requirements with few sources of non-farm income, while at the same time their ability to earn an income from farming was diminishing because the amount of farmland in the Songhuaba watershed area was rapidly decreasing due to the watershed policies.

In short, the studied families' life-course transition towards having children incurred high costs as soon as their children started school. Households that were well-off often had one or more family members working away from home, who provided remittances to help pay for their children's education. Investing in education was seen as a long-term livelihood strategy to ensure that children would have opportunities to gain an income and a decent life when they became adults and had to support their aging parents.

Mobility and immobility – comparison of two generations of migrant workers

People inhabit both biographical time, i.e. they occupy a particular position within their life course, and at the same time are part of and shaped by historical time

(Pilcher 1994). Between two generations of rural migrant workers there are likely to be differences in their mobility throughout their life courses, which gives an indication of how practices, interests, and perceptions of what constitutes a good life are changing for rural dwellers in China. One qualification needs to be raised, namely the new generation of rural migrant workers has yet to live through most transitions within their life courses. Hence, in this section I only discuss mobility practices that are to some extent comparable. Based on existing knowledge concerning the new generation of rural migrant workers (Pun & Lu 2010; Hu 2012), it can be expected that the new generation of rural migrant workers have other goals and motivations for working away from home compared to the old generation, as they are keen to live an urban life. By contrast, the old generation of migrant workers is often portrayed as motivated by the benefits they expect to gain from living in the countryside while labouring for an urban salary, such as the ability to invest in housing, daily consumption, education for their children, or setting up a business (Murphy 2002). Moreover, the new generation of rural migrant workers that longs to escape current rural life is more likely to comprise younger workers than the old generation when they first work away from home or leave to create a life elsewhere.

The data from the four village groups reveal that 30 of the men in the households visited belonged to the new generation of rural migrant workers, i.e. those born after 1980, while 22 belonged to the old generation. In total, six of the women were categorized as old-generation rural migrant workers, i.e. those born before 1980, while the rest, 13, were treated as members of the new generation. The average monthly salary among the new generation of rural migrant workers was CNY 890 (USD 142.818), while the old generation of rural migrant workers in Songhuaba earned CNY 790 (USD 126.759) (Yunnan household survey, 2009).

The new generation of rural migrant workers in the village groups visited was in general younger when they left home to work compared to the old generation. This finding seems to support the notion that, as Yan Hairong (Yan 2003) ardently argues, the countryside and its way of life offers little for young generations of rural dwellers. Further, the findings validate the perception that with the new generation of rural migrant workers there is the formation of a social generation with shared/similar experiences and that has lived through the same historical time. That is, as findings elsewhere indicate (Liu *et al.* 2012), they long to escape their rural origins, but are not able to settle permanently in the cities and are unwilling to return to the countryside. The fact that they were similar in age when they first migrated for work – most were in the age range 17–21 years – shows that they had similar mobility practices and shared an urge to leave their natal communities behind. Further, it is reasonable to argue that for the young men and women belonging to the new generation of rural migrant workers it has become an integral part of their adolescence to move to urban areas after they have completed their education or dropped out of school.

In the case of the old generation of rural migrant workers, their first experience of working more often than not came after they had reached 25 years, which indicates their mobility was initiated due to familial obligations (Yue *et al.* 2010). This was demonstrated in Songhuaba by the fact that 25 out of 28 old-generation migrants contributed remittances to the household. For the members of the new generation, responsibility did not play the same role in motivating them to migrate for work, as revealed by the fact that only 20 sent remittances at the time of the survey (Yunnan household survey, 2009). However, as noted above, one should be cautious about finding overly strong connections between generations and non-remittances, as the particular space inhabited within the life course is just as likely to account for these differences, namely that of adolescence; see Rigg (2007), who argues that as people pass through life courses their priorities, vulnerabilities, and positions change, thus, for example, priorities held during adolescence are likely to be different than those held after becoming a parent.

Household members, including some migrant workers, were asked what factors had motivated their move. They were encouraged to name several reasons and to elaborate on them. The responses revealed that both generations engaged in wage labour to earn money. Further, a larger proportion of the old generation of rural migrant workers in the visited households named lack of enough land as an important consideration, while this was less important for the new generation. In addition, members of the new generation seemed eager to acquire new perspectives and experience urban life, but this was not a major factor for members of the old generation, although some of them named it as a central motivation. Moreover, although earning money was the most important reason for migration for work given by households with old-generation migrants, members of the new-generation households told us that learning new skills and gaining new perspectives was most important to their mobile family members. Additionally, many parents complained about the wasteful habits of their children, who spent all of their urban income on themselves. Their income was not used to meet the need of the household but to fulfil their own wants and desires. The findings presented above at least suggest that there is a quite consistent urge among the new generation to experience urban life.

Both new- and old-generation migrant workers informed that they had left their farms and families because they did not have enough to do. Several families complained that their land had been reduced recently due to the watershed area policies of expropriating farmland for forestry, while members of other families stated that they would go out to work as soon as the government had expropriated their land. In other words, for some there was not enough work on the farm, while quite a few others had found that life at home was too boring.

Examination of members of the new generation's mobility practices within their life courses revealed that the new generation did not initiate their mobility with the intention of keeping one foot on the farm and the other in the city, as members of the old generation did: while the old generation typically intended to *li tu bu li xiang* (leave the land but not leave the village), the new generation intends to *li tu you li xiang* (leave the land as well as the village) (Yang & Guo 1996). Thus, while some members of the households had a joint-family livelihood perspective on their reasons for migration, others had an individualistic outlook on their mobility.

Additionally, the parents' encouragement towards members of the younger generation's education, as evident from the statements of parents and the money spent on education, further enhances the distance of the new generation from agricultural work in Songhuaba. As observed in studies conducted in sub-Saharan Africa and Southeast Asia, which deployed a generational lens during investigations into livelihood transformations (Bryceson 2002; Kelly 2011), rural dwellers have a general disdain for agricultural work, and this is most strongly articulated by the new generations (Rigg 2006). The study conducted in Songhuaba confirms that there is an urge among the new generation to live a different life than the old generation; their mobility is initiated due to individualistic aspirations, and they do not contribute in the same way to the household economy through remittances. At the same time, it should be kept in mind that the young migrant workers are in the adolescent phase of their life course and it remains to be seen whether in the future their mobility biographies, i.e. how their mobility is shaped by transitions within their life courses, will be different or similar to those of the old generation.

The mobility of the new generation of rural migrant workers in Songhuaba is starting earlier than the mobility of the old generation. The motivation to migrate for work is shared between the generations in the sense that everyone wants to earn money, but the new generation is more interested in gaining new perspectives and experiences from their mobility than the old generation seems to have been. With the new generation of rural migrant workers in Songhuaba, mobility seems to have become an integral part of the life-course transition from being part of their parent's household to becoming individual adults.

Conclusions

Through household interviews and participatory mapping in the Songhuaba watershed area, this chapter has explored how transitions within life courses are gendered and shape mobility and immobility. Not only do transitions within life courses of individuals situate them at various positions along the mobility–immobility continuum, they also strongly influence livelihood options and outcomes for the entire household. In particular, the transition towards having children of school age places an extra burden on households with already few resources. The comparison made here between two social generations of rural migrant workers hints at their differentiated mobility practices during adolescence. A comparative perspective on generations of migrant workers shows that we should be cautious about making assumptions regarding the motivations of entire households and their mobility–immobility practices, since they are differentiated by positions within life courses and socio-historical time. The present study shows that while the old generation straddled the rural–urban divide to gain the most from both, i.e. income in the city and consumption in the countryside, members of the new generation are more eager to gain a living and consume in the city, at least while they are single sojourners.

Notes

1   In each village in rural China there are several working teams or groups (*zu*), which often consist of between 30 and 200 households under the same administrative leadership. Each team has a group leader who is assigned tasks by the village committee, such as mediating disputes, improving rural incomes, and organizing labour (Murphy 2002).

2   CNY 1 = USD 0.160470 as of 4 February 2013. All exchange rates mentioned in the chapter have been calculated using this exchange rate.

3   Watersource Department of Kunming, 'Principal Socio-economic Data on Songhuaba Watershed Area', unpublished report, 2004.

4   Some interviews were discontinued due to events in the lives of the agents, such as when children needed to be collected from school. In addition, during some interviews the interviewees decided that they did not want to answer further questions.

5   The age limit was set at 15 years because migrant worker populations are regarded as being in the age range 15–55 years (Murphy 2002).

6   The fieldwork was done for my master's thesis and the research was directed towards the impacts of migration on resource distribution between households. However, much unused data and a different approach to it have provided a rich source of information for this chapter.

References

Bourdieu, P. 1977. *Outline of a Theory of Practice*. Cambridge University Press, Cambridge.

Bryceson, D.F. 2002. The scramble in Africa: Reorienting rural livelihoods. *World Development* 30, 725–739.

Bryman, A. 1987. *Rethinking the Life Cycle*. Macmillan, London.

Bureau of Environmental Protection of Kunming City. 1988. *Multi-subject Comprehensive Investigation of the Protected District of Sources of Water at Songhuaba*. Bureau of Environmental Protection of Kunming City, Kunming.

Chan, K.W. 2008. Internal labour migration in China: Trends, geographical distribution and policies. *Proceedings of the United Nations Expert Group Meeting on Population Distribution, Urbanization, Internal Migration and Development*, 93–122. EAS/WP.206. United Nations, New York.

Chan, K.W. & Buckingham, W. 2008. Is China abolishing the *hukou* system? *The China Quarterly* 195, 582–606.

Cheng, T. & Selden, M. 1994. The origins and social consequences of China's *hukou* system. *The China Quarterly* 139, 644–668.

Davin, D. 1999. *Internal Migration in Contemporary China*. Macmillan, London.

de Haan, A. 1999. Livelihoods and poverty: The role of migration – a critical review of the migration literature. *Journal of Development Studies* 36, 1–47.

De Haas, H. 2010. Migration and development: A theoretical perspective 1. *International Migration Review* 44, 227–264.

De Jong, G.F. & Graefe, D.R. 2008. Family life course transitions and the economic consequences of internal migration. *Population, Space and Place* 14, 267–282.

Donaldson, J.A. 2011. *Small Works: Poverty and Economic Development in Southwestern China*. Cornell University Press, Ithaca, NY.

Ellis, F. 1998. Household strategies and rural livelihood diversification. *Journal of Development Studies* 35, 1–38.

Ellis, F. 2000. *Rural Livelihoods and Diversity in Developing Countries*. Oxford University Press, Oxford.

Ellis, F. & Freeman, H.A. 2005. *Rural Livelihoods and Poverty Reduction Policies.* Routledge, London.

Elmhirst, R. 2002. Daughters and displacement: Migration dynamics in an Indonesian transmigration area. *Journal of Development Studies* 38, 143–166.

Fan, C.C. 2008. *China on the Move: Migration, the State, and the Household.* Routledge, London.

Fan, C.C. & Huang, Y. 1998. Waves of rural brides: Female marriage migration in China. *Annals of the Association of American Geographers* 88, 227–251.

Glenn, N.D. 1977. *Cohort Analysis.* Sage, Beverly Hills, CA.

Halfacree, K.H. & Boyle, P.J. 1993. The challenge facing migration research: The case for a biographical approach. *Progress in Human Geography* 17, 333–348.

Hare, D.A. & Zhao, S. 2000. Labor migration as a rural development strategy: A view from the migration origin. West, L.A. & Zhao, Y. (eds) *Rural Labor Flows in China*, 148–178. University of California Press, Berkeley, CA.

Harris, C. 1987. The individual and society: A processual approach. Bryman, A., Bytheway, B., Allatt, P. & Keil, T. (eds) *Rethinking the Life Cycle*, 17–29. Macmillian, London.

Harvey, D. 2005. *A Brief History of Neoliberalism.* Oxford University Press, Oxford.

Hu, X. 2012. *China's 'New Generation' Rural-Urban Migrants: Migration Motivation and Migration Patterns.* Migration Information Source 2012. http://dx.doi.org/10.2139/ ssrn.1978546 (accessed 14 January 2012).

Jakobsen, T.S. 2009. *Impacts of Labor Migration for Rural Households in a Particular Setting in Southwest China: Resource Distribution and Second-Generation Migrants.* T.S. Jakobsen, Trondheim.

Kelly, P.F. 2011. Migration, agrarian transition, and rural change in Southeast Asia. *Critical Asian Studies* 43, 479–506.

Lee, E. 1966. A theory of migration. *Demography* 3, 47–57.

Liang, Z. 2001. The age of migration in China. *Population and Development Review* 27, 499–524.

Liu, Y., Li, Z. & Breitung, W. 2012. The social networks of new-generation migrants in China's urbanized villages: A case study of Guangzhou. *Habitat International* 36, 192–200.

Lü, C. 2012. *Poverty and Development in China: Alternative Approaches to Poverty Assessment.* Routledge, London.

Mannheim, K. 1952. The problem of generations. Mannheim, K. & Kecskemeti, P. (eds) *Essays on the Sociology of Knowledge*, 276–320, Routledge & Kegan Paul, London.

Massey, D.S. 1988. Economic development and international migration in comparative perspective. *Population and Development Review* 14, 383–413.

Massey, D.S., Arango, J., Hugo, G., Kouaouci, A., Pellegrino, A. & Taylor, J.E. 1993. Theories of international migration: A review and appraisal. *Population and Development Review* 19, 431–466.

Murphy, R. 2002. *How Migrant Labor is Changing Rural China.* Cambridge University Press, Cambridge.

Pilcher, J. 1994. Mannheim's sociology of generations: An undervalued legacy. *British Journal of Sociology* 45:3, 481–495.

Pun, N. 1999. Becoming *dagongmei* (working girls): The politics of identity and difference in reform China. *The China Journal* 42, 1–18.

Pun, N. 2005. *Made in China.* Duke University Press, Durham, NC.

Pun, N. & Lu, H. 2010. Unfinished proletarianization: Self, anger, and class action among the second generation of peasant-workers in present-day China. *Modern China* 36, 493–519.

Rigg, J. 2006. Land, farming, livelihoods, and poverty: Rethinking the links in the rural South. *World Development* 34, 180–202.

Rigg, J. 2007. *An Everyday Geography of the Global South*. Routledge, London.

Skeldon, R. 1997. *Migration and Development*. Longman, Harlow.

Solinger, D.J. 1999. *Contesting Citizenship in Urban China: Peasant Migrants, the State, and the Logic of the Market*. University of California Press, Berkeley, CA.

Solinger, D.J. & Hu, Y. 2012. Welfare, wealth and poverty in urban China: The *dibao* and its differential disbursement. *The China Quarterly* 211, 741–764.

Stark, O. & Bloom, D.E. 1985. The new economics of labor migration. *The American Economic Review* 75, 173–178.

Sun, M. & Fan, C.C. 2010. China's permanent and temporary migrants: Differentials and changes, 1990–2000. *The Professional Geographer* 63, 92–112.

Thao, V.T. 2013. Making a living in rural Vietnam from (im)mobile livelihoods: A case of women's migration. *Population, Space and Place* 19, 87–102.

UNESCO. 2006. *World Data on Education: The People's Republic of China*. 6th ed. International Bureau of Education, Geneva.

Wang, X. 2008. An investigation into intergenerational differences between two generations of migrant workers. *Social Sciences in China* 29, 136–156.

Whyte, M.K. (Ed.) 2010. *One Country, Two Societies*. Harvard University Press, Cambridge, MA.

Xu, Q., Guan, X. & Yao, F. 2011. Welfare program participation among rural-to-urban migrant workers in China. *International Journal of Social Welfare* 20, 10–21.

Yan, H. 2003. Specialization of the rural: Reinterpreting the labor mobility of rural young women in post-Mao China. *American Ethnologist* 30, 578–596.

Yang, Q. & Guo, F. 1996. Occupational attainments of rural to urban temporary economic migrants in China, 1985–1990. *International Migration Review* 30, 771–787.

Yue, Z.S., Li, S.Z., Feldman, M.W. & Du, H.F. 2010. Floating choices: A generational perspective on intentions of rural-urban migrants in China. *Environment and Planning A* 42, 545–562.

Yunnan Statistical Yearbook. 2004. China Statistical Press, Beijing.

Zhu, Y. & Chen, W. 2010. The settlement intention of China's floating population in the cities: Recent changes and multifaceted individual-level determinants. *Population, Space and Place* 16, 253–267.

5 Exploring mobile livelihoods among tribal communities in Odisha, India

Gendered insights and outcomes

Smita Mishra Panda

Introduction

This chapter deals with mobility among tribal communities in Khordha and Sundargarh Districts of Odisha, an eastern state of India. The analysis is based on a study conducted with the objective to understand the gendered nature and process of mobility among tribal women and men in Odisha. A further aim of the study was to examine the shaping of identities and subjectivities from a gender perspective in the context of the two communities.

First, there is a need to distinguish between mobility and migration. Migration is generally referred to as population movements from one place to another for a specific purpose, most often for employment and in the case of women often for marriage. The National Sample Survey Organisation (NSSO) and the census reports by the Government of India are considered the most diligent and reliable sources of statistical information on migration. However, there are no disaggregated data by ethnicity, and the data do not provide any information on the links between women's social contexts, gender relations, or social and/or class relations formed as a result of migration (Agnihotri & Majumdar 2009). Mobility is not only about migration but also underscores different types of movements and forging new relations and identities. Mobility should be understood as movement in social and cultural contexts.

Mobility among tribal communities[1] in India is increasing and visible in changing livelihoods in the communities' original habitats. Outmigration of tribal populations from economically backward states such as Chhattisgarh, Jharkhand, Odisha, and Madhya Pradesh has been taking place in the last three centuries. In the 18th and 19th centuries, the British colonials forced tribal labourers to work in plantation areas, such as the tea estates in Assam. Between 1950 and 1980, Indian tribals migrated to the agriculturally prosperous rural areas of Bihar and West Bengal, primarily to work as agricultural labourers. However, from 1980 onwards, they started migrating to bigger cities in search of employment (Bates & Carter 1998; Jha 2005). In many industrial centres in India, a large proportion of the labour force comprises members of tribal groups, who mainly work as manual and semi-skilled labourers. They also work as labourers in agriculturally prosperous rural areas, where they tend to settle permanently in clustered settlements on land given to them by their employers.

Both tribal women and men are mobile. Mobility among tribal women is generally viewed as wives either accompanying or following their husbands to their place of work. However, it is significant to note that more recently there has been a growing gender-specific demand for labour in both urban and rural areas: 'The global increase in demand for domestic labour is a major dimension of feminization of migration' (Agarwal 2006, 28). In India, employers prefer to employ tribal women for certain types of work; for example, in metropolitan cities such as Delhi there is a demand for young tribal girls to work as live-in domestic workers for urban families. Young girls in their late teens and early twenties are generally preferred from the states of Odisha, Chhattisgarh, Jharkhand, and Madhya Pradesh. A study submitted by the Society for Regional Research and Analysis (2010) to the Planning Commission, Government of India, indicates that in 2009 more than 60 per cent of tribal women in the cities were employed as domestic help, 34 per cent worked as wage labourers, and the remaining 6 per cent had private jobs.

This chapter is organized in seven sections. After the introduction, I describe the methodology used in the study. Thereafter, I describe the conceptual underpinnings of the study, focusing on gender and mobility among tribal communities. In the fourth section, I discuss the situation in the state of Odisha, and the case studies of two districts based on empirical observations. This is followed by an analytical discussion of the different dimensions of gendered mobility among tribal populations. In the sixth section I discuss the gendered outcomes of the mobility in detail. The seventh and final section presents my concluding remarks.

Methodology

The study was conducted in seven villages in Khordha District and six villages in Sundargarh District in the state of Odisha; the locations of the two districts are shown in Figure 5.1.

In the study villages in Khorda District, members of the Sabara tribe live together with members of Hindu caste groups. In Sundargarh District, the study villages had multiple tribes, including Bhuyan, Kharia, Kisan, Gond, Munda, and Oraon. The mobility of tribal women in Khordha can be characterized as seasonal migration within the Odisha state, whereas in Sundargarh women migrate to metropolitan cities outside the state to work as domestic servants. Tribal men in both districts migrate for work mainly to places outside the state. Data were collected through a structured questionnaire survey, focus group discussions, interviews with key informants, and participatory workshops at village level. Key informants in both areas included NGO leaders, teachers, activists, academics, government functionaries at block,[2] district, and state levels, and Panchayati Raj Institution (PRI)[3] members.

In Khordha District, 100 tribal women engaged in seasonal agricultural work and of these, 46 women who worked at 11 stone crusher sites were interviewed individually. In addition, I interviewed 52 tribal men who often migrated to cities

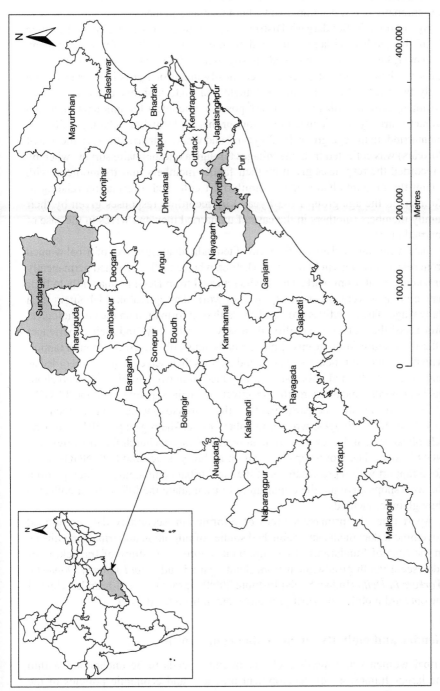

Figure 5.1   Location of the study areas, Khordha District and Sundargarh District in Odisha, India.

outside the Odisha state. Further information was obtained through a structured questionnaire that was completed by both women and men.

By contrast, in Sundargarh District, large numbers of tribal girls and women from the studied villages migrated to metropolitan cities for employment. However, far fewer men migrated, mostly to the urban centres within and outside the state. Female migration comprised mostly unmarried girls in their teens and early twenties. Although data on female and male mobility could have been obtained from the villages, it was not possible to contact the migrants (men and women) directly. For female migration, primary information relating to 26 girls (unmarried, in the age group 14–20 years) and women (married, above the age of 20 years) was collected from the villages through a questionnaire survey, whereby I recorded the responses given by their family members (mostly mothers) with whom the migrants had contact. Similarly, I collected information relating to 20 men (in the age group 21–30 years) by recording responses given by their family members (mothers in the case of unmarried men and wives in the case of married men).

Data were collected also in the form of ten individual narratives of tribal women from selected villages in Sundargarh District, who had either returned permanently or taken a break from work. Those who returned from Delhi permanently to their native villages were either unemployed or worked as agricultural labourers for a daily wage. The narratives provided a wealth of information on the chronological process of the women's mobility, their stay in Delhi city, and their experiences after their return from the city. I made a conscious effort to create enough rapport with the women for them to open up and express themselves (which I recorded as narratives). Additional information was gained from two participatory workshops held in Khordha and Sundargarh respectively, with the support of two local NGOs, CARD and Pragati. The participants in the workshops were tribal women and men from local villages, women members of self-help groups, PRI members, schoolteachers, and a few government representatives, church functionaries, and NGO leaders. The workshops focused on mobility issues and both NGOs had a good rapport with representatives of the local tribal communities. Findings from the workshops gave me the opportunity to triangulate the information collected through other methods.

Apart from the primary sources of information, secondary data comprised government documents and published studies of migration and tribals in Odisha. In the case of Sundargarh, two important reports – 'A study of trafficking of adolescent/youth girls/women from Sundargarh'[4] and *Tribal Women Domestic Workers in Delhi* (Indian Social Institute 2008) – provide a well-rounded view of the outward mobility of tribal girls and women from the district.

Gender and mobility among tribal communities

Tribal women's and men's mobility in India needs to be understood within the larger framework of development practices and economic policies of the country and/or state, structures of inequality and patriarchy, social exclusion, and social and cultural practices that characterize the broader context of the tribal communities. The current model of development in India is perceived as the state allying with private corporations to dispossess local communities of their liveli-hoods. The situation is a paradox that counterposes growth against development (Bhaduri 2007). With changing economic structures and policies within the format of neoliberalist policies, there has been an increase in female labour force participation. While this has no doubt led to a narrowing of the gender gap in economic participation rates, it has not led to commensurate gender equality in pay and status. It is noteworthy that increasing female labour force participation has coincided with an increase in informal and unprotected forms of work (Arza *et al.* 2012).

Despite laws to protect the tribals in India, they are socially excluded and the disadvantages of their class, ethnicity, and gender are part of their everyday lives. Their exclusion is manifested in several aspects, notably the lack of access to agricultural lands and land titles, exploitation in the informal sector (where most tribals are employed), sexual exploitation of tribal women by non-tribals, false implications and arrests of women and men (under accusations of being extremists), and exploitation by moneylenders and others. Tribal exclusion has been further aggravated by failure of land reform policies, indebtedness, and land alienation. The socio-economic and political situation of tribal communities can be best conceptualized by examining the causes of poverty and deprivation. Amartya Sen (2004, 31) suggests that 'to be excluded from common facilities or benefits that others have, can certainly be a significant handicap that impoverishes the lives that individuals can enjoy.' He outlines diverse ways in which social exclusion can cause deprivation and poverty: namely through inequality and relational poverty, labour market exclusions, credit market exclusions, gender-related exclusions and inequality, and social exclusion from health care and food markets. Sen's approach to understanding exclusion resonates with the tribal situation in India in general and Odisha in particular as tribals are the most marginalized and vulnerable groups compared with other communities (Sen 2004). It is estimated that *c.*75 per cent of the tribal population in the state of Odisha live below the poverty level for rural areas recommended by the Planning Commission 2012, i.e. below INR 28.35 per capita per day for urban areas and INR 22.42 for rural areas.[5] The situation in southern Odisha (in Koraput, Kalahandi, and Bolangir districts) is even worse, with approximately 87 per cent of the tribals living below poverty levels.[6]

In India, neoliberalist policies have had a powerful impact on the welfare state. The egalitarian ethic that underlined planned development and change in the welfare state of India is being rapidly decimated. A pre-eminence of markets has emerged, including in the state of Odisha. The state is home to 62 tribal and indigenous communities (23 per cent of the total population of Odisha) and has experienced the impact of the neoliberal policies in a variety of ways. The governmental authorities in Odisha have opened doors to the private sector to access the resources (minerals, forests, land, and water). Odisha has the highest concentration of bauxite (required for aluminium production) and iron ore (required for the production of steel). Ironically, these minerals are concentrated in the tribal areas (in remote rural hill regions) of the state, which has become the favoured destination of mega-national corporations and multinational companies wanting to invest in mineral-based extraction and industrialization.

Tribals generally adopt a combination of livelihoods for their survival and sustenance, which can be described as multilocational (i.e. based in different physical locations and times of the year). For example, they engage in cultivation (settled, swidden, or both) and wage labour close to their habitats, they work in distant places or other locations at varying distances from their homes, and they sell forest products in local markets. Deshingkar and Farrington (2009) refer to this as circular migration, as much of it is seasonal, and based on field evidence in rural India they describe multilocational livelihoods as 'centered on the relationship between migration, agricultural development, geographical location, risk reduction, land ownership, education, skills, age and how this intersects with ethnicity (caste, religion and tribe), gender and power relations' (2009, 18). Multilocational livelihoods also concern mobile livelihoods among communities, such as the tribals under study in this chapter.

Odisha in focus – tribals and mobility

The tribal communities of Odisha are concentrated mostly in the southern and northern parts of the state, in Koraput, Sundargarh, and Mayurbhanj districts. As already mentioned, they comprise *c.*23 per cent of the total population of Odisha (Government of India 2011). The tribes are at various stages of socio-economic development. At one extreme there are tribes that are relatively isolated and inhabit remote, rural hill regions, with their core culture intact, and have little contact with the mainstream population. At the other extreme, there are tribes that have become either Hinduized or Sanskritized by adopting caste traditions or have converted to Christianity and are not distinguishable from non-tribals in the state. However, the majority of the tribals are largely impoverished, dispossessed, displaced, and unemployed, with very few productive assets such as agricultural land. The main tribes are Kondh, Gond, Santal, Munda, Oraon, Bhattada, Bhumij, and Saora. There are 13 primitive tribal groups[7] in the state: Paudi Bhuiyan, Chuktia Bhunjia, Birhor, Bonda, Didayi, Juang, Dongaria Khond, Kutia Khond, Hill Kharia, Lodha, Lanjia Saora, Mankidia, and Soura (Ota & Mohanty 2010). Traditionally, all of the tribal groups were engaged in swidden cultivation, gathering within forests, and different kinds of agricultural production.

Since 1992, neoliberalist state policies have affected the tribals and their natural environments in the name of development, notably in the form of expansion of industries based on mining and natural resource extraction. There is no doubt that the extraction of minerals and their processing will add to the growth of Odisha and the country as a whole, but at what costs? The issue has evoked a debate in the country about the current approach to development, where local tribal communities are likely to lose their livelihood base as a result of the growing extraction-based industrialization and mining, invariably leading to the twin problems of environmental degradation and deprivation of livelihood rights. As a consequence, conflicts between tribals and the ruling classes are the order of the day and the most extreme form currently witnessed is the left-wing extremism (Naxalism), which purportedly has the tacit support of the tribals. There are several development policies targeted at protecting the tribals: Panchayat Extension to Scheduled Areas (PESA) Act 1996 (Issues of India 2011), Schedule V 1952,[8] Non-Alienation of Tribal Lands Act 1956 and Orissa Land Reforms Act 1960 (Ambagudia 2010), and, more recently, The Scheduled Tribes and Other Traditional Forest Dwellers (Recognition of Forest Rights) Act 2006 (the Forest Rights Act) (Campaign for Survival and Dignity n.d.). However, all of these policies seem to have been systematically violated and are largely ineffective in Odisha.

It is estimated that $c.1.5$ million tribals in the state of Odisha have been displaced due to a number of irrigation, mining, industrial, and conservation projects (Kumar 2006). Besides displacement, regular droughts in the western parts of the state force tribals to adopt mobile livelihoods. The mobility of tribals is often expressed in terms of the numbers migrating from a given district, and in the case of Bolangir District (mostly reported and highlighted by media) the number is estimated as $c.200,000$, most of whom migrate to work in brick kilns in Andhra Pradesh and West Bengal. The mobility is annual and estimated to bring in business worth INR 20 million (USD 376,258) per year for the brick kiln owners located outside the state of Odisha. Entire families migrate in order to work in the brick kilns (Daniel 2011). For tribals who have moved to and subsequently settled in caste villages, with no access to forests and agricultural lands, mobile livelihoods have become a way of life, and this aspect is discussed in detail in the following sections. Tribals' mobility takes different forms, namely short-term daily commuting to nearby work sites (e.g. markets, construction sites, and stone crushing sites); seasonal migration to work as, for example, agricultural labourers; and long-term outmigration to work in urban centres.

Tribals' access to productive assets such as land is a crucial indicator of their well-being and vulnerability, and importantly the major reason for their outmigration is a search for alternative livelihoods. In Odisha, tribals have cultivated and managed their natural resources (land, forests, and water) as communal resources for several generations. Most of them do not view land as a 'commodity' that can be bought and sold. Rather, the natural resources, such as trees, plants, animals, ponds, rivers, and mountains, have sacred meanings that are closely intertwined with the tribals' identity as indigenous. Most tribes tend to follow a clan-based land-tenure system that provides customary rights to natural resources (Kumar 2006; Mathur 2009). Over time, communal ownership of resources has given way to individual ownership following the introduction of land settlement. The practice of swidden cultivation (*jhum* or *podu*), which is a way of life for tribals living in the remote hill regions of Odisha, has declined considerably because the tribals are dissuaded by both local and national governments from continuing the practice. Furthermore, much of the land cultivated by the tribals in the scheduled area ($c.74$ per cent) is owned by the state, implying that most of the lands cultivated by the tribals are not privately owned. They may have use rights for those lands only but no individual land titles (United

Nations Development Programme 2008). For example, swidden cultivation in hill slopes with a gradient of less than 10 degrees is recognized by the government as agricultural lands for survey and settlement purposes. However, in practice most of the lands cultivated by the tribals are above 10 degrees.

There has been massive alienation of tribal lands in Odisha. A report by the Ministry of Rural Development reveals that 105,491 cases alleging alienation of 104,742 acres (41,897 ha) of land were filed in 2007, of which only 56,854 acres (22,742 ha) of land have been restored to the tribals (Government of India 2008). In addition, large tracts of land have also been sold through illegal transactions (*benami*) with the tacit support of the government (Ambagudia 2010). According to a report by the Planning Commission, in 2001 a total of 40 per cent of tribals in Odisha lost their traditional sources of livelihood as a result of being displaced due to development projects (Government of India 2002)

Gendered mobility – Khordha and Sundargarh

This section discusses the two case districts, which differ in nature. With respect to Khordha, I focus on women's seasonal migration within the state (rural–rural) and men's movement to cities (rural–urban). By contrast, in the case of Sundargarh, I focus on tribal women's migration to cities to work as domestic workers (rural–urban) and men's migration to urban areas for unskilled and semi-skilled jobs. In both cases, mobility is much higher among women than men in terms of the frequency of the trips made away from their village for work.

Khordha mobility

Although Khordha is not a tribal-dominated district, it has ten blocks with tribal habitations, which had an estimated population of *c.*1.2 million in 2011 (Government of India 2011). The district contains the capital city of Odisha: Bhubaneswar. The predominant tribe in the district is the Sabara. The history shows that the Sabara tribe has moved from the neighbouring district of Nayagarh to some parts of Khordha. The Sabara were initially hired to work as labourers on farms owned by wealthy landlords in the 1930s. Although originally they were provided with land to settle down, most do not own any agricultural land today. The Sabara learnt to plough comparatively late, as they mostly depended on resources from forests for their survival. A typical village inhabited by tribals comprises a tribal cluster (*Adivasi para*) that is set apart from the Oriya caste clusters. The Oriya castes own most agricultural lands in Odisha, which they lease out to the Sabara for sharecropping. The total landholdings of tribals in Khordha amount to only 6 per cent and the rest are owned by non-tribals (Government of Odisha 2012). The Sabara are completely Hinduized through the process of Sanskritization. They emulate all the customs and traditions of their Oriya caste neighbours. In addition, the patriarchal norms and ideologies of the Hindu caste society can be observed among the Sabara.

Much of the ethnographic documentation on tribals of Odisha has not recorded the movements of the Sabara tribe within the state. Over the years, it has become clear that the numbers of female migrants out of Khordha District have increased, especially for seasonal agricultural work in prosperous areas within the state. The trend began in the early 1970s, and today women migrate mainly to the Pipili block villages in Puri District. The mobility of tribals from the study villages in Khordha District is presented in Table 5.1 (women) and Table 5.2 (men). Female mobility occurs within the state and is primarily restricted to agricultural wage labour and stone crushing. By contrast, male mobility extends beyond the state, in search of different types of work, mainly in the unskilled and semi-skilled categories.

In total, 40 per cent of the women in the seven study villages were married, while 15 per cent of men were married. All of the women migrated to the Pipili block villages to work as agricultural labourers, whereas the men migrated to work

Table 5.1 Mobility of tribal women in villages in Khordha District

Village	Number	Average age (years)	Destination place	Occupation
Samantarapur	26	23	Pipili	Agricultural labour, stone crushing, cashew nut picking
Gobindpur	23	24	Pipili	Agricultural labour, stone crushing
Suanlo	12	37	Pipili	Agricultural labour, stone crushing
Girigiria	10	24	Pipili	Agricultural labour, stone crushing, cashew nut picking
Ekdalia	5	38	Pipili	Agricultural labour, stone crushing
Kusupalla	12	22	Pipili	Agricultural labour, stone crushing
Badaberona	12	44	Pipili	Agricultural labour, stone crushing

Source: Survey conducted in Khordha in the period 2010–2011.

Table 5.2 Mobility of tribal men in villages in Khordha District

Village	Number	Average age (years)	Destination place	Occupation
Samantarapur	10	27	Mumbai, Surat, Hyderabad	Construction, truck cleaner, fishing
Gobindpur	8	22	Assam, Delhi, Hyderabad	Construction, family labour, truck cleaner
Girigiria	11	21	Delhi, Mumbai, Hyderabad	Painter, construction
Ekdalia	2	21	Mumbai, Delhi, Chennai	Fishing, construction
Kusupalla	15	25	Chennai, Bangalore, Kerala	Fishing, construction, truck-driver helper
Badaberona	6	24	Assam, Bhutan	Construction, family labour

Source: Survey conducted in Khordha in the period 2010–2011.

on construction sites, in factories, on fishing boats, and in shops in different parts of the country. Married women were able to move outside their village, and then only if they did not have responsibility for looking after young children and had some support from their kin to take care of their household chores during their absence. Married men moved out of their village for work only when there was an urgent need for income, for example, to repay big loans or to help pay for medical treatment of sick parents. In the cities, migrant men lived in groups close to their place of work, in accommodation provided by their employers. In a few cases, men rented accommodation in the cities. Wages for men were in the range of INR 3,000–5,000 per month. A survey (unpublished) of male migration from Khordha villages, undertaken by CARD in 2010 revealed that of the 226 unmarried men from 17 villages of Begunia block in Khordha District, the duration of their stay in the host destination was between 20 days and 24 months. They travelled to, for example, Mumbai, Delhi, Bangalore, Chennai, Surat, Hyderabad, Assam, Bhutan, and Kerala to engage in various forms of unskilled and semi-skilled jobs. The study also revealed that on average, men were mobile only twice, most often before marriage. Further, discussions with members of staff working for CARD (April 2012) revealed that outmigration by unmarried men had declined since 2010, as they preferred to work on road construction sites in Bhubaneswar, where they stayed 15–30 days on average before returning to their villages.

Sabara women migrate in groups to work in villages of Pipili in Puri District in Odisha, located 100 km south of the tribal villages. They travelled twice during the agricultural season, to work during the different stages of the agricultural cycle of paddy, namely for transplantation and weeding, and again at harvest time. On average, the women spent 45 days in Pipili, and in some cases two months, depending upon the availability of work. They were able to earn on average INR 3,000 (USD 56) each time they migrated for work. They tended to save what they earned. Although men were able to earn more in the cities, they failed to save much because they tended to spend most of their income. The average income of men working in the cities was approximately INR 4,000 (USD 75) per month. The channel to Pipili villages has been established for more than three decades. Some of the unmarried women mentioned that their mothers had been part of the movement, when wages were INR 5 (USD 0.09) per day; at the time of the study, wages had increased to INR 130 (USD 2.45) per day, including food. The landlords in the Pipili villages have their own catchment villages from which they draw labour every year. For example, in Panidola village in Pipili, one landlord regularly drew labour from Girigiria village. He organized transportation for the women to travel to Panidola, and provided them with a separate house, food, and entertainment (TV). In addition to accommodation and payment, at the end of the season the landlord also gave them rice, clothes, and coconuts when they departed for their home villages.

Apart from seasonal migration, Sabara women also work at stone crushing sites, which have sprung up along the highway (NH 5) that connects Mumbai and Chennai. The number of crushing sites has increased since the early 2000s, due to a proliferation of construction sites and the demand for stones for concrete construction works in the capital city and elsewhere. The development in the stone crushing business has been primarily fuelled by large-scale investments by the private sector. The sites attract labour from a *c.*35 km radius. Approximately 70 per cent of the women from the seven study villages in Khordha also worked at the crushing sites. At such sites, women are typically engaged either to break stones manually or to carry loads of stone chippings on their head to the crushers.

The owners of the stone crushing company organize the collection of labourers staying onsite and living within the vicinity of the sites by mini-truck or auto-rickshaw. At the time of the study there were four manual crushing sites among the 11 surveyed in Khordha, and the rest were partially mechanized. Women working at manual crushing sites have to break big stones into small pieces, which are then sent to mechanized crushers for further processing. At the mechanized sites, women are mainly engaged to carry loads of small stones, which are unloaded into a machine that converts them into 'metal' (very fine stones required for construction work). The average wage rate is INR 110 for eight hours work per day, and wages are paid weekly. The owner does not provide any facilities for the workers, such as toilets or places to rest. All of the crushers work in shifts (day and night). Approximately 25 per cent of the women work in the evening shift, which starts at 17.00 hours and continues until 23.00 hours. Of the 46 women interviewed, only 11 were single. Women accounted for 90 per cent of the total labour force in the studied crushing sites, and the remaining 10 per cent were men. Men who came from other districts in Odisha tended to stay onsite, whereas the women tended to commute daily and were willing to spend three hours travelling to and from work at the crushing sites (i.e. 1.5 hours each way).

From the findings from the study of the seven villages in Khordha villages, it can be deduced that Sabara women typically engage in multiple livelihoods, namely seasonal agricultural labour in Pipili, work at stone crushing sites close to their villages, agricultural wage labour comparatively closer to their villages, and selling firewood at a nearby market. In a very few villages, among them Champagarh in Ranpur block in Khordha District, women engage in all of the aforementioned ways of securing a livelihood. Typically, the tribals in villages studied in Khordha District adopted a combination of two or three livelihood types. Work availability is highest in the case of stone crushing, where Sabara women tend to work for approximately seven or eight months per year.

The factors responsible for mobility vary for Sabara women and men. There is also slight variation between married women and men in terms of their mobility. In the case of unmarried women, although their priority is to earn some income, migration has the added attraction of giving them the ability to travel and work in groups and enjoy the freedom that it entails. They are able to gain confidence and enhance their bargaining power in the labour market and in their respective communities, whereas unmarried men migrate mainly for fun and exposure to city and urban life. Married women go out to work when their household income is insufficient to meet their needs. In most cases, their husbands either do not work full time or spend their income on alcohol. By contrast, married men migrate for work mainly out of necessity, even when they would prefer to work close to their villages.

Sundargarh mobility

Sundargarh, the second study district, is located in north-west Odisha, bordering the states of Jharkhand to the north and Chhattisgarh to the west. Sundargarh has rich deposits of iron ore, coal, and manganese. The Rourkela region in Sundargarh is an industrial hub and has a major steel plant. Sundargarh District has 17 blocks, covering 1,764 villages, and 58 per cent of the population is tribal. The tribes in Sundargarh include Oraon, Kharia, Bhuyan, Gond, Kisan, Munda, Bhumij, and Khond, most of whom live below the poverty line. According to local NGO activists, the rate of female outmigration among tribals in Sundargarh has been increasing since 1997. The outmigration is mainly referred to as trafficking and *Delhi Chalan* ('sale in Delhi') by media and activists working in the district. The women migrate to Delhi and other metropolitan cities, where they are employed mainly as live-in domestic servants through placement agencies and sometimes through the Church. It is estimated that since the early 2000s, *c.*40,000 girls and women have moved from villages in Sundargarh District to Delhi (discussions with representatives of Pragati, 2011).

Despite industrial expansion in some parts of the district, the majority of the rural population is still dependent on agriculture and collection of products from the forests. The Government has declared the entire district a scheduled area. Approximately 35 per cent of the tribals have converted to Christianity, most of them Munda, Oraon, and Khond. The rest of the tribal population have retained their traditional Adivasi values and norms. In contrast to the Khordha District, the influence of Hinduism is not as strong among the tribes in Sundargarh villages. Traditionally, tribals in Sundargarh have engaged in shifting cultivation, gathering non-timber forest products (NTFPs), and settled cultivation. In addition, they have also sold their livestock (cows, goats, and hens) during the lean months of the year. Although tribals may own 3–5 ha of land, the quality is inferior and not fit for cultivation. As a result, agricultural production is low in most parts of the district, except in the riverine areas where pulses, cereals, and vegetables are grown (Government of Odisha 2010). Many tribals are also employed in the coal and manganese mines and quarry sites, mostly during the non-agricultural season (4–5 months in a year). There is also a strong view that the district has been neglected by both the state and national governments in terms of development inputs, which has resulted in growing poverty and lack of employment opportunities for the tribal population (participatory workshop on the mobility of tribals in Sundargarh, held at Pragati's headquarters in 2010).

The pattern of mobility of tribal women in Sundargarh is entirely different from those in Khordha. Once the girls and women arrive in Delhi, they are taken to the placement agencies. In some cases, they are registered with false names by the agencies to prevent them from being traced in the future. It is estimated that there are *c.*400 licensed placement agencies engaged in the business of coordinating the employment of female domestic workers in Delhi homes. In the case of men, the pattern of outmigration is more or less the same as in Khordha. However, in contrast to Khordha, male migration was not observed in all of the villages from where girls and women had migrated. The numbers of female and male migrants from the study villages in Sundargarh District are shown in Tables 5.3 and 5.4.

An ongoing study conducted by Pragati (see endnote 4) shows that up to 2010, in 11 blocks in Sundargarh, covering 68 *gram panchayats* (GPs, local self-governments at village level), 2,156 women and adolescent girls had migrated for work. The study indicates that 41 per cent of those who had moved to cities were in the age group 14–18 years, 38 per cent were in the age group 19–25 years, 14 per cent were above 25 years, and the rest were below 14 years. Another distinctive feature is that the Christian tribes (i.e. those that had converted to Christianity) in the district seemed to be more mobile than others.

Table 5.3 Tribal female migration from villages in Sundargarh District

Village	Number	Average age (years)	Destination place	Occupation
Diapathara	20	22	Delhi	Live-in domestic help
Ekma	39	18	Delhi	Live-in domestic help
Handipani	20	22	Delhi	Live-in domestic help
Alapaka	16	25	Delhi	Live-in domestic help
Sarajangha	25	22	Delhi	Live-in domestic help
Lakragara	16	23	Delhi	Live-in domestic help

Source: Survey conducted in Sundargarh in 2011.

Table 5.4 Tribal male migration from villages in Sundargarh District

Village	Number	Average age (years)	Destination place	Occupation
Diapathara	20	29	Sundargarh, Keonjhar, Pune, Mumbai	Labourer, driver, truck cleaner, mechanic
Ekma	5	26	Goa, Raipur, Gujarat, Dubai (1 person), Sundargarh	Fishing, construction, office clerk
Handipani	8	26	Delhi, Goa, Karnataka, Sundargarh	Fishing, construction, truck cleaner, labourer
Alapaka	9	25	Delhi, Mumbai, Sundargarh	Painter, construction
Sarajangha	18	27	Goa, Chhattisgarh, Sundargarh	Fishing, construction, cook
Lakragara	4	25	Sundargarh	Construction

Source: Survey conducted in Sundargarh in 2011.

A total of *c*.45 per cent of mobile males were married and had regular contact with their families, whereas only 20 per cent of the unmarried men maintained contact with their families, i.e. made telephone calls and sent remittances for household expenses. Unmarried men did not give money to their families regularly. Education levels among males varied: 20 per cent were illiterate, 25 per cent had received primary level education, 42 per cent middle school education, 12 per cent high school education, and 1 per cent had graduated with a bachelor degree. In contrast to girls and women, there was a considerable amount of male migration within the state.

With regard to female outmigration from the six study villages, 21 girls had returned to their villages and few of them (6) had married. The education levels of the girls who migrated out were varied: 30 per cent were illiterate, 45 per cent had received primary level education, 20 per cent middle school education, and 5 per cent high school level education. The participatory workshops provided me with the knowledge about the role of agents in luring tribal girls and women to the cities.

The Pragati study (see endnote 4) revealed that up to 2010, a total of 723 girls and women had been trafficked and had not returned to their homes, 60 were missing and could not be traced, there had been 345 cases of sexual abuse of which only 38 had been registered, one trafficker had been punished and let out on bail, 56 girls had travelled to Delhi with unknown people, and the identity of 15 traffickers had been established. The majority of the girls had been lured by relatives, neighbours, or friends.

A workshop conducted in Sundargarh with a number of stakeholders brought out in detail the major reasons for both girls' and women's mobility in Sundargarh. In contrast to Khordha, where economic necessity alone was cited as the main push factor for female migration, in Sundargarh there are many reasons for migration, and the insights gained from the workshops and study are worth considering. A summary of female outmigration from Sundargarh is presented in Table 5.5.

Clearly, the rate of female outmigration to Delhi and other cities is increasing due to the hope of a better life and higher levels of income. Young girls (aged 14–20 years) aspire to live in urban areas where they can earn money and experience a sense of freedom. The push factors are mainly low levels of agricultural production, ineffective government programmes, dysfunctional homes, increasing alcoholism among fathers and associated abusive behaviour, and limited opportunities for young girls to acquire skills or income to fulfil their aspirations. In the case of men, clearly the availability of limited opportunities at village level pushes them out of their habitats in search of better income-earning opportunities. The pattern of male outmigration is not the same as that for girls and women. Further, the average age of male migrants is higher than that of female migrants.

Gendered mobility and livelihoods

The gendered dimensions of mobility and livelihoods in both Khordha and Sundargarh districts related to the varied mobility trajectories, the process of mobility, experience in the host destinations (rural or urban), points of conflict,

Table 5.5 Reasons for female outmigration from Sundargarh District

Stakeholders	Main reasons
Panchayati Raj Institution (PRI) members	Continuous drought; the Mahatma Gandhi National Rural Employment Guarantee Scheme (MGNREGS) works unsuitable for women due to hard work and delayed payments; dysfunctional homes (drunkard fathers and bad behaviour towards daughters); increasing industrialization and mining in certain areas have led to the trafficking of girls from the Bonai, Hemgiri, Rajgangpur, and Kotra blocks; girls want more freedom and are attracted to city life; limited opportunities in villages for developing skills; limited livelihood options; increasing demand since 2003 for women and girls to work as domestic help in cities
Girls who had returned from Delhi	To augment household income; influenced by girls who had returned from Delhi (e.g. their clothes, make-up, consumer goods, and cash); influence of *dalals* (women agents); dysfunctional homes; sexual abuse by relatives and known people; lack of interest in furthering their education; the attraction of improving their lifestyle and earning money quickly
Women's self-help group	Limited livelihood options in the villages; continuous droughts and low levels of agricultural production; tribal girls start to attend school relatively late and lose interest in studying; influenced by girls who return after working in cities; drunkard fathers who abuse their daughters; torture by stepmothers; desire to earn money for marriage; no scope for MGNREGS work in the villages; high demand for girls in the age group 8–17 years to work as live-in maids in cities
NGOs	Low levels of agricultural production; inadequate irrigation facilities; fathers agree to send their daughters to the city after receiving advanced payment from the *dalals* (women agents); dowry is a problem in some areas, due to the influence of Oriya castes; discrimination of girls at household level; dysfunctional homes due to alcoholism; influence of girls who return to villages after having worked elsewhere; lack of infrastructure development in the villages; government programmes do not have much impact at ground level
Teachers	The desire to be in the same league as educated urban students; to fulfil their latent potential; shortage of peer group in the villages; faulty government policies; increasing poverty conditions; increasing alcoholism in the family (both parents); gender discrimination at household level

Source: Participatory workshop on tribal mobility from Sundargarh District, held at Pragati, October 2010.

gendered outcomes, and how mobility as a strategy provides tribal households with options for survival and financial stability.

Mobility as social processes

When tribal women from villages in Sundargarh move to metropolitan cities, mainly to the capital city Delhi, they face challenges of new situations in unknown terrain. In the case of tribal women from villages in Khordha, the challenges are much less than those for tribal women from villages in Sundargarh because they are familiar with what to expect in Pipili villages, at stone crushing sites, in agricultural wage work close to the villages, and cashew nut picking. The wages, nature of the work, transportation, and accommodation facilities are all known to the women, whereas tribal women from Sundargarh who move to large cities such as Delhi encounter a lot of uncertainty in terms of their placement as domestic servants. Typical accounts of a woman from Khordha and a woman from Sundargarh are presented in Boxes 5.1 and 5.2 to illustrate the nature of mobility as a social process.

Box 5.1 Khordha District: an account of female mobility

Surekha Naik, a Sabara tribal girl (aged 17 years), had studied up to Grade 6 (i.e. she had completed primary school education). She lived in Girigiria village, in the Bologarh block, Khordha District, and was from a family with six members. The family engaged in sharecropping on 3 mano (5 m^2) of unirrigated land (belonging to an Oriya caste household from the same village). The amount of paddy Surekha's family produced was not sufficient for the entire year. Members of her family also engaged in waged agricultural work in and around their village. Surekha had been travelling periodically to the Pipili area for work in the last two years, together with a group of other girls from her village. They tended go to the same village in the Pipili area, namely Panidola, where they worked for the same landlord. The landlord had arranged transportation to collect the girls from Girigiria. Sometimes the group was accompanied by one girl's brother or husband, but not for the entire period of their stay. Surekha had worked in Panidola for a period of 25–30 days, twice each year. The activities that she typically engaged in were paddy transplantation, weeding, harvesting, and winnowing and threshing (using a machine). She worked for eight hours per day and slightly more during the harvest season. She received INR 130 per day as a wage, together with 1 kg of rice. The landlord had provided accommodation both at the work site and close to his house. He also allowed the girls to watch television in his home. There was no sense of caste difference, and Surekha stated: 'the landlord in Panidola treats us so much better than what we experience back home. He is like a father to me and takes care of all our needs. I feel safe when I am working here.' The landlord gave them extra rice, some fruits, and sarees when they departed after the end of the season. Surekha kept a small portion of the money that she had earned and gave the remainder to her mother, which was approximately INR 2,500–3,000. For the rest of the year, she worked in the fields in which her family sharecropped or as agricultural labourer close to their village.

Box 5.2 Sundargarh District: an account of female mobility

Anita Lakra, an Oraon tribal girl (aged 18 years), belonged to Handipani village in Sundargarh District. She came from a family of five members. The agricultural land owned by Anita's family was not fertile and due to incessant droughts there had been very little production from the land. At the age of 15 years, Anita met a person with whom she, her friend, and another cousin planned to leave for Delhi. Anita did not disclose the identity of the person but apparently he was an agent (dalal) who engaged in recruiting tribal girls and women from Sundargarh to Delhi. The agent, along with Anita and her cousin, were stopped by the police at the railway station at Jharsuguda as they were about to board a train to Delhi. After a few days, Anita went to Delhi with her brother-in-law, who took her to a placement agency. She stayed in the office for one week until a placement was found for her. According to Anita, the living conditions in the office were unhygienic and deplorable. She felt uncomfortable in the office because boys and girls lived in the same room and they were prone to sexual exploitation by the office staff, all of whom were men. Although a member of staff attempted to molest Anita, she was able to escape from him. She also came to know of a woman who had given birth to a baby, whose father was a member of the staff in the office. The man had been unwilling to accept the mother, and therefore the mother had left the baby in the office.

Anita was placed with a family that had ten members living in the same household; her salary was INR 1,200 per month. She was not allowed to leave the house for one year, after which she was able to go out for short periods in daytime. Insufficient food was provided and the workload was heavy. After two years, Anita's brother collected her, and the agency (through which salaries were paid) only paid her INR 7,000 instead of INR 14,400. Anita said: 'the agency people are not honest, as they exploit the girls sexually as well as cheat them by not giving them their actual dues in terms of their salary.' The placement agency deducted certain amounts from girls' salaries, arguing that it was commission for placing them as domestic workers. In addition, Anita was falsely accused of stealing money from the home where she had worked. She said that 'no girl is safe in Delhi, as the agencies will exploit them. It is better to find jobs with independent social networks.'

After her return from Delhi, Anita was not interested in doing household chores and missed city life. She returned to Delhi within a few weeks. Then, her sister convinced her to work for a known family. Anita's salary was fixed at INR 3,500 per month. However, she had to return to her village due to severe health problems. She received the salary due to her. Anita handed the entire amount over to her mother. Thereafter, she did not want to return to Delhi and instead planned to marry and settle down.

The two cases presented in the text boxes provide a brief insight into what happens in different places (i.e. in rural–rural and rural–urban movements). It is noteworthy that although tribal women in Delhi face many problems, the number of girls and women moving to the city has not declined. The attraction of working in Delhi pesists still and my study revealed a few cases (seven) where girls from villages in Sundargarh had been treated well by the families with whom they lived as domestic servants. Their salaries were paid regularly and the girls could visit their home villages once per year at Christmas. This finding is contrary to the information obtained during my study survey, discussions with members of civil society, and development workers in Sundargarh, who always portrayed girls and women as being exploited in the city.

In the case of Khordha District, there is a high demand for tribal labour in the rural areas of Odisha. Tribal women in villages in Khordha always move in groups, either to work as agricultural labourers in Pipili villages at the stone crushing sites located along the highway (NH 5) between Mumbai and Chennai, or to do wage work in and around their villages during the agricultural season, which for rice cultivation is July–December. They feel safe and secure as a collective, and this gives them strength. Girls and women who have worked in Pipili villages seem to possess a strong bargaining power due to the high demand for their labour. The landlords (Oriya castes) in Pipili are unlikely ever to want to engage local labour for agricultural work in the fields because they are much less able compared with tribal girls and women from Khordha villages. Sabara women's strong bargaining power is reflected once they return to their villages. They demand higher wages for the number of hours they work at the stone crushing sites and in agricultural fields close to their villages. The local landlords are aware that they cannot afford to ill-treat the girls and women, especially during the peak season, when the demand for labour is high. Sabara women have been able to establish a strong independent identity for themselves. They have also been successful in creating social capital and building village-level alliances that facilitate their well-being in mobile livelihood situations. By contrast, tribal women from Sundargarh have less bargaining power once they arrive in Delhi or in other cities. They pass through a chain of agents, including a placement agency at the end of their journey to Delhi, where they tend to be exploited the most. Once placed in homes as domestic servants, their bargaining power and freedom is further curtailed. For example, they are given *rotis* (Indian bread) as their staple diet, instead of rice. They are abused physically and verbally if they are unable to deliver the desired services. In many cases, they are made to work long hours without much food and rest. In contrast to the situation for tribal females in Khordha, tribal women in Delhi are unable to come together as a group in the city. They tend to be isolated, although they are referred to as tribals or *Adivasis* from Sundargarh villages. Their individual bargaining strength is very low. Some of them lose their identity as they may be registered with an agency under a false name. In addition, many have forgotten their mother tongue (Sadri) and can only speak Hindi (the language spoken in Delhi). In many cases, the placement agencies are run by people from the same tribal group as those they recruit, but they tend to exploit female members of their own community once the girls and women have arrived in the city. Due to the absence of any social capital in the city, tribal girls and women continue to be exploited in the informal sector market in Delhi.

Tribal men from both study districts tend to have similar experiences. Unmarried men move out in order to broaden their experiences, become independent, and have an income. By contrast, married men become mobile through economic necessity. City life is attractive for unmarried tribal men because they can enjoy their freedom and spend money as they wish. Since they do not feel obliged to give money to their parents, they buy clothes, mobile phones, music systems, and alcoholic drinks. Although city life is hard, they do not seem to mind too much as long as they are able to find work and earn some money. In the cities, they tend to live and work in groups and consequently do not feel insecure. Married men send remittances to their homes to repay debts, build houses, and invest in agriculture.

Mobility – strategy for livelihoods

In Khordha, both women and men combine several types of livelihood for their survival. Women, especially, are able to create livelihoods for themselves by combining a number of alternative forms of work. Traditionally, they gathered products from forests and engaged in some agricultural wage work. Over the years, forest cover has declined in the district and tribals have been forced to adopt other livelihood means. Today, women engage in multiple livelihoods for survival of their households. Men engage in one or two activities. In Sundargarh, women find it difficult to secure employment in the district itself. Very few women are inclined to move to other parts of the state, unlike tribal women in Khordha. The younger unmarried women prefer to move to the cities where there is potential for long-term employment. In other places, work may be seasonal and tribal girls and women are not satisfied with such work. Men are mobile for employment both within the state and outside the state. Income is not fixed in the case of tribal women in Sundargarh. In cases where there is a steady flow of remittances from cities, a household can expect to receive INR 1,500–2,000 (USD 28–38) per month for expenses. Although some families in home villages in Sundargarh (12–15 per cent) have been able to improve their economic status within two years due to the receipt of remittances, there has not been much visible improvement among the rest of the families, whose daughters work in the cities. In the case of Khordha, all families with girls and women engaged in mobile livelihoods are able to eat for the entire year, buy two or three sets of clothes, and save some money for the future (e.g. for marriages, repairs to houses, and agricultural investments). However, very few (15 per cent) are able to acquire assets by, for example, buying land, vehicles, or household goods. Money is also spent on the education of tribal children. Some women are frustrated when their husbands or partners take their hard-earned money or their daughters' money and spend it on alcohol. Men's excessive drinking invariably leads to domestic violence and currently, with the support of the local NGO, tribal women in Khordha are raising such issues publicly in order to find ways to address the problem. Such situations also highlight that although women seem independent and empowered, they do not always have a say in their household's expenditure. This may be due to the influence of the neighbouring Hindu castes, whose patriarchal norms, ideology, and stereotypes have seeped into Sabara tribal society.

Gender-specific mobility

The villages in the two study districts, Khordha and Sundargarh, clearly show that mobility is gendered. The patterns of mobility for women and men are different. There are differential choices in employment options. In addition, there are gender-specific demands for labour in different employment sectors. For example, Khordha tribal women are in high demand for seasonal agricultural labour in prosperous areas of the state. Similarly, Sundargarh tribal women are in demand for domestic work by an increasing number of placement agencies in Delhi. In the case of Khordha, the demand is because wealthy landowners in agriculturally prosperous areas of the state are unable to source labour from local villages. Moreover, those who are available are not efficient at completing the tasks. Therefore, landlords prefer to employ tribal women from villages *c.*100–120 km distant to work in their fields. Similarly, in Sundargarh, tribal women are sought after by placement agencies in Delhi. In addition to the usual push and pull factors underlying mobility, the patterns of integration of tribal women in the labour market and their occupational concentration in few sectors can be understood in two ways: the social and economic vulnerability of tribal women in Delhi; and the social and economic status of employers who consider that live-in domestic help can facilitate the maintenance of their status, as in most cases both husbands and wives work outside the home. The general perception among members of the middle class in Delhi is that tribal women are most trustworthy and the cheapest to employ. Tribal women are usually single and seek domestic work due to poverty, low levels of education, and lack of skills. In addition, they have shown their ability to work hard at domestic tasks that many others would consider demeaning (Kujur & Jha 2008).

Similarly, tribal men are employed in certain specific types of jobs such as fishing, factory work, construction work, stone crushing, road construction work, security workers, painters, truck drivers, and truck cleaners. Very few men are employed in the skilled category. However, it is interesting to note that in contrast to tribal women, tribal men have not been able to carve a niche for themselves in the labour market. This is reiterated to a great extent by the difference between women and men in terms of the frequency of their mobility. In both Khordha and Sundargarh, tribal women are more mobile than men (i.e. they make more trips to their place of work). Whereas, for example, in Khordha, unmarried men migrate out a few times before they marry, after marriage they are only mobile in cases of severe economic necessity. In Sundargarh, male migration occurs in some areas and the frequency of their movements is much less compared to those made by women. Thus, gender constitutes mobility and mobility is constituted by gender.

Mobility outcomes – survival and stability

As mentioned earlier, Sabara women in Khordha villages move and work in groups and their collective strength and bargaining power is high. Their experience is positive and they look forward to migrating for seasonal work. Although the work at the stone crushing sites is hard, Sabara women find the year round availability of work and timely payment of wages (weekly) attractive. Married women who work at the stone crushing sites have much higher bargaining power at home due to their contributions to their household's economy. A Sabara woman whose husband drank alcohol and was rarely at home took care of a family of six single-handedly, and stated: 'My children can go to school and we eat well.'[9] Sabara girls are in demand for marriage as they are considered hard working and financially independent.

Sundargarh tribal women's experiences in Delhi may not seem to be positive compared with Sabara women from Khordha. They feel alienated from their own culture and people because of their isolation and fear of losing their job, sexual harassment, being victimized as a consequence of being suspected of theft, and of not being accepted by their families in their home village, especially if they become unmarried mothers (discussions emerging from participatory workshops in Sundargarh). The women fear social stigma and do not want to face members of their village community. Many of them move to Delhi without notifying their parents directly, and such women experience the greatest fears of not being accepted by their family when they return. However, my study survey revealed that all women who returned had been accepted by their family members. Instead, the problem they face upon their return concerned their potential for marriage. Men are reluctant to marry girls who return from Delhi: '*Yei Jhia mane bhalo nuhanti*' (these girls are not good). Although tribal culture allows girls and boys to choose their partners, due to Hindu influence the freedom of choice is changing fast and increasingly parents arrange marriages for their daughters or sons. By contrast, unmarried men are highly sought after by women once they return to their villages. Meena, who had returned from Delhi two years earlier at the time of the interview, said: 'Men are not considered to be "polluted" and think they can also make some material demands during marriage [dowry]. They behave like *Babus* [big officers], despite being unemployed.' Men expect that they should be treated well by their families because they have been exposed to city life and have imbibed modern values, which are considered superior to tribal values.

The villages in Khordha are notable for the increasing trend in the consumption of alcohol and domestic violence among the Sabara tribals, especially where women earn some income. I came across 22 families where the conflict in the family concerned money earned by women which was used to purchase alcohol for men. When women ask their husbands to earn an income, they are often physically abused. At times, the insecurity of male spouses is manifested in drinking bouts and physical violence against their wives. A woman leader from Girigiria village lamented 'many of the married women in the stone crushing sites work out of necessity, as their men do not bring home any income and instead spend a lot of money on drinks.' Sabara women may have gained considerable control over their material lives, but there are certain deep-seated patriarchal values that often remain unchallenged. Furthermore, paid employment is a necessary condition to challenge intra-household hierarchies but not enough to change power relations completely (Kabeer 2000).

After their return to their home village, unmarried men in Khordha do not want to contribute to household expenses. Instead, they demand good food and alcoholic drinks at home. It is a common sight in Sabara villages to find young men moving around smartly dressed with mobile phones in their hands or listening to music through earphones. If mothers show any unhappiness about their sons' acrimonious behaviour, the sons threaten them, saying 'I will commit suicide' or 'I will leave home and never come back.' Parents succumb under such pressures and tend to give in to their sons' demands. When questioned about their sons' behaviour, mothers responded by asking 'Who will give us water when we die?' (a Hindu ritual performed on a funeral pyre by sons after the death of their parents). The Sabara women of Khordha are strongly influenced by Hinduism, whereby sons are given preference over daughters and are more highly valued.

Concluding remarks

The gendered outcomes of the mobility of tribals from villages in Khordha and Sundargarh districts and the pursuit of tribal people's livelihoods in different urban and rural locations has undoubtedly changed the nature of their vulnerability. Tribal women in both districts are able to create mobile livelihoods, although there are limited options available to them, which often hinders their occupational mobility. Female mobility from Khordha shows that women are able to offset their vulnerable conditions to some extent because they are able to bargain in the labour market. They are also able to narrow the social distance between themselves and non-tribals at village level. Despite the change, Sabara women from Khordha are concentrated in jobs that are considered to rank the lowest in the labour market. Their condition can be regarded as little more than subsistence, where income from female mobility is crucial to support the households. In contrast to Sabara men, women have been able to create a niche for themselves, where the demand for their labour remains a permanent feature in Khordha District and beyond. With regard to the trends in employment among tribals in Khordha, there is an emerging process of feminization of labour. Apart from agricultural labour, women's employment at the stone crushing sites underscores the point that there is increasing participation of tribal women in the workforce, which invariably is not reflected in government statistics.

Female mobility from tribal areas of Sundargarh may seem to open up many opportunities as it is mostly rural–urban migration. However, the study revealed very clearly how tribal women's agency is curtailed because they are unable to exercise their free will in choices relating to consumption, values, and behaviour in the urban settings. There are several oppressive structures at work that are exploitative in nature in the informal sector market, namely agents who take the girls and women to Delhi, police, placement agencies, and even the homes where they are placed as domestic workers. Tribal women are exposed to complicity, coercion, and control exercised by such oppressive structures, all of which makes it difficult for them to make any claims for a better life. They are viewed as helpless workers who can be exploited in the city because they have limited options for occupational mobility due to lack of appropriate education and skills. This is clearly a situation where tribal woman workers are moulded by 'patriarchal forces which control, regulate and direct how, where and how much a woman should work' (Banerjee 2011, 195). Furthermore, their situation can be interpreted as rural marginalization to urban vulnerabilities. The stability of tribal women is at stake in Delhi. They are trapped by unscrupulous agents and lack freedom in the city. They continue to remain marginal despite moving to Delhi. Since they are unable to come together in groups, tribal women continue to be vulnerable and weak in many ways. Although some have the option of returning to their villages, they are not certain of family and community acceptance. In addition, marriage within their community becomes difficult. By contrast, tribal men do not seem to be in a vulnerable position in their host destinations.

The research conducted in both study districts in Odisha suggests that the tribals are able to obtain only minimal resources for their survival. Conditions are not sufficient to create a sense of self-worth, where the tribals can participate in the social, cultural, economic, and political transactions of society with a certain degree of confidence. If such conditions continue to prevail, there is every chance it will take many generations for the tribals to achieve anything approaching equality in society.

Notes

1   The Constitution of India has used the term 'tribe' to label the indigenous communities in the country, which constitute 9 per cent of the total population.
2   A block is a level of local government comprising a group of *gram panchayats* (local self-governments at village level).
3   The 73rd Constitutional Amendement Act 1992 of the Government of India created Panchayati Raj Institutions (PRIs) as tiers (village, block, and district) of self-governance below the states in the federal set-up.
4   Pragati, 'A study of trafficking of adolescent/youth girls/women from Sundargarh', mimeo.
5   INR 1 = USD 0.019.
6   K. Kumar, 'Displaced and dispossessed: a brief paper on tribal issues in Orissa', mimeo, 2006
7   The constitution of India defines primitive tribes as those with a declining or stagnant population, lower level of literacy, pre-agricultural level of technology, and are economically backward. They are considered to be most vulnerable among the tribal population of the country.
8   The Schedule V areas in Odisha are: the entire districts of Mayurbhanj, Sundargarh, Koraput, Rayagada, Nabarangpur, and Malkangiri; Kuchinda tahasil in Sambalpur District; Keonjhar, Telkoi, Champua, Barbil tahasils in Keonjhar District; Khondamal, Balliguda and G. Udayagiri tahasils in Kandhamal District; R. Udaygiri tahasil, Gumma and Rayagada block in Parlekhemundi tahasil in Parlakhemundi Sub-division and Suruda tahasil in Ghumsur Sub-division in Ganjam District; Thuamul Rampur and

Lanjigarh blocks in Kalahandi District; and Nilagiri block in Baleshwar District. The scheduled areas contain almost 70 per cent of the forest areas of Orissa, but form only 44 per cent of the state area. Schedule V of the constitution of India guarantees to its indigenous people, rights over their lands. Source: www.lawmin.nic.in/coi/contents.htm (accessed 14 February 2013).

9   All quotations from interviewees have been translated from the local language, Oriya, by the author Smita Mishra Panda and Manju Prava Dhal (CARD).

References

Agarwal, A. (ed.) 2006. *Migrant Women and Work*. Sage, New Delhi.

Agnihotri, I. & Majumdar, I. 2009. Dusty trails and unsettled lives: Women's labour migration in rural India. *Indian Journal of Gender Studies* 16, 375–399.

Ambagudia, J. 2010. Tribal rights, dispossession and the State in Orissa. *Economic and Political Weekly* 45, 60–67.

Arza, C., Braunstein, E., Goulding, K. Cook, S. & Razavi, S. 2012. *Gendered Impacts of Globalisation: Employment and Social Protection*. UNSRID Research Paper 2012–3. UNRISD, Geneva.

Banerjee, N. 2011. A note on women as workers. Banerjee, N., Sen, S. & Dhawan, N. (eds) *Mapping the Field: Gender Relations in Contemporary India*, 192–212. Stree, Jadavpur.

Bates, C. & Carter, M. 1998. Tribal migration in India and beyond. Prakash, G. (ed.) *The World of the Rural Labourer in Colonial India*, 205–247. Oxford University Press, New Delhi.

Bhaduri, A. 2007. *Growth, Distribution and Innovations: Understanding Their Inter-relations*. Routledge, London.

Campaign for Survival and Dignity. n.d. www.forestrightsact.com (accessed 11 February 2013).

Daniel, U. 2011. *Migration in Western Odisha: Learning and Intervention*. Aide et Action, Odisha.

Deshingkar, P. & Farrington, J. 2009. *Circular Migration and Multilocational Livelihood Strategies in Rural India*. Oxford University Press, New Delhi.

Government of India (GoI). 2002. *Orissa Development Report*. Planning Commission, Government of India, New Delhi.

Government of India (GoI). 2008. *Annual Report: 2007–2008*. Ministry of Rural Development, Government of India, New Delhi.

Government of India (GoI). 2011. *Provisional Population of Orissa: Totals, Orissa Series 22*. [Census 2011] Government of India, New Delhi.

Government of Odisha (GoO). 2010. *District Plan of Sundargarh*. Planning and Coordination Department, Government of Odisha, Odisha.

Government of Odisha (GoO). 2012. *Economic Survey of Odisha (2011–2012)*. Directorate of Economics and Statistics, Bhubaneswar. www.odisha.gov.in/p&c/Download/Economic_Survey_2011_12.pdf (accessed 13 February 2013).

Indian Social Institute. 2008. *Tribal Women Domestic Workers in Delhi*. Indian Social Institute, New Delhi.

Issues of India. 2011. *Panchayat Extension to Scheduled Areas (PESA) Act, 1996*. http://socialissuesindia.wordpress.com/2011/08/04/panchayat-extension-to-scheduled-areas-act-or-pesa-1996/ (accessed 11 February 2013).

Jha, V. 2005. Migration of Orissa's tribal women: A new story of exploitation. *Economic and Political Weekly* 40:15, 1495–1497.

Kabeer, N. 2000. *Bangladeshi Women Workers and Labour Market Decisions: The Power to Choose.* Vistaar Publications, New Delhi.

Kujur, J.M. & Jha, V. 2008. *Tribal Women Domestic Workers in Delhi.* Indian Social Institute, New Delhi.

Kumar, K. 2006. *Dispossessed and Displaced: A Brief Paper on Tribal Issues in Orissa.* Vasundhara, Bhubaneswar.

Mathur, H.M. 2009. Tribal land issues in India: Communal management, rights and displacement. Asian Development Bank (ed.) *Land and Cultural Survival: The Community Rights of Indigenous Peoples in Asia,* 163–192. Asian Development Bank, Manila.

Ota, A.B. & Mohanty, B.N. 2010. *Population Profile of Scheduled Tribes in Orissa.* Scheduled Castes and Scheduled Tribes Research and Training Institute, Bhubaneswar.

Sen, A. 2004. *Social Exclusion: Concept Application Scrutiny.* Critical Quest, New Delhi.

Society for Regional Research and Analysis. 2010. *Migration of Tribal Women: Its Socio-economic Effects – An In-depth Study of Chattisgarh, Jharkhand, M.P. and Orissa.* Planning Commission, Government of India, New Delhi. http://planningcommission.nic.in/reports/sereport/ser/ser_mig.pdf (accessed 13 February 2013).

United Nations Development Programme. 2008. *Status Report: Land Rights and Ownership in Orissa.* UNDP, New Delhi.

6 Mobility patterns and gendered practices among Soliga people in Karnataka, India

Anitha Venkatesh and Veena N.

Introduction

Social scientists have studied indigenous migration from political and cultural perspectives in order to understand changes in market integration and how such changes affect indigenous populations in terms of their health, knowledge preservation, and hunting and land-clearance practices (Godoy 2001). Many theories concerning indigenous peoples relate to their rural to urban migration. Early studies showed that migration was a matter of individual choice and undertaken mainly due to desires to increase income by seeking employment opportunities in urban areas (Todaro 1969). Under the new economics of labour migration, population mobility is seen as a set of risk-diversification strategies (Stark & Bloom 1985).

Young and Doohan (1989) argue that migration models are not applicable to the study of indigenous peoples' mobility because they assume that economic importance is a major predictor of mobility. Migration models exclude circular patterns of mobility, often the most common form of mobility among indigenous people (Young & Doohan 1989; Young 1990). According to Taylor and Bell (2004a), the mobility patterns of indigenous populations are fundamentally a product of changing relationships between indigenous cultures and the nation state(s). Taylor and Bell (2004b) also suggest that an inherent assumption of migration models is that people only move to increase their income. However, their suggestion is inappropriate in the context of indigenous populations that prioritize family and ancestral land above employment opportunities.

Mobility was important for indigenous peoples even before development policies were put into effect, but has been overlooked by migration theories. Studies of the aspects of indigenous peoples' mobility are important because their mobility is not only linked to survival, but also to traditional mobility practices, kinship, and culture (Hamilton 1987). Existing ethnographic research indicates that certain cultural, structural, and historical factors have a bearing on the rate and patterns of indigenous mobility (Prout 2009). Young and Doohan (1989) describe indigenous populations' mobility as a phenomenon that reflects the setting within which people live – a specific cultural situation described as a culture of mobility to maintain relationships between places, cultures, and kinships.

Discussions of indigenous mobility practices have focused on external forces, such as the impact of policies (Taylor & Bell 2004a; Prout 2007).

Cresswell (2010) notes that basic differences in mobilities are central to any hierarchy and have given rise to politics of mobility. Hence, studying the processes of mobility and immobility could shed light on shifting power relationships. Further, mobility and immobility are implicated in the creation, reinforcement, and change in the meanings and practices of gender (Valentine 1989; Koskela 1997). Enforced immobility or denial of the right to mobility keeps women in a subordinate position and sustains unbalanced gender relations (Hanson 2010). The latter point is central to any analysis of how mobilities modify gendered practices (Cresswell & Uteng 2008). The manner in which such mobility practices transform gender roles and gender relationships should be investigated in indigenous mobility literature, and the research presented in this chapter is a contribution in this respect.

The Soliga's place and culture

Biligiri Rangaswamy Temple Wildlife Sanctuary is located in the Biligiri Rangana Hills (BR Hills) in the Chamarajanagara District in southern Karnataka, 90 km south-east of Mysore and 180 km south-west of Bangalore (Kothari 2007) (Figure 6.1). Chamarajanagara is known for its forest resources and has a high population of forest-dwellers. Scheduled Tribes (as recognized under the Constitution of the Indian Republic) make up 11 per cent of the population of the district (Government of Karnataka 2006), and include 28,000 Soliga (in 2,403 families) living in 57 forest villages called *podus* (tribal settlements). The Soliga live within the sanctuary that was created in 1972, at which time it covered an area of 322.4 km^2. In 1987, it was extended to 540 km^2 (Kothari 2007).

The Soliga, whose name translates as 'people of the bamboo', formerly harvested forest products and engaged in hunting and shifting cultivation (Poojar 2005). They speak Soliganudi, an ancient form of Kannada, the official language of Karnataka. The Soliga have lived deep within the forests of the BR Hills for centuries, and they maintained their traditional nomadic life until 1980 (Veena N. *et al.* 2006). Women, men, and children all went hunting and gathering together, and in that way young children learned about the trees and animals that provided them with food and protection. Soliga women would move within the forest with their husbands, in groups with other women, or alone. They sourced all their firewood, food, and medicines from the forest, such as *Amla* (Indian gooseberry), herbs, mushrooms, root vegetables, medicinal plants, and honey.

Soliga society was patriarchal and men were the heads of the villages, communities, and judicial committees. However, couples lived in nuclear households in farmsteads that were some distance apart from each other, and family and children were central in their lives. Accordingly, within each family, women and men shared all tasks, such as childcare, hunting, gathering, and cooking. Traditional practices such as attending village festivals, funerals, marriages, and visiting sick family members are still regarded as very important

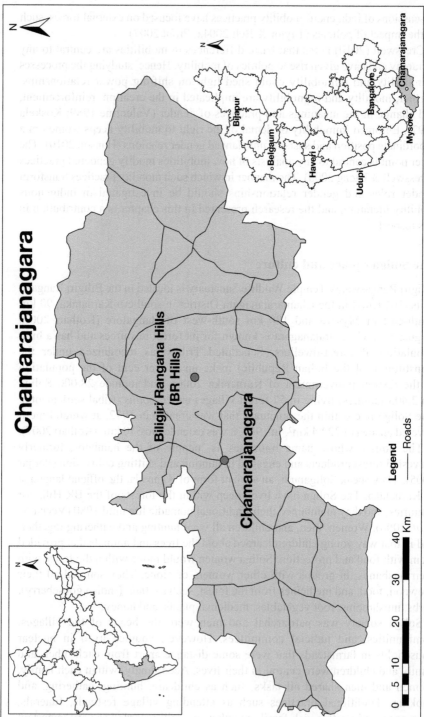

Figure 6.1 Location of the study area, the Biligiri Rangana Hills (BR Hills) in Chamarajanagara District, southern Karnataka.

occasions and normally both women and men are involved in them. Despite constant mobility within the forests, the tight bonds of family and kin structure are maintained. Traditionally, there was neither a dowry system nor discrimination against female children within Soliga communities. Furthermore, despite the patriarchal system, women had freedom of mobility. For the Soliga, mobility continues as a cultural practice today.

At the beginning of the 20th century, the Soliga's interaction with the external world was limited to pilgrims on their way to temples in the BR Hills and to traders who bartered non-timber forest products (NTFPs) for cloth and trinkets. As the demand for forests increased, Karnataka Forest Department became a major factor in the lives of the Soliga towards the end of the 20th century. The authorities treated them with contempt as unclean, uncivilized forest-dwellers. They exploited the Soliga and forced them to work for low wages. The authorities also burnt the Soliga's houses, forced them to leave without any compensation, and resettled them in areas lacking access to forest resources. People who lived in villages near to forests shared a similar attitude towards the Soliga. For example, they exploited the Soliga by paying them pittances for NTFPs. They also feared the Soliga because they lived among ferocious animals in the forest, and labelled them sorcerers and magicians who could cast spells and harm others. Politically, the Soliga were ignored and therefore received few benefits from the state.

Development, mobility, and the status of women

There is a considerable body of literature on the status of India's forests and those living within them. Traditionally, indigenous people were highly mobile, often moving to gather forest products and to hunt, and later started to practise shifting cultivation. When India was under British rule, the practice of shifting cultivation was made illegal and pressure was placed on indigenous people to cease their traditional practices (Ramesh & Guntipilly 1997). The post-independence forest laws did not particularly benefit indigenous people. The Government of India passed a law banning shifting cultivation in order to protect forest resources (Gadgil & Guha 1992). Most of India's forests were declared reserve forests. It was illegal to cultivate land in such forests or to collect timber from them. Indigenous people were displaced from their traditional lands to settlements where they could not continue with their traditional occupations, habitat, and livelihoods (Walter & Paranjpye 1997). The compensation and rehabilitation provided to indigenous people did not benefit them or help to improve their economic and social status. Rather, their marginalization increased. The transition from nomadic and semi-nomadic ways of life to a more sedentary form of living has had consequences for the Sogila's mobility practices, which in turn have affected their culture, kinship, and gender relationships (Vijayalakshmi 2003).

Most indigenous communities in India have ceased their nomadic ways of life in the forests and mountains and have settled in specific places (Walter & Paranjpye 1997). It is difficult for indigenous people to acquire full-time waged work close to their settlements. Instead, they have to travel long distances of *c.*20–25 km to collect forest products. Forced displacement and outward migration affect both men's and women's mobility. Increased infrastructure and market facilities provide employment opportunities for tribal people, and consequently traditional forms of land use and livelihoods have changed (Deshingkar & Farrington 2009). Much research on the tribal population in India is focused on migration and seasonal migration, as large numbers of tribal people have migrated to more prosperous rural and urban areas for employment opportunities (Deshingkar & Start 2003; Deshingkar 2006).

Although better infrastructure and communication facilities have led to increased mobility to urban centres, settled cultivation has changed the social structure in Soliga homes and villages. Today, the Soliga are entirely dependent on rainfall, different types of landownership, and labour sharing (Rasul & Thapa 2003). Also, the division of labour has become more defined and men and women take responsibility for different tasks. Women continue to do most of the agricultural work, but their contribution is undermined by low returns from smallholdings (Vijayalakshmi 2003). Therefore, they have to subsidize their household income by engaging in wage labour (Bose 2006). In common with other indigenous women, Soliga women perform a wide range of activities and are mobile as daily, temporary, and/or seasonal labourers.

Most indigenous communities have been displaced by government-led modernization projects and laws governing the conservation and protection of biodiversity and wildlife.[1] Due to lack of land, unemployment opportunities, and basic facilities in the places where they were resettled, indigenous people have had no other choice but to increase their level of mobility. For example, some indigenous women have to walk or travel increasingly longer distances, whereas others have ceased to be mobile because the men in their families migrate out of the villages (i.e. the resettlement villages). In Soliga community, the entire family is mobile together, inside the forest on a daily basis and outside the forest on a seasonal basis. As the distances travelled daily increase, women with small children no longer join their husbands in the forests. Instead, they stay at home with their children while the men go in search of honey, timber, and fruits. Moreover, in the absence of women and children, men tend to travel longer distances, leaving women to take care of other members of their households. This has resulted in gender differences in the daily mobility practices for domestic, economic, and social purposes. As a consequence, the perspectives, experiences, and aspirations of Soliga men and women have also changed.

In February 2004, an official memorandum was issued that banned the collection of NTFPs for commercial use. However, the ban was not implemented in the BR Hills until April 2006 (Setty *et al.* 2008). This was probably due to ongoing correspondence between Karnataka Forest Department and the Government of India. Karnataka Forest Department argued that many tribes considered that collection of NTFPs for commercial use was a bona fide practice. Another reason for the delay might have been that local officers were in charge of implementing the ban (Reddy cited in Sandemose 2009). After the ban was implemented, the Soliga could not enter the forests to collect NTFPs for domestic use. Their mobility outside the BR Hills was limited because they were isolated and found it difficult to adjust to the outside world. A Tiger Task Force commissioned by the Government of India reported that although the purpose of the ban was to increase the level of protection of already protected areas, the major consequence had been an escalation in conflicts between local people and park authorities (Government of India 2005).

Methodology

The research findings presented in this chapter are part of a research project on changing mobility among indigenous people. The findings are drawn from one focus group discussion and 22 interviews with Soliga women and men, both mobile and not mobile, and NGO staff, as well as direct observations and informal discussions with NGO workers and villagers. Intra-household interviews were conducted with both men and women in each case.

Since the early 1980s, two NGOs – the Ashoka Trust for Research in Ecology and the Environment (ATREE) and Vivekananda Girijana Kalyana Kendra (VGKK) – have been working to improve health and educational facilities in the BR Hills. The VGKK runs a hospital, school, and hostel for indigenous people, where researchers can stay, and ATREE runs a research station. Soliga people, especially women, in the BR Hills are not comfortable about speaking to outsiders, and therefore NGO workers facilitated our visits to Soliga villages and interviews. Research questions were posed in the local language, Kannada. Three villages were selected for data collection based on their history of mobility practices and past and present experiences of mobility: Muthukane Gadhai, Chikka Bangale Podu, and Doddha Bangale Podu:

1   Muthukane Gadhai village is located 6 km east of the ATREE research station. At the time when the study was conducted, the village had 80 houses and a population of *c*.400. The Soliga had lived there for 40 years and had received land rights from the Government of Karnataka. However, they did not have the right to sell the land and could only transfer it to family members. Their main occupations were the collection of NTFPs, wage labour, and work for local NGOs and on coffee plantations. Both men and women were mobile as daily labourers.

2   Chikka Bangale Podu village is located 10 km east of ATREE research station. At the time of the study, there were 60 households and a population of almost 300. Most villagers did not have land rights and their main occupations were the collection of NTFPs, trading in flowers and herbs both within and outside the BR Hills, and working for local NGOs and as daily labourers for Karnataka Forest Department. Women were not involved in daily wage labour because their mobility was controlled by men. Further, only men traded flowers and herbs which was done outside the BR Hills. The economic status of the households and women in the village was lower compared to the other two study villages.

3   Doddha Bangale Podu village is situated *c.*20 km north-east of ATREE research station. At the time of the study, there were 150 households, with a population of 600. The village is close to Biligiri Rangaswamy Temple, and therefore women could sell firewood to earn INR 100–200 each week.[2] The main occupations were agriculture, the collection of NTFPs, selling firewood, and wage labour. There were mixed mobility patterns in households. Members of households with land were more mobile than those from households without land. Those who were mobile worked as wage labourers within and outside the BR Hills. Both men and women participated in wage work. However, jobs were scarce and work was only available three or four times per month, and therefore the villages normally depended on the forest for their food supplies.

The villagers had been displaced from their original settlements since 1980. Prior to their displacement, their main sources of livelihood had been shifting cultivation, hunting, and gathering forest products. Following displacement, they lost their traditional habits and livelihoods, but men and women were able to continue to move freely within the forest surrounding the villages in order to collect forest products. In mid-2012, the Government of Karnataka started a food scheme to provide nutritious food for Soliga tribal people in all villages.

Data were collected in the period October–December 2012. We focused on collecting data on each interviewee's age, the location of their house, and the availability of land for their household. Of the 22 interviews, 10 were held with men and 12 with women, who were interviewed in order to understand mobility practices and gender relationships in the study villages.

The respondents were in the age group 20–80 years, and most had completed primary education. Those with the highest levels of education were from Muthukane Gadhai – a man who had completed Grade 10 (normally completed by the age of 15 years) and a woman who had completed Grade 8 (normally completed by the age of 13 years). In-depth interviews were conducted and supplemented with direct observations and a focus group discussion. The focus group discussion involved eight women, some mobile and some not mobile, in order to understand mobility and immobility patterns, experiences, and perceptions among women.

Mobility, livelihood, and tradition

After the implementation (in 2004) of the government ban on the collection of NTFPs, indigenous people could not enter the forests to collect NTFPs for domestic or commercial use. Many Soliga were forced to find other sources of income and livelihood. One option was to harvest coffee beans in other places, i.e. outside BR Hills. A further option was daily wage labour in adjacent towns. Some people were employed by the two NGOs, while others took up trading: 'Every year, for five–six years, our family would migrate to coffee plantations, where we worked from January to April' (Jade Gowda, male, 40 years, Muthukane Gadhai).[3] According to Jade Gowda, his family's mobility was circular migration rather than seasonal migration. Due to his attachment to his land and traditions, he returned home as quickly as possible.

Lakume Gowda (aged 60 years) worked as a daily labourer in forest plantations to supplement the income from his 2 ha of land, on which he grew coffee. He said: 'It is difficult to earn money as a daily labourer although the wage is between 150 and 200 rupees [INR] per day.' However, mobility outside the BR Hills was more problematic because outsiders cheated indigenous people. In common with Lakume Gowda, Kethamma found it difficult to live outside the BR Hills because it would be more expensive: 'We don't like to migrate to other places for work as temporary or seasonal migrants. When we stay outside, daily expenses are high, whereas in the forest we can collect forest products for our daily needs' (Kethamma, female, 26 years, Muthukane Gadhai).

Madhamma (female, aged 40 years), from Doddha Bangale Podu, had 3 ha of land. Although the land was in her father's name, she had grown coffee on it because she did not have any brothers who would have taken responsibility for the land. However, the income from the land was not sufficient for her family's needs and she engaged in daily wage labour within the BR Hills to manage their daily needs. She had never migrated beyond the BR Hills for work, although she informed that younger people, especially those with an education, preferred to migrate outside to access better employment opportunities.

> We have two hectares of land where we can grow coffee. Normally, my husband and I are both involved in daily labour within the BR Hills, but the availability of jobs is limited and we usually have only eight to twelve days of work per month. Mobility within the BR Hills is part of our culture, and changes in government policy cannot change it.
>
> (Kethamma, female, 26 years, Muthukane Gadhai)

The Soliga have a strong sense of commitment to their traditions and kinship structures, which form a basic part of their identity. Specific places in the BR Hills, including springs, specific trees, and certain places, are sacred to them and visiting such places repeatedly renews their commitment to their culture and tradition: 'We don't like to migrate to other places for work as temporary or seasonal migrants, although we can earn some extra money, because it is difficult for us to leave our home' (Kethamma, female, 26 years, Muthukane Gadhai).

The sentiment expressed by Kethamma was echoed also by a young man who had been educated to a comparatively high level:

> I finished my degree [BSc] five years ago and I work at ATREE. Although I can get a job in the city, I don't like leaving home. We were born and brought up here. We have our own tradition and culture and our values and priorities.
>
> (Jagadish, male, 26 years, Doddha Bangale Podu)

Although people with small parcels of land can supplement their income by engaging in wage labour and although educated people can work for NGOs, Soliga that are both uneducated and landless find it very difficult to make ends meet: 'We don't have any land, so my husband sold flowers near the temple every day. Three months ago, elephants destroyed his shop. Now, he does not have a job, and it is very difficult to manage my family's expenses' (Lakkamma, female, 27 years, Doddha Bangale Podu).

Some women have also taken up trading, even though is not a traditional occupation. Jade Madhamma lived near the temple and sold firewood, flowers, herbs, and medicinal plants:

> For the past five years, my husband has been travelling to work at construction sites, but he spends most of his money and doesn't send much money home. I have two children, so to manage household expenditure I collect fuel in the forest and trade flowers near the temple.
>
> (Jade Madhamma, female, 38 years, Doddha Bangale Podu)

Sørensen and Olwig (2002) note that improved accessibility to the outside world has an impact on indigenous populations' mobility. The respondents in our study said that despite better infrastructure and transport facilities, the Soliga do not often use vehicles because they consider them expensive and unsafe:

> We normally use few vehicles to travel within the BR Hills. In fact, we carry firewood and NTFPs on our head instead of using vehicles. Men use bicycles to carry heavy loads. We normally walk 15 to 20 kilometres per day. Buses are expensive and walking is safer than using transportation.
>
> (Focus group discussion, woman from Muthukane Gadhai)

> Now we have access to road and transportation facilities, we can travel to town and buy things that we need. We could not do it 30 years ago. Due to constraints of money, time, and information, we use transportation for social activities like shopping, meeting people, attending events, rather than to commute to work.
>
> (Focus group discussion, woman from Muthukane Gadhai)

Gender, culture, and mobility

Women's traditional freedom of movement within the BR Hills has been curtailed by the Government of India's legislations implemented by Karnataka Forest Department. In addition, mobility within the forest has become risky because the Forest Department tends to arrest and harass those caught in violation of the law. Subsequently, there has been a change in Soliga women's mobility:

> I used to be involved in the collection of NTFPs and firewood in the forest and there were no restrictions on my mobility. When government polices stopped us from entering the forest, we lost our livelihood. Now, my husband restricts my mobility. I never travel alone to town. I cannot even shop or visit

my relatives without him. He wants me to take care of the house and domestic animals, and cook for him. I don't have any freedom, any mobility, or any decision-making power to buy even small necessities from the market.

(Madevi, female, 30 years, Doddha Bangale Podu)

We were isolated from mainstream society inside the forest before 1980. After the laws and development projects entered the BR Hills, we started interacting with mainstream society. We have a strong culture and tradition, we respect women, and [traditionally] we don't practice dowry giving and domestic violence, but recently, both [practices] have started in our communities due to external exposure. It [the exposure] also impacts on gender roles within the household. Men used to help us in cooking and taking care of children, but now they think it is completely women's work. The burden on women has increased.

(Focus group discussion, woman from Doddha Bangale Podu)

In contrast, Kethamma, from Muthukane Gadhai, held the opinion that men did not control her mobility when she went to collect forest products or other necessities on a daily basis. However, the majority of the other women (eight) informed that when they engaged in wage labour outside the home, their mobility was restricted. Other women said their mobility was restricted only if they wanted to travel outside the forest:

My husband and I worked outside in 2009 because of lack of job opportunities in the BR Hills. After two months, we returned to the BR Hills. Now, he does not allow me to work as a labourer. He feels that if I earn money, he might lose his status in the household and community.

(Akkamma, female, 28 years, Chikka Bangale Podu)

My husband doesn't allow me to work on my neighbour's land. So, sometimes we eat only once a day. My female neighbours are mobile and work at coffee plantations and for the Forest Department as daily labourers. They earn between 150 and 200 rupees [INR] per day. Although I wanted to travel with them and could earn more money that way, my husband does not like me doing this. I only collect wood and sell it sometimes. Now, my children are grown up and I want them to be better educated, but my husband takes them to the forest to collect Non-timber forest products such as honey and Indian gooseberry.

(Lakkamma, female, 27 years, Doddha Bangale Podu)

It is evident from the above quote that women have lost their decision-making power with regard to their children's education. Further, mobility outside forest areas leads to increased interaction with mainstream Indian society, which tends to look down on women in general and all indigenous people. Hence, indigenous women positioned at the intersection of class, caste, and gender are vulnerable to exploitation in three ways. Daily wages are lower for women than for men doing the same work and this has degraded women's position in society and reduced the value of their work. Hence, women's options are diminishing, and many women now have little decision-making power within their respective households:

> Although I earn only a small amount of money, I don't want to work outside the BR Hills as a labourer. I feel secure within our community and people. It is not safe for single women outside the BR Hills.
>
> (Lakamma, female, 33 years, Chikka Bangale Podu)

> As daily labourers, men can earn 200 rupees [INR] and women earn 150 rupees [INR] for the same work.
>
> (Kethamma, female, 26 years, Muthukane Gadhai)

> I don't like to work as a labourer outside the BR Hills because it is not safe. There is violence and insecurity. In the forest, we are free to move without any restrictions on time and place. If we migrate to other places, we lose our independence, freedom, and mobility.
>
> (Kethamma, female, 26 years, Chikka Bangale Podu)

Traditionally, women and men shared household chores, cooking, and childcare in nuclear families. With exposure to the outside world, both women's and men's notions of gender roles have changed and today women are largely responsible for household work and childcare:

> I do not restrict women from going out and earning money, but I don't do household work. That is women's work. Women are good at managing money, so I don't take any money from my wife. I don't give her any money either. I spend my earnings for my own needs.
>
> (Lakume Gowda, male, 60 years, Muthukane Gadhai)

> My husband works at a forest plantation as a daily wage labourer when jobs are available. Otherwise, he just stays at home. I look for jobs close to home, as my husband does not help me with household chores and childcare. When I was earning, I had more bargaining power with my husband and I could make him share household work and had a say in decisions regarding household needs.
>
> (Jangamma, female, 25 years, Doddha Bangale Podu)

Thus, the relatively egalitarian gender relations within Soliga society have given way to clearly demarcated gender roles and women hold a strongly subservient position both within the family and society. They have not only lost their decision-making power over their children's education but also their bargaining capacity with regard to family income. They are seen merely as housekeepers and homestead workers, not as partners in their respective communities and in Soliga society in general:

> When we were unable to enter the forest, we started working as labourers at construction sites outside the BR Hills. My husband started drinking more and he now spends all his money on himself. I have to support the household myself. Life was better when we stayed within the BR Hills.
>
> (Jogamma, female, 33 years, Doddha Bangale Podu)

> My husband does not have a job, and doesn't allow me to work as a labourer. So it is very difficult to manage my family's expenses. We eat two times a day and sometimes only once a day. I don't have much bargaining power compared to women who earn money.
>
> (Lakkamma, female, 27 years, Doddha Bangale Podu)

Since there was no 'income' to be earned, the concept of men as breadwinners was not recognized among the Soliga. Today, the notion is gaining ground, along with the practice of giving dowry, domestic violence, addiction to liquor, and other social problems. Women who are more mobile than other women have greater bargaining power concerning their children's education, health, and household assets:

> After we were displaced from the forest, we got six hectares of land. We grow coffee and do not work anywhere other than our field. I am more secure and have better economic status than others in the community. I have more bargaining power and more mobility within the household and in the community. I also send my children for higher education. My husband respects my decisions with respect to household expenditure and children's education. He works at ATREE and I am in charge of our land and income from that, so I have more bargaining power. However, performing all these tasks places a huge burden on me.
>
> (Sharadha, female, 32 years, completed Grade 6,[4] Doddha Bangale Podu)

> Women don't walk long distances to carry water, fuel, and fodder. Their life has become easy. They also get jobs with NGOs so they have exposure to interact with outsiders, unlike before. Most are involved in Sangas [self-help groups for women to make small savings) so they can keep their earnings in bank accounts and manage household expenditure.
>
> (Nanjanna, male, 70 years, Muthukane Gadhai)

Due to their childcare obligations, women tend to seek employment closer to home than men do (Chapple 2001), even though they earn less. Compared to men, women spend more time on household activities and have less leisure time, which further limits their mobility (Hanson & Hanson 1981; Pas 1984; Lu & Pas 1998).

In summary, married Soliga women have comparatively less mobility than single women. Their domestic and social mobility within the BR Hills is not restricted, but restrictions are placed on their economic activities within and outside the BR Hills. Women with greater exposure to the outside world have more land rights and knowledge of cash crops such as coffee and, therefore, they have more bargaining power with respect to their time and income and can use their mobility for economic gains.

Conclusions

Taylor and Bell (2004a) state that indigenous mobility is a changing relationship between mobility practices and interactions with institutional structures, with particular types of mobility processes underlying particular circumstances, settings, and situations. In the case of the Soliga, loss of access to forests due to government regulations has negatively impacted their forest-based livelihoods and well-being. Lack of access to forest resources has curbed their mobility in the dense forests of the BR Hills and by adversely affecting their food security it has had an impact on their nutrition, health, and well-being. Hence, the Soliga living in the BR Hills are forced to seek livelihoods elsewhere, among mainstream Indian society. Thus, it is evident that legislation has resulted in a major change in the mobility patterns of forest-dwelling people.

When the Soliga move out of the forest, they are exploited and discriminated against, especially in the case of women. In addition, the mobility of Soliga women has been impacted by violence against them and lack of security for their lives, bodies, and property. Such violence and insecurity are endemic in patriarchal India and discourage independence and mobility, and instead promote women's purdah (seclusion from public spaces) and dependence on men. Exposure to the patriarchal and misogynistic norms and patterns of mainstream Indian society has increased male dominance and the subjugation of women in Soliga society. Various studies have shown that migration and mobility patterns affect indigenous peoples' cultures and kinship structure (Young & Doohan 1989).

Cresswell (2010), Hanson (2010), and Cresswell and Uteng (2008) have pointed out the gendered implications of the processes of mobility and immobility in creating, reinforcing, and changing the meanings and practices of gender. In the case of the Soliga, mobility in the forest empowered Soliga women who traditionally worked alongside men to support, nurture, and educate their children. In contrast, mobility outside the forest has disempowered Soliga women, who have become solely responsible for household work and childcare. Their mobility is not only controlled, but also enforced. The women are also expected to maintain the norms of decency and respect that mainstream patriarchy imposes on women. Finally, Soliga women are forced to accept degrading positions through being paid less than men for doing the same work. Thus, mobility and immobility are used to create, enforce, and retain Soliga women in a subordinate position. As Cresswell (2010) notes, basic differences in mobility between women and men are central to the creation of a hierarchy between them.

Hence, a change in the law governing the exploitation of the forests through the collection of NTFPs not only reduced the Soliga's status from being 'people of the bamboo' to daily wage labourers, but also further disempowered Soliga women within their communities (in which earlier they had thrived in relatively egalitarian gender relationships). The sharp change in the Soliga's mobility patterns has played a critical role in the process of degradation and disempowerment of women. If mobility is conceptualized as a capability (Kronlid 2008), it is clear that the capabilities of Soliga women have been limited by the imposition of institutional structures and processes.

Notes

1   S. Satish and E. Schaengold, 'Indigenous peoples and biodiversity conservation: Emerging issues in India', paper presented at the conference on Displacement, Forced Settlement, and Conservation, University of Oxford, September 1999. A synopsis of the proposed paper can be downloaded from: http://repository.forcedmigration. org/pdf/?pid=fmo:1951 (accessed 9 February 2013).
2   INR 53 = USD 1 (January 2013).
3   The interviews were conducted in the local language, Kannada, and translated by Veena N.
4   Grade 6 is normally completed at the age of 12 years. However, not all children start school at the age of five or six years, and therefore Sharadha could have been between 12 and 15 years of age when she dropped out of school.

References

Bose, A. 2006. Empowering Soliga tribes: 'Sudarshan model' of Karnataka. *Economic and Political Weekly* 41, 565–566.

Chapple, K. 2001. Time to work: Job search strategies and commute time for women on welfare in San Francisco. *Journal of Urban Affairs* 23, 155–173.

Cresswell, T. 2010. Towards a politics of mobility. *Environment and Planning D: Society and Space* 28, 17–31.

Cresswell, T. & Uteng, T.P. 2008. Gendered mobilities: Towards an holistic understanding. Uteng, T.P. & Cresswell, T. (eds) *Gendered Mobilities*, 1–14. Ashgate, Aldershot.

Deshingkar, P. 2006. *Internal Migration, Poverty and Development in Asia.* ODI Briefing Paper 11. Overseas Development Institute, London. www.odi.org.uk/publications/ briefing/bp_internal_migration_oct06.pdf (accessed 30 January 2013).

Deshingkar, P. & Farrington, J. 2009. *Circular Migration and Multilocational Livelihood Strategies in Rural India.* Oxford University Press, New York.

Deshingkar, P. & Start, D. 2003. *Seasonal Migration for Livelihoods in India: Coping, Accumulation and Exclusion.* ODI Working Paper 220. Overseas Development Institute, London. www.odi.org.uk/publications/working_papers/wp220.pdf (accessed 30 January 2013).

Gadgil, M. & Guha, R. 1992. *This Fissured Land: An Ecological History of India.* Oxford University Press, Delhi.

Godoy, R. 2001. *Indians, Markets and Rainforests: Theory, Methods, Analysis.* Columbia University Press, New York.

Government of India. 2005. *Joining the Dots.* The Report of the Tiger Task Force. Project Tiger, Union Ministry of Environment and Forests, New Dehli.

Government of Karnataka. 2006. *Karnataka: Human Development Report 2005*. Planning and Statistics Department, Government of Karnataka, Bangalore.

Hamilton, A. 1987. Coming and going: Aboriginal mobility in north-west South Australia, 1970–71. *Records of the South Australian Museum* 20, 47–57.

Hanson, S. 2010. Gender and mobility: New approaches for informing sustainability. *Gender, Place & Culture: A Journal of Feminist Geography* 17, 5–23.

Hanson, S. & Hanson, P. 1981. The impact of married women's employment on household travel patterns: A Swedish example. *Transportation* 10, 165–183.

Koskela, H. 1997. 'Bold walk and breakings': Women's spatial confidence versus fear of violence. *Gender, Place, and Culture* 4, 301–319.

Kothari, A. 2007. Conservationists vs. conservation. *The Hindu* 26 August 2007.

Kronlid, D. 2008. Mobility as capability. Uteng, T.P. &. Cresswell, T. (eds) *Gendered Mobilities*, 5–34. Ashgate, Aldershot.

Lu, X. & Pas, E.I. 1998. Socio-demographics, activity participation and travel behaviour, *Transportation Research Part A* 33, 1–18.

Pas, E. 1984. The effect of selected socio-demographic characteristics on daily travel behaviour. *Environment and Planning A* 16, 571–581.

Poojar, I.C. 2005. *Biodiversity Education for Indigenous Communities: Education for a Sustainable Future*. Center for Environment Education, Ahmedabad.

Prout, S. 2007. *Security and Belonging: Reconceptualising Aboriginal Spatial Mobilities in Yamatji Country, Western Australia*. PhD thesis. Macquarie University, Macquarie Park, NSW.

Prout, S. 2009. Security and belonging: Reconceptualising aboriginal spatial mobilities in Yamatji Country, Western Australia. *Mobilities* 4, 177–202.

Ramesh, M.K. & Guntipilly, F. 1997. A critique of the Karnataka Resettlement of Project – Displaced Persons Act, 1987. Fernandes, W. & Paranjpye, V. (eds) *Rehabilitation Policy and Law in India: A Right to Livelihood*, 202–214. Indian Social Institute, New Delhi.

Rasul, G. & Thapa, G.B. 2003. Shifting cultivation in the mountains of south and Southeast Asia: Regional patterns and factors influencing the change. *Land Degradation & Development* 14, 495–508.

Sandemose, P. 2009. *Local People and Protected Areas: The Ban of NTFP Collection For Commercial Use and Effects on Cash Incomes and Livelihoods of the Soligas in BR Hills, India*. www.umb.no/statisk/noragric/publications/master/2009_pernille_ sandemose.pdf (accessed 9 February 2013).

Setty, R.S., Bawa, K., Ticktin, T. & Gowda, C.M. 2008. Evaluation of a participatory resource monitoring system for nontimber forest products: The case of *Amla* (*Phyllanthus* spp.) fruit harvest by Soligas in South India. *Ecology and Society* 13, Article 19. www.ecologyandsociety.org/vol13/iss2/art19 (accessed 9 February 2013).

Sørensen, N.N. & Olwig, K.F. 2002. *Work and Migration: Life and Livelihoods in a Globalizing World*. Routledge, London.

Stark, O. & Bloom, D., 1985. The new economics of labour migration. *American Economic Review* 75, 173–178.

Taylor, J. & Bell, M. 2004a. Introduction: New world demography. Taylor, J. & Bell, M. (eds) *Population Mobility and Indigenous Peoples in Australasia and North America*, 1–10. Routledge, London.

Taylor, J. & Bell, M. 2004b. Conclusion: Emerging research themes. Taylor, J. & Bell, M. (eds) *Population Mobility and Indigenous Peoples in Australasia and North America*, 262–267. Routledge, London.

Mobility patterns and gendered practices 133

Todaro, M. 1969. A model of labor migration and urban unemployment in less-developed countries. *The American Economic Review* 59, 138–148.

Valentine, G. 1989. The geography of women's fear. *Area* 21, 385–390.

Veena N., Prashanth, N.S. & Vasuki, B.K. 2006. *Our Forest, Our Lives: 25 Years of Tribal Development*. VGKK (Vivekananda Girijana Kalyana Kendra), BR Hills, Karnataka.

Vijayalakshmi, V. 2003. *Scheduled Tribes and Gender: Development Perceptions from Karnataka*. Working Paper 128. Institute for Social and Economic Change, Bangalore.

Walter, F. & Paranjpye, V. (eds) 1997. *Rehabilitation Policy and Law in India: A Right to Livelihood*. Indian Social Institute, New Delhi.

Young, E. 1990. Aboriginal population mobility and service provision: A framework for analysis. Meehan, B. & White, N. (eds) *Hunter-Gatherer Demography: Past and Present*, 186–196. Oceania Monograph 39. University of Sydney, Sydney.

Young, E. & Doohan, K. 1989. *Mobility for Survival: A Process Analysis of Aboriginal Population Movement in Central Australia*. North Australia Research Unit, Australian National University, Darwin.

7 Gender vulnerabilities of resettlement and restricted mobility of ethnic groups in northern Laos

Kyoko Kusakabe and Sengkham Vongphakdy

Introduction

In northern Laos, ethnic groups have traditionally relocated their villages in order to find fertile land, flee war, escape natural disasters and the risk of diseases, and avoid internal conflict. However, since the 1990s, ethnic peoples' mobility has changed because the state has taken greater control over their movements in the name of security and development. De Wet (2006, 191) quotes Koenig as suggesting that 'involuntary resettlement is also impoverishing because it takes away political power, most dramatically the power to decide about where and how to live.'

Turton (2006, 14) defines those affected by forced resettlement as

> 'development-induced displaced persons' who have been allocated a specific area within their own country in which to resettle and who have been provided with at least a minimum of resources and services in order to re-establish their lives. The term may also apply to those who are resettled by government-sponsored programmes that use resettlement as a method of rural development and/or political control.

In the case of Laos, only the latter half of the Turton's definition applies, since, as we show in this chapter, some villages have not received even the minimum in terms of resources and services. After the ethnic groups were relocated, their access to the forests was further restricted by the introduction of rubber concessions and increasing pressure on land from other ethnic groups that had occupied the settlement areas for longer periods of time. Hence, in the case of those who were resettled, their impoverishment occurred not only as a result of being displaced, but also because they were forced to stay; they could neither return to their former place nor move elsewhere. Traditionally, ethnic groups in northern Laos have used mobility to escape poverty. Whenever land was scarce and there was conflict with other groups, they would move elsewhere. However, it is no longer possible for them to use such strategies. This chapter analyses the vulnerability of women and men under resettlement programmes and rubber concessions in northern Laos. We argue that women and men experience vulnerability differently and that women's vulnerability is closely related to their restricted mobility.

Oliver-Smith (2006, 141) states 'to be resettled is one of the most acute expressions of powerlessness because it constitutes a loss of control over one's physical space'. Cernea (1996) notes eight processes that lead to the impoverishment of resettled populations: landlessness, joblessness, homelessness, marginalization, increased morbidity, food insecurity, loss of access to common property, and social disarticulation (i.e. dismantling of communities' social organization structures). In northern Laos, lack of access to basic resources and services and the introduction of rubber concessions where they have resettled have not only deprived them of their access to land and the forests, but have also further limited their access to the forest in the newly resettled area in Luang Namtha Province. Landlessness and lack of access to upland fields forced women especially to collect non-timber forest products (NTFPs) and engage in wage labour. At the same time, the dispersal of relatives into different villages has decreased options for women to leave their children in care when engaging in income-generating activities. Hence, a combination of landlessness and social capital make life and adjustment to resettlement difficult for women.

Women experience displacement differently from men (Tan *et al.* 2005; de Wet 2006). When displacement is the result of a state project, women usually receive fewer benefits from the state than men.[1] In addition, the social changes and changes in livelihoods have a greater effect on women, and they end up spending more time working than before. Walter Fernandes (see endnote 1) found that in India tribal women more often became jobless and landless after resettlement. Due to their loss of access to land following displacement, they were deprived of any control over productive resources. Fernandes adds that due to patriarchal practices, the women were less able to take advantage of the new opportunities in the place of resettlement, hence, their dependency on men increased. A similar phenomenon has been identified by Bisht (2009). Wisner *et al.* (2007) point out that the stress of displacement could lead to increased domestic violence. De Wet (2006) notes that resettled people have to depend more on cash sources of income. However, as Walter Fernandes (see endnote 1) points out, when women are excluded from the market economy, it is difficult for them to establish new livelihoods (see also Tan *et al.* 2005 for a discussion on how women become more impoverished than men as a consequence of resettlement). Bisht (2009, 314) argues that women's lack of economic independence and social autonomy leads to the 'risk of being excluded from the process of rebuilding everyday routines'. This echoes what Cernea (1997) calls 'social disarticulation', in which space, place, and time are disturbed and experienced as discomfort. In this chapter, we argue that restricted access to forest resources in northern Laos has affected women's and men's livelihoods, and women have been excluded from most of the important decisions about moving their village in order to survive. Similar findings regarding women's exclusion have been reported by Bisht (2009) from a study conducted in India. We would like to add on the element of daily mobility to this discussion and argue that what makes the gender differences in the effect of resettlement is how their mobility patterns are constructed.

Resettlement programmes and economic concessions in northern Laos

Since the late 1990s, the state has ordered ethic groups in the mountains of northern Laos to live in places along roads where it is easier for the authorities to access them. The reason given for resettlement programmes is that they will facilitate drug control and the elimination of poppy cultivation, and will promote development and the provision of social services. The international community has contributed to such sedentarist policies of the Lao People's Democratic Republic by providing support to resettled communities in terms of infrastructure, such as roads, water supplies, and schools. Forced relocation had been carried out earlier, in the 1980s, as part of anti-insurgent operations (Evrard & Goudineau 2004), when the state had feared that isolated ethnic groups would become integrated with groups of insurgents and therefore had tried to control the scattered groups so that the insurgents (anti-socialist government groups) would not be able to access them. The government designated protected forest areas and prohibited ethnic groups from cultivating open upland in those areas. The state also demarcated forest areas to be allocated to each village, so that the villagers could only farm uplands within their designated area. The area demarcation was not necessarily based on the needs of the villagers, nor was the resettlement of villages necessarily planned according to the availability of upland areas. Many resettled communities have been left to fend for themselves and look for new upland areas to farm and other sources of income to make ends meet.

More recently, Chinese investment in rubber plantations increased and plantations cover large parts of the forested area in northern Laos (Shi 2008). The agreement made between the Lao government and investors is that the rubber plantation investors need to make an agreement also with local communities to provide them with rubber seedlings and/or infrastructure developments in the villages. However, there have been problems in the implementation of the agreements because the regulations are very weak. In addition to rubber, Chinese companies have introduced maize production. Chinese agricultural invest-ment in rubber plantations has created a demand for agricultural labour. Today, the relocated ethnic groups are heavily dependent on casual work linked to agriculture.

In the 1970s, when the main focus in Laos was the struggle for national liberation, ethnic groups in the country were officially classified in three main categories comprising a total of 68 ethnic groups. In 1998, the Lao government classified ethnic groups into 49 subgroups, and into four different language groups – Lao T'ai, Mon-Khmer, Chinese-Tibetan, and Hmong-Ewmian – on the basis of language, historical background, and custom, tradition, and culture. The study area, Luang Namtha Province, consists of five districts, with *c.*360 villages, 25,000 families and 163,000 people and 17 ethnic groups (UNESCO 2008). In

Luang Namtha, the largest ethnic group is the Akha (25.1 per cent), followed by the Khmu (24.5 per cent), Tai Lue (12.2 per cent), Tai Dam/Daeng/Khao (10.1 per cent), Hmong (5 per cent), and Lahu (3.6 per cent) (UNESCO 2008).

Most of the ethnic groups have traditionally practised semi-nomadism and circular itinerancy (Evrard & Goudineau 2004). Ovesen (2004) notes that the first immigration of highlanders (including Hmong and Akha) was in the early 19th century, due to conflict and oppression in southern China, but their immigration did not have a large impact on lowland Laos, since they occupied only the high mountain areas. However, since the1950s, their mobility has been of a very different nature. During the American War (Vietnam War) and subsequent civil war, there were huge movements of population in the highlands: in 1979, up to 730,000 people were relocated (Taillard cited in Evrard & Goudineau 2004). Even though Luang Namtha was conquered by the Pathet Lao (army) in 1962 and the revolution army was victorious in 1975, the displacement of highlanders in Luang Namtha continued because anti-revolutionary armies still occupied the province, especially in the south-west. In order not to let the anti-revolutionary army gain support from the highlanders, from the 1970s to the 1990s the Lao government moved the highlanders to places along the roads where they could monitor them and cut their ties with the insurgents. In total, 50–85 per cent of the villages and families were displaced (Evrard & Goudineau 2004). Evrard and Goudineau (2004, 939) quote Evrard as describing such mobility as 'resettlement-induced forms of mobility'.

In the 1990s, the displacement of highlanders continued, but then under the name of development. Initially, the Lao government claimed to 'bring development to the mountainous areas' (Evrard & Goudineau 2004, 944), but in 1985 it changed its policy and instead moved the highlanders down to places near the roads and towns. The resettlement (*chatsan asib khong thi*, i.e. establishment of permanent occupations) was not announced as an official policy of the Lao government until recently, but has been practised on the ground as part of rural development projects since the 1990s (SOGES 2011). Apparently, a further reason for the resettlement was to stabilize shifting cultivation and eradicate opium cultivation. The policy on shifting cultivation was announced in 1996 (Cohen 2000). The situation was compounded by the Lao government's 'focal site' strategy, which was reaffirmed during the period 1998–2002, and aimed to direct development efforts towards specific geographical areas (Cohen 2000). The development efforts have since been implemented with tacit approval from foreign aid agencies (Rigg 2007; Evrard 2011).

However, the Lao government was sensitive about uncontrolled and/or disorganized migration (Evrard & Goudineau 2004), as is evident from the Prime Ministerial Executive Order No. 36 Article 13 (SOGES 2011). According to Meingsawanh Mekonsy, Head of the Department of Interior Affairs of Luang Namtha Province, some highlanders were moved by the government, but some were deported by district authorities; for example, in the late 2000s, Hmong people were deported back to Vietnam and Luang Prabang, and Tai Dam people were deported back to Muang Long.[2]

Prime Ministerial Executive Order No. 36 states that provinces and districts need to resettle villages for socio-economic development and national security purposes, and Article 3 specifies who should be resettled (SOGES 2011). The programme focuses particularly on places where villages are difficult to access, are scattered, where the people are poor, where they live on steep slopes and in watershed areas, where they are engaged in illegal activities (opium poppy cultivation or illegal hunting), where villages are under development projects (such as dam, mining, and industrial areas), and located in sensitive areas such as borders (i.e. they are important for national security). The programme also states that resettlement areas will provide land for those who are displaced to make a living, access to roads and water, and will encourage different ethnic groups to live together. Mountain dwellers' level of dependence on natural resources has been underestimated (SOGES 2011), and this clearly reveals the state's priority on infrastructure development such as dams and mines above carefully balancing the environment and people's livelihoods with development.

Several studies have been conducted on the impact of the resettlement pro- grammes in Laos (Cohen 2000; Evrard & Goudineau 2004; Baird & Shoemaker 2007; High 2008; Mann & Luangkhot 2008; Petit 2008; Evrard 2011; SOGES 2011) and most of them cite the negative impacts. Holly High (2008), whose study relates to southern Laos, argues that resettlement did not necessarily create a worse situation for the resettled population, and it was unthinkable for villagers to return to their former villages. Cohen (2000) notes that the mortality rate has increased among villagers who were relocated, especially the child mortality rate, and he blames the deteriorating water supplies and sanitation, and the increase in incidences of malaria at lower altitudes. Petit (2008) claims that there is lack of access to land for newly resettled people and this has led to food security problems. Evrard and Goudineau (2004) find that such difficulties in adjusting to new places has led to further mobility and increased slash-and-burn agriculture, which is ironic since the purpose of resettlement is to stabilize the practice.

In addition, there has been an increase in economic concessions in Luang Namtha Province since the early 2000s. Rubber has been planted in Luang Namtha since 1994 (Shi 2008). Some ethnic peoples have been taught how to plant rubber from the villagers in Had Ngao. Since around mid-2000, large-scale rubber projects have emerged (Shi 2008). Most of the economic concessions granted by the government for rubber production are owned by Chinese investors. The National Land Management Authority (2009) notes that in 2009 *c.*30,000 ha was under rubber plantations in Luang Namtha. Among the approved land lease projects, half were foreign investments, almost all of them were Chinese investments, and more than 80 per cent were for the production of rubber (National Land Management Authority 2009).

The Lao government made a Memorandum of Understanding with China in 1997 and since then the total amount of trade with China has been increasing. According to the Lao Statistics Bureau, in the year 2005 bilateral trade was worth USD 1.331 million, which by 2008 doubled to USD 2.630 million.[3] The Lao People's Democratic Republic encourages investment in rubber and, for example, sugarcane, cassava, and corn, as 'alternative crops' (i.e. alternative to opium poppy crops) and provides subsidies for such investment from the Opium Replacement Special Fund (Shi 2008). The investment in the production of rubber is by far the largest investment and accounts for 22 approved investment projects out of 33 investment projects. Plans were made for 22,640 ha of rubber plantations by 2010, and a production rate of 600,000 tons of rubber by 2015.[4] Land under concession has to be registered under the land registration scheme. However, due to a tradition of relocating when the need arises, indigenous people do not have any registered uplands, even though they pay taxes according to the size of the upland fields that they cultivate. Hence, they are unable to claim rights to use land when the government grants concessions. Although direct relocation as a result of economic land concessions is rare (as mentioned by SOGES 2011), private companies' claims to exclusive rights to certain lands and expansion of economic concessions restrict villagers' access to upland fields.

One of the requirements governing the use of land for rubber plantations is that degraded forests should be used instead, not pristine forests, in order to avoid contributing to deforestation. However, on many occasions, forests converted to rubber plantations under economic concession are not as degraded as the developers claim. As a consequence of weak monitoring, some concessions plant rubber in a different place from the place that was given approval or over a larger area than approved (National Land Management Authority 2009).

No displacement as a result of economic concessions has been reported, but during our fieldwork we heard that after villagers had been resettled, one of the original village areas had been converted into a rubber plantation. Even though rubber plantations have not contributed to displacement, they have affected the villagers' livelihoods and vulnerabilities, as we discuss later (in the section headed 'Changes in livelihoods'). As Evrard (2011) points out, contrary to what is normally perceived, poverty is more difficult to understand among highlanders due to their historical, cultural, and social constructions of their practices, which also shape how they react differently to external shock. Further, Toyota (2003) notes the importance of recognizing the variation that exists within groups and contradictions between individuals. We followed a similar perspective in our study, noting the varied responses and strategies that the highlanders demonstrated in the face of resettlement. Mann and Luangkhot (2008) claim that resettlement affects women differently in different locations, and the difference relates to whether they continue to cultivate in fields near their original village. We explore this point further in this chapter, and analyse how different livelihood choices have different impacts on women and men.

Fieldwork

The fieldwork was carried out by the authors (of this chapter), assisted by enumerators. We contacted the planning department in Luang Namtha Province via the Public Works and Transportation Institute (PIT) and were then referred to the district authorities. In turn, the district authorities recommended villages that had been moved in recent years under the government's resettlement programme. We (the authors) made reconnaissance visits to the villages in Luang Namtha District and Viengphoukha District, and selected eight villages (five in Luang Namtha District and three in Viengphoukha District) on the basis of the villagers' history of mobility and to obtain a balance in terms of the respondents' ethnic diversity. In this chapter, we discuss five of the eight villages: Namtalang Tai (a Khmu village), Namkap Tai (a Musuer, Lenten, and Khmu village), Nammat Mai (an Akha village), Namsa (an Akha village), and Sopthout (a Lenten village) (Figure 7.1). The data were collected between August 2010 and January 2012.

After several open-ended interviews had been conducted in each village, with people of different age and sex, a semi-structured questionnaire was developed, which focused on the changes in livelihoods and mobility patterns that had occurred since the villagers' arrival in their respective villages. The respondents were selected from anyone who had ever married. As far as possible, both the husband and the wife in each family were interviewed, except when only one spouse was available. Furthermore, we aimed for a balanced sex ratio, i.e. 50 per cent female interviewees and 50 per cent male interviewees in each village. Respondents were selected from villagers who were available in the village on the day that we held the interviews. In Namkap Tai, we interviewed 24 men and 20 women (from 28 households); Sopthout, 17 women and 17 men (from 19 households); Nammat Mai, 20 men and 17 women (from 21 households); Namsa, 23 men and 24 women (from 27 households); and Namtalang Tai, 15 men and 17 women (from 19 households). In addition to the questionnaire survey, in-depth interviews were conducted, mainly focusing on middle-aged women who had experienced relocation several times. We held in-depth interviews with one man and three women in Sopthout, one man and six women in Namkap Tai, three women in Nammat Mai, one man and three women in Namtalang Tai, and one man and four women in Namsa. The interviews were conducted partly in Thai and partly in Lao, recorded and translated by students of an ethnic higher secondary school in the province. The semi-structured questionnaire results were analysed using SPSS Statistics Version 20, while the recorded interviews were translated and analysed for their content and context, focusing on the interviewees' expressions.

The respondents were in the age range 15–73 years, and most of them had received very little formal education. The average number of years spent attending school was approximately two years for men, and less than one year for women. The highest educated man came from Namtalang Tai, who had received ten years of education, while the highest educated woman came from Nammat Mai and had received eight years of education. The households in the study villages had between six and eight members on average. Musuer households in Namkap Tai were larger than households belonging to other ethnic groups, and the average for all study villages was 8.2 persons. However, households were often scattered in different uplands and only came together during their New Year celebrations. The largest household, in Namsa village, had 19 members (all Akha).

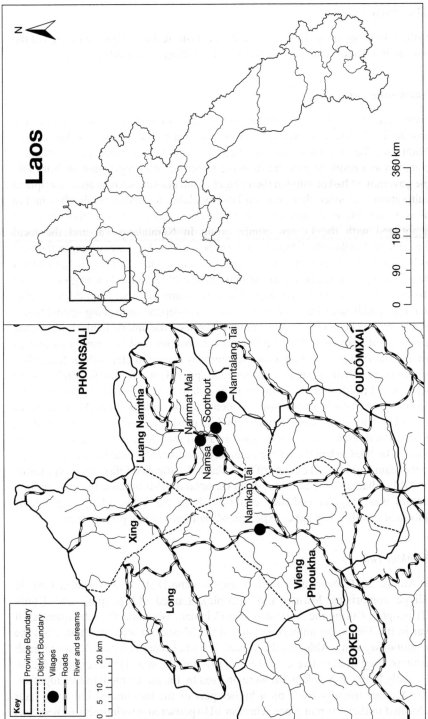

Figure 7.1 Location of the study area in Luang Namtha Province, Lao People's Democratic Republic (Lao PDR).

The study villages

In the following subsections we describe the historical development of each of the five study villages, with special focus on the villagers' mobility.

Namtalang Tai

Namtalang Tai in Luang Namtha District was formerly a Lenten village, but around 1997, Khmu people moved in from Nam Pik village, *c.*4 km east of Namtalang Tai. The move was not directly under the government's resettlement plan, but as a result of pressure from the government's programme. In Nam Pik, the government had prohibited the villagers from opening up new areas for upland cultivation, and since there was no land available for paddy fields, they had to move to new places to cultivate rice. Therefore, a group of leaders from Nam Pik negotiated with the Lenten ethnic group in Namtalang Tai and the local government to allow the Khmu to move to Namtalang Tai. Lenten people continue to live in the northern part of the village (19 households, 110 people) and Khmu people occupy the southern part (38 households, 290 people). Due to good soils in the village, the rice yields are high. The earliest arrivals from Nam Pik were able to secure paddy land, but latecomers have had to depend on farming upland fields. However, it is becoming more difficult to work on the upland fields. In 2007, the government granted a 900 ha rubber concession on land covering a large area around the village. When the Chinese company started to plant rubber trees, they promised to construct an all-weather road, provide water and electricity, build schools and residential areas, and provide 600 trees per household. However, the company only made minor improvements to the village land. After the trees around the village were cut down in 2007, to make way for the rubber plantation, a large flood in the same year washed away all the paddy fields and some of the houses. In 2008, when the rubber company constructed a road linking the village to the main highway, all but one of the villagers' cattle died following an epidemic. In 2011, villagers were unable to farm the upland fields because the precipitation pattern was irregular and they could not burn the fields. Many respondents informed that they had never experienced shortages in rice prior to then.

Namkap Tai

In August 2010, Namkap Tai, in Viengphoukha District, was a mixed ethnic village comprising Musuer (387 people), Lamed (43 people), and Khmu (21 people). During the American War (Vietnam War) and the subsequent civil war in the 1960s, the authorities moved the Musuer to separate them from the revolutionary army. Although the Musuer households normally lived apart in small hamlets, they tried to live close together during the war. However, the Musuer currently living in Namkap Tai were ordered by the government to live together. The Musuer initially lived on a higher part of the mountains, but were later relocated to their current place when an EU-sponsored development project was implemented in Namkap Tai in 1997. The location was originally a Khmu village, but during the war, the Khmu fled to the district centre or provincial centre. By the time the Musuer had been moved into Namkap Tai, the surrounding forest was already barren and the Musuer were forced to open upland fields in distant places. The World Food Programme's Food for Work programme allowed the Musuer to develop paddy fields near the village. However, since the land available for development was not sufficient to enable the Musuer to grow enough produce to feed their families, many sold the developed paddy land to lowland Laotians and returned to practising upland farming during the years 2003–2004. The Lamed people arrived in Namkap Tai in 2005, under the government's resettlement programme. Whereas in their former place, Nale District, the Lamed had lived in close proximity to each other, none of the villages in Luang Namtha District could accommodate all of them and therefore they were forced to disperse and settle in different villages alongside different ethnic groups.

There are two types of rubber plantation around Namkap Tai: one is managed by urban Laotians, and the other is a Chinese rubber concession. The Chinese concession started operations in the years 2005–2006, when local villagers were hired to work in the plantation for LAK 25,000 (USD 3.3)[5] per day. Whenever the Chinese wanted to fell trees in order to open up the plantation, they were accompanied by many representatives of government authorities to ensure that the work would not be disrupted by protests from the villagers. By 2010, the rubber plantation covered 34 ha.

Nammat Mai

Nammat Mai (also know as Nammat Somboon) is an Akha village in Luang Namtha District. In 2010, the village comprised 35 households and had a total population of 207 people. The elderly members of the village informed that the villagers had originally moved from China to Xing District; in 1966, the members of 58 households moved from Xing District to Luang Namtha District by walking for ten hours. In 1991, due to conflict among male youths, they moved to Namchien village in Luang Namtha, which they reached by walking for seven hours. The conflict had become so severe that one of the youth groups had broken away and decided to leave, forcing all of their relatives to follow, even though the women and elderly did not have any problems with each other.

In Namchien, the villagers had a total of 50 ha of paddy land with good access to water. The village is located on a trekking route and the government has set up a tourist house in the village, where the villagers can take care of tourists and earn some income from providing the service. In the same year that the tourist service was started around 1993, there was an epidemic in Namchien and almost half of the population died. In 2006, partly under pressure from the government to relocate to a place near an all-weather road and partly because of the many deaths in the village, the villagers decided to move to Nammat Mai. However, the government's promise of paddy land was not fulfilled and the villagers had to buy land on which to build their houses. Lack of clear land demarcation by the district government led to conflicts with those living in the neighbouring village of Tai Dam. The Akha's claim to land was weak because they were latecomers. Three years after the Nammat Mai villagers had planted rubber trees near their village, the Tai Dam reclaimed the land. The Akha lost the land, the rubber trees, and three years' worth of labour that they had put into the plantation.

Namsa

Namsa is an Akha village in Luang Namtha District. In August 2010, there were 32 households and a total population of 179 people. The village elders informed that the villagers had originally come from Muang La in China. They moved to Luang Namtha District in the late 1930s. In 2005, under the resettlement programme, the government wanted the villagers to move to Plang village. The government officers told them that if they wanted to remain living in remote areas, the government would not be able to support them. Namsa people had perceived the communication as a threat and had therefore decided to move. However, they found that Plang was located too far from the nearest town and subsequently moved to Namsa in 2007. Namsa is located on Lenten village land. The Akha have been able to establish their residences in the village, but as there is nowhere for them to farm near the village, they continue to farm their upland fields in Plang. In addition, they raise their livestock in the village (Luang Namtha District) they had lived in before moving to Plang, as there is more forest there. Since they are latecomers to the area, they have less access to land. They also experience more difficulties in collecting sufficient quantities of NTFPs because there is less forest around the village.

Sopthout

Sopthout is a Lenten village in Luang Namtha District, although several Khmu families live in one part of the village. The Khmu had initially moved to the area to work in the local rubber plantation and later decided to settle down there. In 2010, Sopthout had 32 households and a population of 179 people; 23 households were Lenten, seven were Khmu, and two were Tai Deang. The villagers formerly lived on the other side of the nearby river, but in 1994, district authorities ordered them to move to the present location, where road access is better and schools are located. In 2006, the land around Sopthout was converted to rubber plantation, which is owned by a Chinese company. There is no land suitable for rice cultivation in Sopthout; instead, the villagers are dependent on upland fields. However, as a consequence of rubber plantation, there is limited availability of upland areas suitable for cultivation. In addition, part of the rubber plantation occupies Sopthout's reserve forest, which affects the availability of NTFPs. Workers from the neighbouring Oudomxay (Oudômxai) Province were hired to work on the rubber plantation, not local people. Further, the company responsible for the plantation had promised the villagers that they would invest in infra-structure for them, but the infrastructure did not materialize, despite the village leaders petitioning the district authorities to force the company to honour its promises. The village is located on an eco-tourism route running through the district, and because it is located along the nearby river the villagers are able to sell souvenirs to tourists who arrive by boat as well as those who arrive by car, although the amount of income earned from tourism is very meagre.

Changes in livelihoods

The changes in villagers' livelihoods in the study area have changed mainly as a consequence of their move to new locations and due to the increase in rubber plantations. In response to varying land pressure, some have had to reduce the amount of upland fields they cultivate, some have increased the amount, and some have substituted their increasing need for cash income by collecting NTFPs or working as hired labourers. In the following, we demonstrate how the burden of the changes has been borne unequally by women and men.

Upland cultivation in Namtalang Tai has decreased (Table 7.1), partly because the government restricts the villagers from opening up new upland fields, partly because most of the land around the village has been converted to rubber plantations, and partly because many villagers have shifted to rice cultivation; among the participant households, only three did not cultivate rice. However, the flood in 2007 that followed the rapid felling of trees to open up land for rubber plantation devastated their paddy fields, and since then many villagers have had to depend on collecting NTFPs and resorting to farming some upland fields in order to make ends meet. In Namtalang Tai, villagers reported that in 2011 it had not been possible for them to cultivate the uplands because irregular rainfall that year had made it impossible to burn trees to open up the fields:

> When it was flooded, I could not do anything. The house had to be rebuilt. I do not know how to describe, but we just lived like that. We depended on our relatives . . . At that time, we already had paddy land, but it was also lost. Nothing was left in the paddy. That year, I just kept on crying. Nothing was left . . . Never did we experience flood. Only that year was [land] flooded. The year there was flood was the same year as the beginning of the rubber plantation. There was great damage. The government did not give us anything. Villagers think that it [rubber plantation] is related but those who did the cutting do not think like that.
> (Ngun, female, 40 years, Khmu, from Namtalang Tai)[6]

In common with Namtalang Tai, Sopthout suffered from irregular rainfall and similarly the amount of upland available for cultivation had decreased, i.e. there was no more upland available for the villagers to cultivate because all of the land around the village had been converted to rubber plantations: 'When we were in the old Sopthout [village], we did upland farming in nearby places because there was a lot of land. Now our uplands are in far away places' (Mun, female, 56 years, Lenten, from Sopthout).

Table 7.1 Average change in upland production, NTFPs sold, and income from hired labour in the study villages (percentage change from the time prior to resettlement to the time when the study was conducted)

Village	Upland field		NTFPs sold		Income from hired labour		Households with income from hired labour	
	%*	+/–**	%	+/–	%	+/–	%	+/–
Namkap Tai	8.2	–	8.9	+	63.2	+	50	+
Sopthout	51.2	–	45.6	–	2051	+	325	+
Nammat Mai	15.2	+	11.9	+	756	+	500	+
Namsa	15	+	6.5	+	925	+	500	+
Namtalang Tai	29.4	–	65.9	+	85.9	–	50	–

Source: Questionnaire survey.

Notes: *Percentage of change from the base year (see below);
 **+ = increased, – = decreased.
 Income from NTFPs sold and hired labour has been adjusted by the CPI (Consumer Price Index). It was difficult to specify the base year, but each village's cutting year for the 'before' and 'after' situation was estimated as follows. The base years for Namkap Tai and Sopthout were set around 2005 (when the Lenten ethnic group moved into Namkap Tai) and when the rubber plantation started in Sopthout village; the base years for Nammat Mai and Namtalang Tai were set around 2006 (when the villagers of Nammat Mai moved to their current location and when a road was constructed to connect Namtalang Tai to the nearest highway); and the base year for Namsa was set around 2007 (when the villagers moved to their present village). The figures are based on recall data. In Namtalang Tai, only three households did not have any paddy land, and those that had paddy did not have to depend much on cultivating upland fields or working as hired labourers.

Due to the shortages of land available for rice cultivation and because it is more difficult for the villagers to collect NTFPs, they have become heavily dependent on earning an income by working as hired labourers:

> After they did the rubber plantation, collecting forest products was difficult. They have brought a lot of labourers from outside and these workers collected a lot of NTFPs, and they ate them all. So, the villagers have nothing left. Now, it is not possible to look for food in the forest. We can only be hired as manual labourers and get cash to buy things to eat. If there is no [work for] hired labour, there is nothing to do, and we do not have any income. We have to work as hired labourers to survive.
>
> (Ngiao, female, 43 years, Lenten, from Sopthout)

Despite the difficulties of making a living, it is difficult for the villagers to leave Sopthout:

> We cannot move anymore. We need to stay on here to live. Before, there was land everywhere, but now there is no land. They have already divided the

land. They have planted rubber trees in all of the area. Other places, there is no land anymore . . . So, we need to stay here. My children and grandchildren need to stick in this place too. We are not going anywhere.

(Ngiao, female, 43 years, Lenten, from Sopthout)

In contrast to Namtalang Tai and Sopthout, the impacts of the rubber plantations were not as direct in the other three study villages (Namkap Tai, Nammat Mai, and Namsa). However, the restrictions on land use has made it impossible for the villagers to take advantage of the growing opportunities in rubber plantations or any other opportunities following the introduction of the government resettlement programme.

Villagers in Nammat Mai have increased the area covered by their upland fields because they have gained access to markets where they can sell their rice. In addition, they have increased the amounts of NTFPs collected and spend more time working as hired labourers in order to meet their increasing needs for cash incomes after moving to the resettlement village on a road that gives them better access to markets and towns. However, since they do not have access to land near their village due to the uncertain demarcation of land belonging to Nammat Mai and the neighbouring village of Tai Dam, they are not able to plant rubber trees or make any other investments on land around their village. Hence, they need to depend on a temporary short-term income from the collection of NTFPs and working as hired labourers:

When we came here, we planted rubber on the land, but when it was around three years old, the Tai Dam came and told us that this is their land and reclaimed the land. So, we lost the rubber trees and we only have 300 rubber trees left. When we moved here, the *Muang* [district authorities] came to eat here, but they did not tell us that this is Lao land. So, we have decided to farm *hai* (upland fields) there. We are not able to discuss with the *Muang*, because we do not know Lao language and do not have an education.

(Hong Bo, male, 60 years, Akha, from Nammat Mai)

Villagers in Namsa, too, have experienced restrictions on their access to forested land around their village and instead have to farm the uplands in their former village. They have to increase their collections of NTFPs and work as hired labourers in order to finance their new settlement and cover their increased expenditure due to living near markets. Since 2011, they have had to rely increasingly on non-farm income, because irregular rainfall prevented them from opening up their fields. Life in the resettlement area has become difficult for some:

All the people want to do paddy [rice cultivation]. The Lenten have already occupied the flat land . . . and do not let us use it. That is why our villagers have to do a lot of rubber [plantation work], because they do not have any paddy [land].

(Fu Do, female, 65 years, Akha, from Namsa)

In Ta Sen Ka [the former village], we always had enough rice. Here, we do as much *hai* as possible, but do not have enough rice. We only get large stems but there is little rice produced. There is no land to do *hai* anymore.

(Na Ku, female, 50 years, Musuer, from Namkap Tai)

We go to Nammai (the former settlement) to look for forest goods. It takes three hours to go to Nammai. Sometimes we go to the forest for two nights. Now, there is a lot of people [who] go to the forest, but cannot find anything. Before, we could look for rabbits and rats to eat, but now we cannot find [any]. I do not plant rubber [trees] because we do not have enough labour.

(Cha Le, male, 63 years, Musuer, from Namkap Tai)

To summarize, resettlement and the development of rubber plantations have forced those living in the study villages to change their livelihoods. All of the villagers had experienced restrictions on their ability to access forested land and had to supplement their income by collecting NTFPs and working as hired labourers. The changes to their livelihoods have been exacerbated by their restricted mobility: 'Over there in Bako, I stayed at the *hai* most of the time and little in the village. Here, the *Kantun* (local authority) told us to stay at the village, so we stay there most of the time' (Na Nga, female, 40 years, Musuer, from Namkap Tai).

Our findings raise the question of whose workload increased after resettlement. As shown in Table 7.1, in recent years there has been a major increase in the number of households that engage in work as hired labourers, with the exception of villagers from Namtalang Tai, the majority of whom were able to earn their income from rice cultivation. In the other villages, whereas previously mainly men engaged in work as hired labourers, after resettlement women were increasingly engaged in hired labour work (Table 7.2).

The respondents in Namsa informed that while mainly men worked as hired labourers, in terms of frequency, women were hired more often and

Table 7.2 Members of households in the study villages that worked as hired labourers before and after resettlement, by gender

Village	Before resettlement		After resettlement		Total number of respondents*
	Men	*Women*	*Men*	*Women*	
Namkap Tai	13	7	17	19	44
Sopthout	7	3	21	11	34
Nammat Mai	1	1	15	20	37
Namsa	4	4	33	13	47
Namtalang Tai	1	0	1	4	32

Source: Questionnaire survey.

Note: *The total number who worked as hired labourers does not correspond with the total number of respondents.

on average were hired an additional seven times. This was also the case in Sopthout:

> There is much more work for women in the new village. When we are near the town, we want to buy this and that. Then, we need money. Then, whenever we have time, we will go for [work as] hired labour . . . When going for hired labour, I go much more than my husband. [A] Chinese company hires labour. My husband will go only one or two days a month, not often, like me. As for our rubber plantation, my husband works on it more than me.
>
> (Shoang Tu, female, 25 years, Akha, from Namsa)

Working as hired labourers and contributing to the family finances sometimes reflected women's comparatively weak position within their family. For example, a widow who lived with her married sister worked as a labourer more often than other villagers because she needed to demonstrate her ability to contribute to her family:

> We go for [work as] hired labour and get money, but spend money to buy rice and all is gone. Every year, we go and get 20,000 kip [c.USD 2.5] for hired labour. My sister also goes but I go more than others.
>
> (Na Chi, female, 45 years, Musuer, from Namkap Tai)

A similar trend was observed in the collection of NTFPs (Table 7.3). In all of the study villages, women had increased their frequency of collecting NTFPs compared with men. By contrast, in Sopthout and Nammat Mai, villagers' access to the forest had become more and more restricted, and therefore both women and men had reduced the frequency of their visits to the forest to collect NTFPs. In the case of Namsa, men were increasing their investments in paddy land and rubber plantations, even though access to land was limited. By contrast, women were responsible for collecting NTFPs and making ends meet in the short-term. In general, the length of time that women spent on collecting NTFPs per day had increased (Table 7.3), which indicates that in all relocated villages it is becoming more difficult for villagers to access forest products:

> Being women is more difficult [than being a man]. Cooking is done by women, and men do not help. Weeding is done by women. Men say that they are tired and quit early. Cooking, fetching water, and cooking rice are all done by women.
>
> (Na Nga, female, 40 years, Musuer, from Namkap Tai)

> After rubber plantations was opened, there was no forest, and . . . [it has been] more difficult to look for things to eat. Before, we looked in any place there was forest, now everywhere we look is rubber plantation. Everywhere is other people's land.
>
> (Mun, female, 56 years, Lenten, from Sopthout)

Table 7.3 Average changes in the frequency of collecting NTFPs in the study villages and the length of time spent collecting on each occasion

| Village | % change in frequency of collecting NTFPs (no. of times) | | | | % change in time required for collecting NTFPs per time (hours) | | | |
| | Men | | Women | | Men | | Women | |
	%*/times**	+/-***	%/times	+/-	%/times	+/-	%/times	+/-
Namkap Tai	27/ 14.7–18.7	+	183/ 4.9–14	+	22/ 2.4–2.9		16/ 1.4–1.6	+
Sopthout	13/ 42.6–36.9	−	52/ 60.5–28.9	−	38/ 0.94–0.58	−	0/ 0.64	n/a
Nammat Mai	14/ 79.7–68.9	−	8/ 97.5–89.5	−	39/ 1.4–1.9	+	11/ 2–2.2	+
Namsa	14/ 95.3–82.4	−	23/ 97.6–119.8	+	4/ 1.6–1.7	+	23/ 1.0–1.3	+
Namtalang	35/ 75.8–102	+	42/ 83.1–118	+	141/ 0.8–2		53/ 1.2–1.9	+

Source: Questionnaire survey.

Notes: *Percentage of change, either increase or decrease from the base year (see Table 7.1 for an explanation);
**actual changes in frequency;
***+ = increased, − = decreased.

Dispersed relatives

The resettlement of villages in northern Laos has often created friction among the villagers. In some villages, the inhabitants separated and went to different places, as in the case of Nammat Mai and Namsa, and the Lenten in Namkap Tai village. On many occasions, women had to follow their husband's family to their new settlement and were separated from their parents and siblings. This not only caused suffering, especially in the case of young, newly married women, but having fewer relatives created practical difficulties in terms of childcare arrangements:

> When we work on our [local] rubber plantation, we have to bring the children if there is no one to look after them. Sometimes, I carry my child on my breast when I work. . . . The only time I cannot bring my children is when we are opening *hai* and burning *hai* [because it is dangerous]. When I collect vegetable and bamboo shoots, I can bring the children. I only bring the smallest baby with me, and I have to carry the baby when I dig bamboo shoots. It is difficult and makes me sick all the time. . . . When I go for hired work, I do not bring the children. It is not that the employer does not allow us to bring them, but it is too cumbersome if the child is with me. When the neighbour woman or father-in-law is not around, I cannot leave the child. I do not know how well the others will look after the child, so I dare not leave the child with them.
>
> (Mi Pe, female, 29 years, Akha, from Namsa)

Thus, not only were there fewer relatives around, but also women of all ages in the settlement villages spent more time earning money and hence did not have time to look after other women's children. However, the type of income-generating work (hired labour and short, frequent trips to collect NTFPs) enables women villagers to make arrangements with their neighbours for short-term childcare:

> When I am old, other people come to ask me to look after their children. The children that I look after are not children of my children, but the neighbours' children. When the mother goes to the forest or collects bamboo shoots and vegetables, they will ask me to look after their children. When they come back, they will give some forest foods that they have collected. Here, it is easier to ask others to look after children. It takes only a short time to collect bamboo shoots in this village, so we only have to ask others to keep an eye on our children for a short period of time.
>
> (Fu Do, female, 65 years, Akha, from Namsa)

Changes in mobility and decision-making patterns

Although women's workloads have increased since resettlement and although their daily life spent managing household, childcare, and farm work has been affected as a result of resettlement, they are excluded from the original decision-making process to move their respective villages, as Bisht (2009) also found in a similar study in India. One of the women from Namsa said:

> I do not have any involvement in the decision to move here. It was the village elders who decided to move. It is not possible to tell them that we do not like this and that decision. There are only men who will decide. Women will talk among themselves, but cannot decide.
>
> (Mi To, female, 67 years, Akha, from Namsa)

Even though it was against their will, they were forced to follow their husbands and parents-in-law:

> Wherever the husband takes me, I have to be with him. Actually, I want to be with my parents, but I cannot because women have to follow husbands. As a woman, I cannot take care of my parents. So, I have to come with my husband. Since we came here, I have been to Na Cho [her parents' village] only once. I want to go and visit more often but I do not have time. My brothers come to visit me very often.
>
> (Shoang Do, female, 37 years, Akha, from Namsa)

Women felt frustrated by such male domination:

> If I were a man, I would be a strong leader. I would make sure that half of all the land would be for us [by negotiating with Tai Deang], but I am not a man, so I will not be able to do so . . . Akha women say anything, men do not listen. They think that our opinion is not important . . . Everything is up to men. If a man cannot go [to negotiations] and talk well, then that man does not have any ability! I have my opinion and suggestions, but since I am not a man, I cannot go to negotiations.
>
> (Mi Tu, female, 57 years, Akha, from Nammat Mai)

Despite women's frustrations and their increasing role in supporting their family, resettlement has further weakened their decision-making power in their household. Figures 7.2 and 7.3 show how, since resettlement, men have increasingly become the main decision-makers concerning crop selection and children's education, especially in the latter case because such decisions have important implications for financial investments. Women tended to think that they are involved in decision-making more than men perceive is the case. However, in our study, both women and men had noted the tendency for women's decreasing involvement in household decision-making after resettlement (Figures 7.2–7.9).[7] Such deterioration in decision-making power has been partly due to the widening gender gap with respect to access to information and exposure to the outside world.

Figure 7.10 shows that men in the studied villages have drastically increased the frequency of their trips to the district or provincial market, whereas women have decreased the number of trips they make to the markets, with the exception

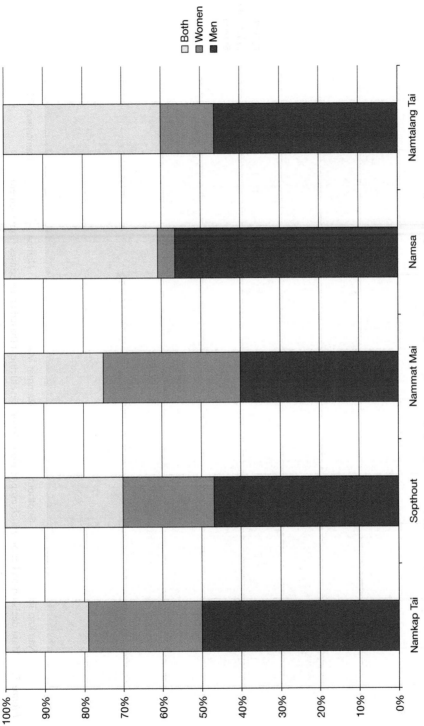

□ Both
▨ Women
■ Men

100%
90%
80%
70%
60%
50%
40%
30%
20%
10%
0%

Namkap Tai   Sopthout   Nammat Mai   Namsa   Namtalang Tai

Figure 7.2 Main decision-maker on which crop to plant, before resettlement (based on responses from men).

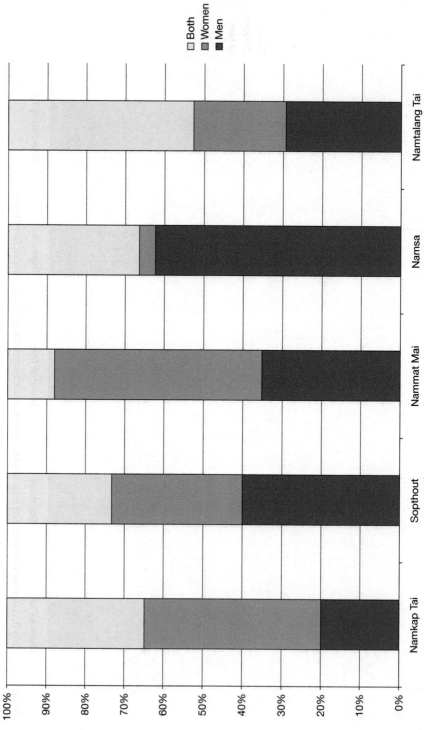

Figure 7.3 Main decision-maker on which crop to plant, before resettlement (based on responses from women).

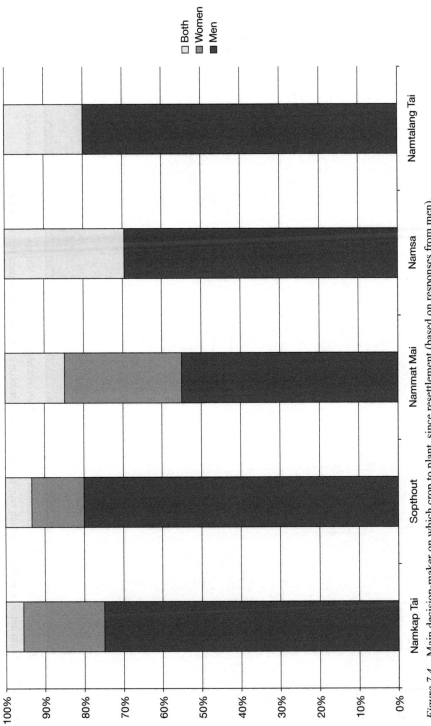

Figure 7.4 Main decision-maker on which crop to plant, since resettlement (based on responses from men).

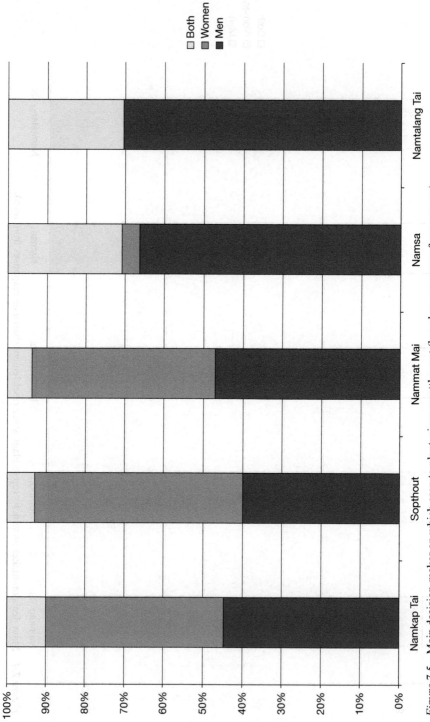

Figure 7.5 Main decision-maker on which crop to plant, since resettlement (based on responses from women).

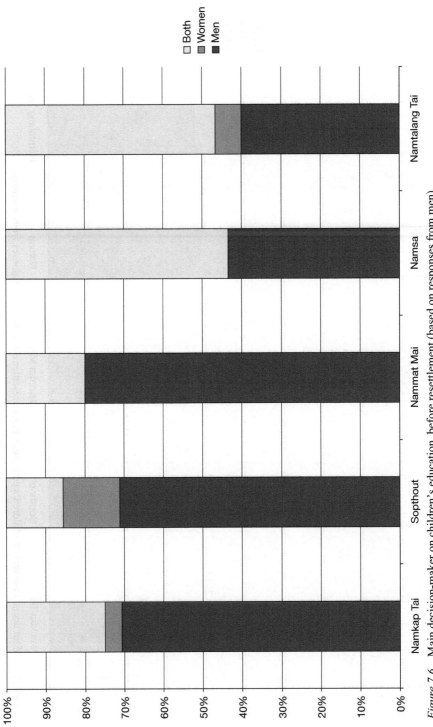

Figure 7.6 Main decision-maker on children's education, before resettlement (based on responses from men).

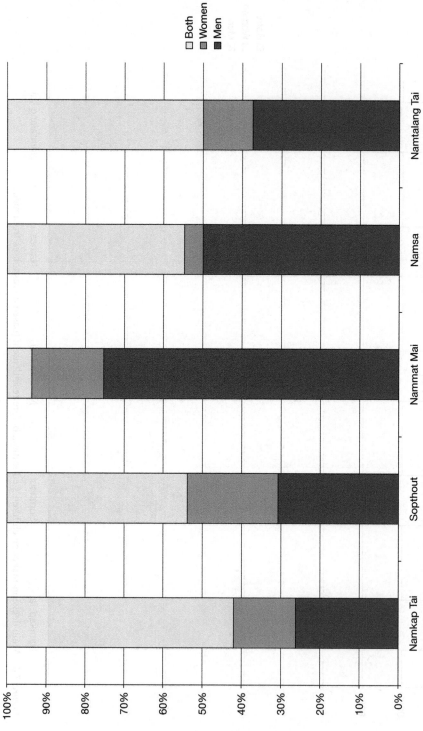

Figure 7.7 Main decision-maker on children's education, before resettlement (based on responses from women).

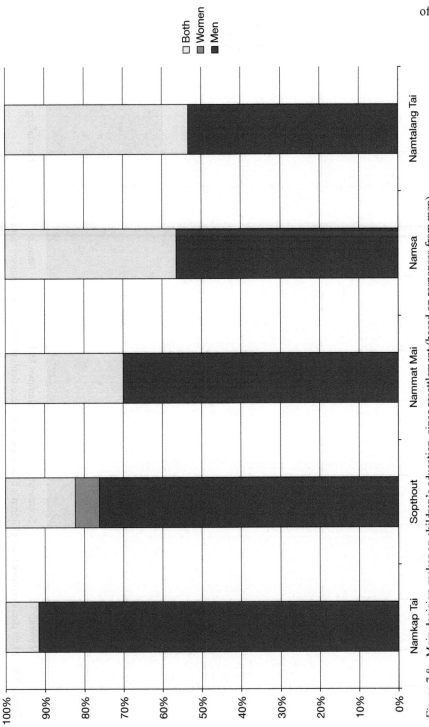

Figure 7.8 Main decision-maker on children's education, since resettlement (based on responses from men).

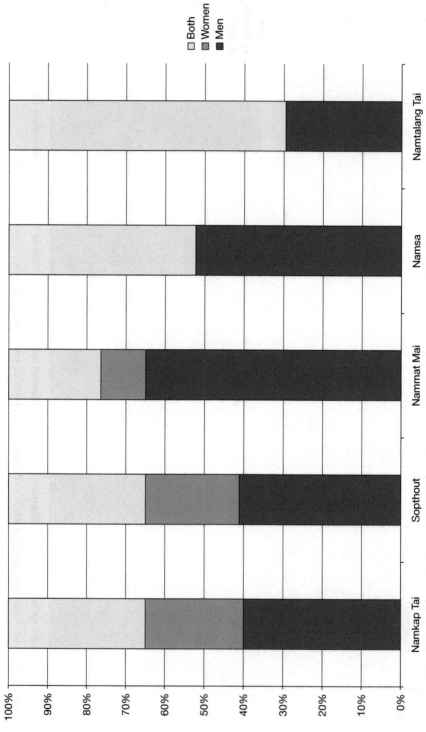

Figure 7.9 Main decision-maker on children's education, since resettlement (based on responses from women).

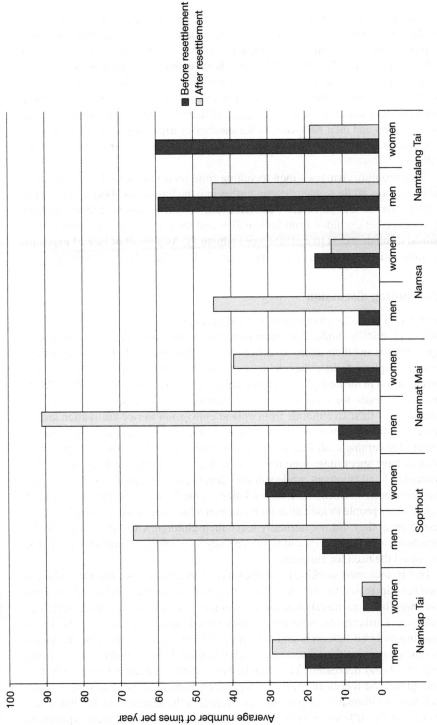

Before resettlement
□ **After resettlement**

Average number of times per year

Namkap Tai   Sopthout   Nammat Mai   Namsa   Namtalang Tai

men   women   men   women   men   women   men   women   men   women

Figure 7.10 Frequency of going to market before and since resettlement, by village and sex of respondents.

women in Nammat Mai. Instead, women ask their husbands to buy items from the markets. In addition, since resettlement, men have had access to motorbikes, which makes it easier for them to reach the markets than women, none of whom could ride a motorbike. Before resettlement, both women and men walked to the markets, which sometimes could take a whole day and therefore they would have to stay overnight. Even today, many women will walk to the markets if their husband does not take them on the back of their motorbike. In Namtalang Tai, both women and men had reduced the number of trips they made to the market because merchants from outside the village regularly open a small market in the village.

Such mobility changes – men travelling from their village to the provincial or district centre, while women venture further into the forests to collect NTFPs or are hired as agricultural labourers – can have long-term implications because women will be further excluded from information and the type of exposure that can be gained through access to markets (see endnote 1). As a result of lack of exposure to information, women have a weaker voice in household decision-making.

Concluding discussion

In northern Laos, the government's resettlement programme and the expansion of rubber plantations under economic concessions has restricted villagers' use of upland fields and their ability to collect NTFPs. This has led to lower yields from farmers' upland fields; the yields may also have been affected by irregular precipitation in the new places. The resettlement of villages near a road has led to increased needs for cash income. Furthermore, for villagers to weather the transition of their livelihoods from upland cultivation to rice cultivation and/or work on rubber plantations, they have to earn more cash income. The responsibility for earning cash income has fallen upon the women. Since resettlement, women have spent more time than men collecting NTFPs and have more often worked as hired labourers, while still attending to all their household chores. Since they have been distanced from their relatives, it has been more difficult for women to find other people to look after their children while they work. Although prior to resettlement they did not normally leave their children with other villagers, the increased need for NTFPs and to earn money by working as hired labourers has increased the need for childcare.

Due to increased workloads, women have less time to visit markets, whereas men have increased the number of trips they make to markets. Although men can use motorbikes to travel to markets, women generally do not have access to vehicles. Furthermore, whereas women spend more time outside the home working as hired labourers and collecting NTFPs, and have become the major income earners in their respective households, their decision-making power in the households has decreased. This may be because they are not familiar with their new place and therefore prefer to depend on men, who generally have more exposure to information, especially since access to the nearest town has improved. Moreover, the differences between men and women in terms of their exposure to the outside world, and hence their opportunity to access information, may mean that the knowledge gap between women and men is increasing. Thus, the resettlement programme and rubber plantations have resulted in increased workloads for women, with possible long-term implications for women in terms of the increased amount of time they spend collecting NTFPs from forests.

Resettlement and the rubber plantations have decreased women's power in their household by forcing them to engage in activities that are more restricted in terms of their mobility. The restriction has been threefold. First, by restricting their access to forests, it has become more time-consuming for women to collect NTFPs and farm uplands. Second, by making it difficult for villagers to make long-term investments in paddy or rubber plantations, the villagers do not have any choice but to depend on generating income more quickly from other sources. Third, through linking the villages to roads and to the markets, men with access to means of transportation have benefitted more than women, which has further strengthened the gendered division of labour. Living near to a road has also resulted in the villagers' increased need for cash income, which has placed pressure on women to earn more by working as hired labourers and collecting more NTFPs.

Our findings have confirmed the findings from other studies that have revealed that displaced people suffer from landlessness, joblessness, food insecurity, loss of access to common property, and social disarticulation (e.g. Cernea 1997). Our findings have also confirmed that women suffer disproportionately from restricted access to land and disruption to their social network, and struggle to 'rebuild everyday routines', as Bisht (2009) also has pointed out. When their former routine is disrupted, women are faced with increasing responsibility for feeding their family. Although women in the study area were financially independent, they were burdened by their economic responsibilities and their mobility was restricted by their limited access to forests and upland fields. Moreover, they are unable to make use of new opportunities in the resettled area, not because of lack of an education or resources compared to men, but because their traditional roles within their family restrict and control their mobility to the mountains. The women's disadvantages stem most from their restricted mobility and the resulting lack of access to information, exposure, social networks, and employment opportunities. Living near to roads does not improve their access to markets. On the contrary, it has increased the gender gap in terms of future livelihood opportunities. As Massey (1993, 62) states, 'mobility and control over mobility both reflect and reinforce power.' Women's exclusion from markets is a reflection of their weaker power compared to men, which in turn further disadvantages them (see endnote 1).

In this chapter, we have argued that in order to understand gender differences resulting from forced resettlement we not only need to look at the villagers' access to land and employment, but also their mobility patterns. As a consequence of villagers in northern Laos being resettled near roads, the relative difference in mobility between women and men can have a long-term effect on gender relations and women's capacity to adapt to the changing natural and economic environment.

Notes

1   W. Fernandes. 'Development-induced displacement: The class and gender perspective'. Paper presented at the International Conference on The Emerging Woman in the Indian Economy, Christ College, Bangalore, 26–27 November 2007.
2   Presentation by Meingsawanh Mekonsy on 7 May 2012 at Luang Namtha District Hall.
3   'Import and Export Statistics by class of commodity with 2 digits', www.nsc.gov.la (accessed 13 April 2013).
4   Data on trade with China obtained from the Ministry of Commerce, 26 November 2010.
5   1 USD = LAK 7900.
6   The names of all interviewees quoted in this chapter are pseudonyms.
7   Both women and men perceive their role in decision-making differently. Men believe they take the majority of the decisions, whereas women consider that decision-making is more equitable and that they have an almost equal role in the process. For this reason, we decided to question women and men separately for their opinions, rather than just ask heads of households.

References

Baird, I.G. & Shoemaker, B. 2007. Unsettling experiences: Internal resettlement and international aid agencies in Laos. *Development and Change* 38, 865–888.

Bisht, T.C. 2009. Development-induced displacement and women: The case of the Tehri Dam, India. *The Asia Pacific Journal of Anthropology* 10, 301–317.

Cernea, M.M. 1996. Understanding and preventing impoverishment from displacement – reflections on the state of knowledge. McDowell, C. (ed.) *Understanding Impoverishment: The Consequences of Development-induced Displacement*, 13–32. Berghahn Books, Oxford.

Cernea, M.M. 1997. The risks and reconstruction model for resettling displaced populations. *World Development* 25, 1569–1587.

Cohen, P.T. 2000. Resettlement, opium and labour dependence: Akha-Tai relations in northern Laos. *Development and Change* 31, 179–200.

de Wet, C. 2006. Risk, complexity and local initiative in forced resettlement outcomes. de Wet, C. (ed.) *Development-induced Displacement: Problems, Policies and People*, 180–202. Berghahn Books, Oxford.

Evrard, O. 2011. Oral histories of livelihoods and migration under socialism and post-socialism among the Khmu of northern Laos. Michaud, J. & Forsyth, T. (eds) *Moving Mountains*, 76–99. UBC Press, Vancouver.

Evrard, O. & Goudineau, Y. 2004. Planned resettlement, unexpected migrations and cultural trauma in Laos. *Development and Change* 35, 937–962.

High, H. 2008. The implications of aspirations. *Critical Asian Studies* 40, 531–550.

Mann, E. & Luangkhot, N. 2008. Study on women's land and property rights under customary or traditional tenure systems in five ethnic groups in Lao PDR. www.laolandissues.org/wp-content/uploads/2011/12/Women-Land-Rights-Study-Liz-Mann-et-al.pdf (accessed 2 February 2013).

Massey, D. 1993. Power-geometry and a progressive sense of place. Bird, J., Curtis, B. Putnam, T., Robertson, G. & Tickner, L. (eds) *Mapping the Futures: Local Cultures, Global Change*, 60–69. Routledge, New York.

National Land Management Authority, Land and Natural Resources Research, and Information Center. 2009. *Report: Findings of The State Land Lease and Concession Inventory Project in Luangnamtha Province*. Lao PDR, Vientiane.

Oliver-Smith, A. 2006. Displacement, resistance and the critique of development: From the grass roots to the global. de Wet, C. (ed.) *Development-induced Displacement: Problems, Policies and People*, 141–179. Berghahn Books, Oxford.

Ovesen, J. 2004. All Laos? Minorities in the Lao People's Democratic Republic. Duncan, C.R. (ed.) *Civilizing the Margins: Southeast Asian Government Policies for the Development of Minorities*, 214–240. Cornell University Press, London.

Petit, P. 2008. Rethinking internal migrations in Lao PDR: The resettlement process under micro-analysis. *Anthropological Forum: A Journal of Social Anthropology and Comparative Sociology* 182, 117–138.

Rigg, J. 2007. Moving lives: Migration and livelihoods in the Lao PDR. *Population, Space and Place* 13, 163–178.

Shi, W. 2008. *Rubber Boom in Luang Namtha: A Transnational Perspective*. GTZ, Vientiane.

SOGES. 2011. *Resettlement in Laos: Final Report*. 6 August 2011. Framework Contract Commission 2007 Lot Nr 4, Contract no. 2010/253997. SOGES, Turin.

Tan, Y., Hugo, G. & Potter, L. 2005. Rural women, displacement and the Three Gorges Project. *Development and Change* 36, 711–734.

Toyota, M. 2003. Contested Chinese identities among ethnic minorities in the China, Burma and Thai borderlands. *Ethnic and Racial Studies* 26, 301–320.

Turton, D. 2006. Who is a forced migrant? de Wet, C. (ed.) *Development-induced Displacement: Problems, Policies and People*, 13–37. Berghahn Books, Oxford.

UNESCO. 2008. *IMPACT: The Effects of Tourism on Culture and the Environment in Asia and the Pacific: Alleviating Poverty and Protecting Cultural and Natural Heritage through Community-based Ecotourism in Luang Namtha, Lao PDR*. UNESCO, Bangkok.

Wisner, B., Fordham, M., Kelman, I., Johnston, B.R., Simon, D., Lavell, A., Brauch, H.G., Oswald Spring, U., Wilches-Chaux, G., Moench, M. & Weiner, D. 2007. *Climate Change and Human Security*. 15 April 2007. Radix – Radical Interpretations of Disaster. www.radixonline.org/cchs.html (accessed 26 December 2012).

8 Concluding discussion

Ragnhild Lund

The overall objective of this book is to document the gendered dimensions of increasing connectivity and mobility among indigenous men and women in India, China, and Laos by focusing on the complex changes that people face with rapid infrastructure improvement and commercialization/industrialization in the places where they find their livelihoods. Fresh empirical insights that may nuance our understanding of mobilities are presented.

Inspired by Cresswell (2011), we have identified the following interconnected dimensions to understand the mobilities of the studied indigenous peoples: mobility as social processes, mobility as livelihoods, mobility as voluntary to forced, and mobility as gendered. The themes permeating all the chapters draw essence from an understanding that movement (or lack of movement) does not possess any inherent meaning, but needs to be understood and elucidated as a socially contextualized phenomenon through both material and discursive representations and practices (Uteng, Chapter 2; see also Haraway 1988; Sheller & Urry 2004). In this book, several of the chapters rely on Kronlid's (2008) understanding of mobility as capability, that given socio-spatial constraints may explain people's ability to move or not, depending on gender, ethnicity, class, and location, as we find here.

We also find that changes in spatial mobility patterns affect individual and collective options and actions, thus producing varying terrains of social mobility. Today, people's mobility is increasingly influenced and forced by external forces – namely, the state and the market – which people have little control over or are increasingly facing difficulties in negotiating. At the same time, we have documented here how mobility is not new to most indigenous peoples, as displacement of indigenous peoples has taken place repeatedly throughout history. Hence, there has been stability within traditional movement at the same time as recurrent, seasonal mobility has constituted movement within this stability.

Although we have raised and documented some pertinent mobility issues of contemporary Asia, it is now time to reflect critically on some of them and how they relate to and provide insights into present mobility discourses. We like to think that the knowledge produced may add value to present development policies and practices. Hence, there is a need to revisit the major findings, key analytical concepts, and methods that we present in this book.

Migration and mobility

A major finding in the three countries where our research was conducted is that rural lives are becoming increasingly delocalized, households coexist in multiple locations, and livelihoods are becoming less engaged with farming and more with wage labour in mining, industry, and cash cropping. Furthermore, urbanization and urban lifestyles put a squeeze on the already marginalized and vulnerable, and in the case of China are decisive for citizens may return to their homeland as retired and/or elderly. Therefore, we find that just using such terms as 'migrant' and 'migration' does not capture the full extent of peoples' mobilities. Rather, we have learnt that human mobility is not about moving from one starting point to an end point, but about the range of movements in time and space. Both migration and mobility are embodied and contextualized movements, but by studying mobilities one can capture the fluidity of peoples' practices that form their everyday social lives, and the expansion or restriction in their choices. A focus on mobility also captures the complexity of movements, the inequalities of movements, and how movements are gendered.

We found contextual variations in peoples' movements. In India, labour migration takes place at a large scale, but exploring mobilities provides a more nuanced picture of the processes of 'de-territorializing' of previously tribal areas. We have gained insights into what happens to tribal people's livelihoods in the new economy and how there is a trend for tribal people to move from marginalized rural positions to vulnerable urban situations. In China, the 'floating rural population' moves back and forth between countryside, home, and urban residence. In a life course perspective on mobility, we understand how people's perceptions and ability to move change from one generation to the next. Simultaneously, we find that there is a generational shift as young people, particularly young couples with children in school age, move to the city, possibly permanently. We have also learned how people strategize in their choices to be mobile. While first-generation migrants pool money and send resources back to their ancestral villages, young migrants try to set up new lives in the cities. In Laos, indigenous people's mobility has been severely constrained by the state's resettlement projects and economic concessions for cross-border investment. With limited access to land, indigenous people are devising new ways to make a living. However, these new livelihood strategies have gendered effects. While men go to markets and towns and venture into forms of new livelihood investments, women have to go to forests for their daily needs. Such gender disparity in exposure to the outside world affects women's decision-making power in households.

Mobility, immobility, and moorings

We find that increasingly mobilities are intertwined with immobility ('moorings', as defined in Western literature by Urry 2007). Urry (2007) suggests that mobility studies will be further strengthened by analysing the dialectical relationship of moorings and mobilities. Only by doing so may one chart out geographies of exclusion (Uteng, Chapter 2).

Our empirical findings show that processes of exclusion relate to both mobility and immobility. We find that immobility – what makes a person stay put – is as much about traditions of keeping that person at bay as it is about new movements which make them develop new livelihood options (forced or not). Acknowledging the importance of stability within movement and movement within stability, as opined by Halfacree (2012), we have developed knowledge from the different locations to understand the relationship between movement and moorings. We find there are some essential differences among the different sites in the three countries and they are embedded in different contexts and socio-spatial relations. For example, the Chinese findings show that because of the fixity of the *hukou* system, people at the end of their working life tend to return to their ancestral lands. Rural populations have no security, pension schemes, or social benefits in the cities. Their future is hence quite uncertain, and therefore investing in the hometowns has become a possible exit option from life in the city (see also Wang & Gu in press). We realize that people's moves are made consciously, as they do not just move from one place to the other but often move back and forth, partly depending on their citizenship rights and access to social benefits. Laos represents forced resettlements and increasing control of people's movements initiated by the state and foreign companies. If we pursue the metaphor of 'moorings' (as the place where one secures a vessel), we realize that the previous ability to move freely, as in the old economy, has since become restricted. The fact that mobility has become a restricted good shows that the ties to the 'ancestral bay' are about to break. However, even if the mooring has become disconnected, people generally see potential in moving. In India, tribal people have already become permanent villagers, but as marginalized, secondary others. Their routes of mobility have changed from subsistence shifting cultivation to seeking wage work in the informal and formal economies. This happens while whole communities are being increasingly displaced due to rapid urban expansion, large-scale development programmes, mining, and industrial development. Hence, the transition to a fully-fledged market economy is rapidly becoming a reality for various tribal groups (where they tend to be exploited), and, except for dreaming of the past glory of abundant resources in clean and beautiful environments, mooring appears less significant and is reduced to the imagination.

What these examples show is that mobility and immobility are not binary opposites but interconnected dimensions. At the same time, the socio-political dimensions of mobility enable us to understand the complexity of the mobility-immobility nexus. As documented in most of the cases discussed in this book, external institutions such as the state, corporate societies, and local governments lead to multiple forms of mobilities that are influential for how women and men can seek new livelihoods. Therefore, we understand the need to study the relationship between mobility, immobility, and development. As Adey (2010) says, mobility is fundamentally a lived relation – it is an orientation to oneself, to others, and to the world.

Resettlement, displacement, and re-territorialization

Uteng (Chapter 2), by referring to the burgeoning literature on mobilities, also underscores the importance of investigating the role of states as actors in the production of mobilities, immobilities, and moorings of displaced people, and by unravelling the events of displacement and how the state enforces, encloses, precludes, and enables the mobility of the displaced. We have documented how resettlement and displacements are major causes of mobility, and generally implemented by the state and corporate sector. In India, displacements have led to deplorable situations for tribal men and women because their habitats have been destroyed. In Laos, people's movements are increasingly controlled by the state, while in China the control is becoming somewhat looser as the *hukou* system has become less rigid. However, in all three countries, people still try to continue some of their traditional farming practices, but under increasingly difficult situations; and therefore many people seek new means of livelihoods. Such findings challenge the inferences of James Scott (2009), who maintains that indigenous peoples in Southeast Asia are constantly on the move. We find that although mobility is enabling, it is a restricted good. In all countries in globalized production, mobile labour is utilized as a means of production, but restrictions on access to social security also restrict permanent settlements.

Hence, the findings from our research show that, despite countrywise differences, many similarities are found in terms of mobility, and the present processes of social change indicate that mobilities in Asia are affected by processes working across different scales, which imply fundamental re-territorialization of land and resources that are largely irreversible nationally and regionally. Hence, the interplay of social and spatial mobilities affects people negatively, as they have limited choice of options and therefore find themselves in disadvantaged positions in the labour market, especially in the case of indigenous women.

Gendered mobilities become increasingly feminized

Gendered mobilities represent the embodied experiences of movements of indigenous peoples. Subsequent to contextual and structural changes, such as patriarchy and new socio-economic realities, we find that mobilities are gendered in new ways. For example, the mobility of indigenous peoples has become gender-specific, as women and men seek different types of work. For example, young women are preferred in certain types of informal employment in both rural and urban areas. This is amply demonstrated in the chapters on the mobility of tribal people in India (Chapters 5 and 6). Pushing women and men into different positions makes them challenge conventional gender norms (Chapter 7). In Laos, there is a problem that relatives become dispersed due to resettlement; in India, tribal women organize themselves into work collectives and engage in wage work far away from their place of origin; in both Laos and China, agriculture is feminized; and in both China and India, women become involved in new sectors of the economy as domestic workers, prostitutes, entertainers, agricultural labourers, and industrial workers. It is evident that rather than being an issue of power struggle within the confines of the household, women's access to new roles and spaces may become less dictated by local cultures and traditional social practices. Such a change has the potential to both empower and disempower women in mobility situations.

Nevertheless, we find that even though young women and men move out of their homes and villages to cities, where they distance themselves from traditional culture and norms, women's options at the home place are still dictated by local traditions and norms, particularly when it comes to maintaining their reproductive activities. For example, the China case shows that mobility patterns change among the generations and traditional gender roles are being reproduced differently among old and young people. The older generations of migrants tend to plough back resources into the household in the countryside and men move mostly on a seasonal basis. Middle-aged women remain in the countryside, farm, and look after young children and the elderly. We find that the new economy extends women's reproductive roles. By contrast, the young-generation migrants move away for several years, sometimes never to return, particularly if their children need better schooling. In trying to make a good life in the city, young people have become more assertive and more aware of their rights. Similarly, in one study area in India (Khordha), tribal women's groups assert their identity for better social acceptance in the villages where the population is predominantly Hindu caste groups. This primarily happens because women gain new knowledge, powers, and presence in new public spaces. However, the opposite is the case in mobilities from the other study area, Sundargarh, where there is a loss of identity and disempowerment socially.

The impact on women's lives of major restructuring in the global economy by the neoliberal political agenda is well documented by researchers (e.g. Elson 1991; Lie & Lund 1994; 2005; Sassen 1998; UNRISD 2005; Pearson 2007), who have shown how the drive for profit in the global economy has treated female labour as a commodity. Increasingly, women have to find paid work outside their home and community (Kabeer 2007; Pearson 2007; Azmi & Lund 2009), leading to feminization of labour. Furthermore, global demands for agricultural and mineral products have pushed developing economies away from producing food and wage goods for their own people, resulting in deteriorating traditional livelihoods and increasing the burden of poor women and men seeking food, shelter, and other essentials. Chant (2010) argues that the links between gender and poverty are oversimplified and underproblematized. According to her, we need to rethink the 'feminization of poverty' and address the 'feminization of responsibility'. Our findings add to the above discourses by showing how gendered mobilities encompass the whole economic and social system on a global scale, and show how indigenous women and men are stuck in a position of poor, marginalized, and secondary others. It is important that women's labour has become a commodity and causes women to remain in poverty. However, due to economic restructuring and different politico-spatial relations it is also evident that marginalized people remain as secondary citizens due to the implementation of policies related to their constraints and impetus to move. This is particularly well documented in the Indian case (Chapter 5). Due to their lack of education and low status, tribal women particularly move from marginalized positions in the countryside to vulnerable positions in the cities. Their rights as citizens are not protected at times in new destinations or in mobile livelihood situations with respect to, for example, wages, identity, health insurance, access to legal recourse, housing, and other basic services. Such findings underscore the significance of mobility in accessing new employment opportunities.

Mobile methodologies

Mobility is a way of engaging with and understanding the world analytically (Adey 2010). This book pays attention to the variety of experiences and expectations among culturally diverse Asian contexts. Our research sites have been dispersed, and each portrays different social transformations. Hence, in our work we have developed methodologies that are partly mobile and partly stationary. We have been able to deal with the country-specific and unique, while at the same time we have been able to move beyond through experiencing the fields of others. Thus, our methodology is in some way affected by the researchers' own mobilities. We do not follow one field, but we study several co-existing fields. This has led to different exposure to information among the research partners and cross-fertilized our fields. The fact that the team of researchers behind the making of this book also brings substantial interdisciplinary and multicultural research experience has created a productive tension in cross-cultural encounters and made us increasingly self-reflexive.

Lessons learnt and the way forward[1]

Marching ahead with modernization at the cost of the negative consequences of resultant mobilities will in effect jeopardize all efforts being targeted at development. This book illustrates the diverse range of influences that 'development' has exerted in reshaping mobilities, thereby carving out, in many cases, deformed social fabric, agencies, entitlements, roles, and capabilities. To this end, the book posits that mobilities as a constituent factor for development should be decoded at multiple levels. The following are some of the important arenas for unpacking 'mobilities' that present an already fertilized ground for direct policy interventions:

- Mobilities as an encoded belief system, its prescriptions for movement along gendered faults: How can these be harnessed in order to empower women?
- Mobilities as a platform for accessing varied social and economic functioning in highly segregated societies: How can existing and newly emerging mobilities be positively strengthened for accessing new opportunities?
- Mobilities as a structuring mechanism for both 'everyday life' and 'life-changing events': What kind of 'mobilities' will emerge from a specified type of development intervention?

- Mobilities as a direct outcome of the development decisions taken by coalitions of multinational companies and government authorities: How can an analysis of resultant 'mobilities' be inbuilt in the pre-planning of development projects?
- Mobilities as a bearer of disjointed mechanisms between physical planning, economic planning, bureaucracy, and infrastructures: How can the displaced be effectively (physically) settled either onsite or offsite? How can their changed livelihood structures be absorbed or an alternative structure be proposed as part of the development plan itself?
- Mobilities as a historical reference point to unpack how similarly affected mobilities have been dealt with in other parts of the world with special reference to indigenous populations: Are there 'positive' accounts of displacement and effective resettlement plans that have been reviewed and found to be effective in delivering sustainable solutions?
- Mobilities as a code for deciphering a divorce between history, traditional movements, and contemporary forms of movement occurring due to the neoliberal practices: What are the positive and negative changes?
- Mobilities as a decisive but missing factor for designing – comprising land use and transport planning, community development, economic development, urban design, community activism, and empowerment.

As a most basic policy recommendation, the cases presented in this book suggest that understanding development should be assimilated with an agenda on mobilities detailing 'mobility needs' and 'mobility gaps'. Policies should be designed to address the distribution of existing and potential mobility resources within a population. This will also serve to understand the ways in which mobilities could be networked to reduce environmental, economic, and social costs. Monitoring should be made an essential part of development and potential as well as actual mobilities, and the controlling factors and resultant outcomes should be assessed.

At the beginning, this kind of data gap should be addressed through developing appropriate methodologies. First, available data on mobilities in the Global South are scant. When it comes to collecting data on a complex theme such as mobilities, the problems are many and varied. It should be borne in mind that data would ideally need to be segregated at the level of gender, activities, spatial expanse, economic groups, and affected populations/displaced populations. Gender analyses, in particular, should reveal how time-space-resource distribution is taking place within and among groups. Second, a cohesive approach needs to be built to linking 'soft' or qualitative information to 'hard' data. This could aid in developing a model that corresponds much more to 'everyday functioning' than one that is a rigid set of indicators. Inspiration could be drawn from the methodology pursued by the authors of this book, which encompasses qualitative and quantitative methods in multiple sites, and which facilitates cross-country comparisons. Third, mobility-gap analyses should form an inevitable part of resettlement programmes. An explanation of the gap figures, for example, in terms of movements generated by different types of households, would shed light on the distribution of mobility opportunities among the respective groups and genders. The issue of mobilities should be built as a systematic component in the rehabilitation operations from the inception stages. From a gender-empowerment perspective, it is an essential element to integrate women's experiences through making women active agents of the planning processes. This in turn means that knowledge should be collected directly from women affected by planning, through an ongoing process, which the authors of this book have been primarily occupied with. It is advisable that future research studies measure the costs and effectiveness of specific change alternatives for various purposes.

This book in essence has advocated broadening the scope of understanding mobilities through analysing the 'lived world' of mobilities, how it unfolds, and the possible interventions required with special reference to developing countries. A crucial element of unpacking mobilities, especially in the Global South, is that the understanding, analysis, or strategies need to be visited regularly, reaffirmed, and refined. This book has explored the idea through the cases of India, China, and Laos. Positioning itself in the domain of gendered mobilities, the book furthers a hope that similar research endeavours can aid in carving out effective policies for a sustainable future.

Note

1   This section is a revision of a text provided by Dr Tanu Priya Uteng, planner and mobilities studies expert. Dr Uteng has built on some of the policy recommendations she proposed in the report *Gender and Mobility in the Developing World* (Uteng 2012).

References

Adey, P. 2010. *Mobility.* Routledge, London.

Azmi, F. & Lund, R. 2009. Shifting geographies of house and home – female migrants making home in rural Sri Lanka. *Journal of Geographical Science* 57, 33–54.

Chant, S. (ed.) 2010. *The International Handbook of Gender and Poverty: Concepts, Research, Policy.* Edward Elgar, Cheltenham.

Cresswell, T. 2011. Mobilities. Agnew, J.A. & Livingstone, D.N. (eds) *The Sage Handbook of Geographical Knowledge*, 571–580. Sage, London.

Elson, D. 1991. *Male Bias in Macro-economics: The Case of Structural Adjustment.* Manchester University Press, Manchester.

Halfacree, K. 2012. Counter-urbanisation, second home, and rural consumption. *Population, Space and Place* 18, 209–224.

Haraway, D. 1988. Situated knowledges: The science question in feminism and the privilege of partial perspective. *Feminist Studies* 14, 575–599.

Kabeer, N. 2007. *Marriage, Motherhood and Masculinity in the Global Economy: Reconfigurations of Personal and Economic Life.* IDS Working Paper No. 290. Institute of Development Studies, University of Sussex, Brighton.

Kronlid, D. 2008. Mobility as capability. Uteng, T.P. & Cresswell, T. (eds) *Gendered Mobilities*, 5–34. Ashgate, Aldershot.

Lie, M. & Lund, R. 1994. *Renegotiating Local Values: Working Women and Foreign Industry in Malaysia.* Curzon Press, Richmond.

Lie, M. & Lund, R. 2005. From NIDL to globalization: Studying women workers in an increasingly globalized economy. *Gender, Technology and Development* 9, 7–30.

Pearson, R. 2007. Beyond women workers: Gendering CSR. *Third World Quarterly* 28, 731–749.

Sassen, S. 1998. *Globalization and Its Discontents.* The New Press, New York.

Scott, J. 2009. *The Art of Not Being Governed: An Anarchist History of Upland Southeast Asia.* Yale University Press, New Haven, CT.

Sheller, M. & Urry. J. 2004. The new mobilities paradigm. *Environment and Planning A* 38, 207–226.

UNRISD (United Nations Research Institute for Social Development). 2005. *Gender Equality: Striving for Justice in an Unequal World.* UNRISD, Geneva.

Urry, J. 2007. *Mobilities.* Polity Press, Cambridge.

Uteng, T.P. 2012. *Gender and Mobility in the Developing World.* World Bank, Washington, DC. https://openknowledge.worldbank.org/handle/10986/9111 (accessed 29 January 2012).

Wang, Y. & Gu, G. Forthcoming. Home perception and home making strategy: The struggle of rural urban migrant women in Beijing and Shanghai. Wang, M., Kee, P. & Gao, J. (eds) *Transforming Chinese Cities.* Routledge, London.

Index

For Product Safety Concerns and Information please contact our
EU representative GPSR@taylorandfrancis.com Taylor & Francis
Verlag GmbH, Kaufingerstraße 24, 80331 München, Germany